The Philippine Islands
Vol.-40

by
Ed. Emma Helen Blair and
James Alexander Robertson

Double 9
BOOKS

The Philippine Islands
Vol.-40
by Ed. Emma Helen Blair and James Alexander Robertson

ISBN: 978-93-59399-37-9

Published by

DOUBLE 9 BOOKS

2/13-B, Ansari Road
Daryaganj, New Delhi – 110002
info@double9books.com
www.double9books.com
Tel. 011-40042856

ABOUT THE EDITOR

Emma Helen Blair (1869-1951) was an American historian and author known for her significant contributions to Philippine history and also scholarship. Born on July 19, 1869, in Ohio, she pursued her education at Ohio Wesleyan University and later at Columbia University. Blair's passion for history and research led her to collaborate with James Alexander Robertson, an esteemed scholar, in editing and compiling "The Philippine Islands, 1493-1898" series. This monumental project spanned fifty-five volumes and covered the colonial history of the Philippines from the 16th to the 19th century. The comprehensive series showcased her expertise in meticulously examining and also presenting historical documents and narratives. Her work significantly contributed to a deeper understanding of the Philippines' complex past and its interactions with various colonial powers. Her commitment to historical accuracy and attention to detail earned her a reputation as a meticulous and reliable historian. Beyond her contributions to Philippine history, and main thing that Emma Helen Blair also authored "The Philippine Policy of Secretary Taft" and co-wrote "A History of the Philippine Islands" with Robertson. Both of these works further demonstrated her dedication to scholarship and the exploration of the Philippines' political and social developments.

James Alexander Robertson was born in Corry, Pennsylvania, in 1873. He was the sixth of eight children born to Canadian parents who became naturalized citizens of the United States after moving to Corry in 1866. His father, John McGregor Robertson, was a builder from Verulam, Ontario, close to Peterborough. His mother, Elizabeth Borrowman Robertson, immigrated to Canada as a child from her native Scotland. When Robertson was seven years old, his mother died. After three years, he and his family relocated to Cleveland, Ohio, where James finished his secondary education. In 1892, he enrolled in Adelbert College at Western Reserve University for graduate study. He studied in Romance languages, majoring in Old French, and received his Bachelor of Philosophy degree from Western Reserve University in 1896.

CONTENTS

Preface

In the present volume but one document appears in the chronological order of events in the islands; it is short, and is mainly concerned with the ecclesiastical disputes which had been only partly quieted with the death of Archbishop Pardo. The rest of the volume is occupied by an ethnological appendix, which presents the observations of early missionary writers—Jesuit, Augustinian, and Franciscan—on the native peoples and their customs and beliefs. Due allowance being made for their ecclesiastical standpoint, these writers may be considered excellent authority on this subject—especially Combés, who was one of the Jesuit pioneers in Mindanao.

The document first mentioned above is a letter from a Manila Jesuit, relating events in that city during the year 1690–91. As in the lifetime of Pardo, there are dissensions between the ecclesiastical and the secular powers, the former represented by Bishop Barrientos, acting ruler of the archdiocese; the latter by the Audiencia until July, 1690, and after that by the new governor, Zabálburu. The bishop attempts to remove by force some of his prebends from the Augustinian convent, but is foiled by the vigilance of the friars. Being opposed in this scheme by the auditors, Barrientos excommunicates them, a proceeding which they ignore. At the coming of the new governor, his favor is adroitly obtained by a military officer named Tomás de Endaya; and the auditors are for a time treated insolently by both. Zabálburu soon shows, however, that no one can govern him; and he displays much egotism, contemns the religious, and oppresses the Indians with exactions for public works.

The Jesuit Colin, one of the pioneers in the Philippine missions, furnishes in his Labor evangélica (Madrid, 1663) a valuable account of the native races and their customs. He makes some attempt to trace the origin of the Malayan tribes, which he places, for most, in the islands of Sumatra and Macasar (or Celebes), and for some in the Moluccas. The Negritos came, he thinks, from Farther India, and possibly from New Guinea also. A chapter is devoted to the alphabet, mode of writing, and languages in use among the Filipínos. Colin praises their quickness and cleverness; some of them act as clerks in the public offices at Manila, and of these some are capable of taking charge of such offices; and they are competent printers. Colin discourses at length upon the native languages—admiring the richness and elegance of the Tagálog—and upon their mode of bestowing personal names. He then proceeds to describe their physical appearance, dress, ornaments, treatment of hair and teeth, and tattooing; their food, customs in eating, and modes of making wine; their songs and dances; their habits of bathing. Their deities, religious observances, and superstitions are recounted—including the worship of spirits, ancestors, idols, and phenomena of nature—and their ideas of the creation, and of the origin of man. Their mortuary customs include the employment of hired mourners, the embalming of the corpse, the killing of slaves to accompany the soul of the deceased, and a taboo imposing silence. Colin gives an account of their limited form of government (its unit the barangay); their laws, criminal and civil, with their penalties (among which appears the ordeal); the different ranks of society, and the occupations of the people; their weapons and armor; their marriages and divorces, and punishments for adultery. He also recounts their customs in adoption of children, inheritance of property, and slavery. Similar information is furnished by another Jesuit writer of note, Francisco Combés, on the native peoples of Mindanao and other southern islands, in which he spent twelve years as a missionary. He enumerates the several tribes and their distinctive characteristics; of these the Lutaos (or Orang-Laút, "men of the sea"), the chief seafaring and trading tribe, have acquired an ascendancy over the others which is comparable to that of the Iroquois among the North American Indians. Combés describes their mode of warfare, and ascribes to their aid the supremacy of Corralat over the other Moro chieftains, since their wars are of little importance except when waged by the sea-routes. These Lutaos of the coast hold in a sort of vassalage the Subanos, or river-dwellers, who are slothful, ignorant savages, treacherous and cowardly. Combés next praises "the noble and brave nation of the Dapitans," a small tribe who migrated from Bohol to Mindanao; he relates their history as a people, and why they changed their abode, and how they have always been the loyal friends and followers of the Spaniards. The virtue and ability of their women receives much praise. Combés discusses the origin of the Mindanao peoples, and sketches the general characteristics of each, and their mutual relations. According to our author, the Joloans and Basilans came from Butuan, in northeastern Mindanao; and the history of this migration is related in some detail, as well as the way in which the Joloans became so addicted to piracy.

Combés proceeds to recount the beliefs and superstitions current in the southern islands. Paganism prevails in them; but the southern coast of Mindanao, and Basilan and Joló, are Mahometan. Curious legends are related of the founder of the latter religion there, who is reverenced almost as a divinity; but those people know little of Mahomet's religion save its externals, and are practically "barbarous atheists." The people are largely governed by omens; they sometimes offer sacrifices to their old-time idols, but these have little real hold on them. Sorcery has great vogue among them, and Corralat and other powerful chiefs excel in it; this is one source of their ascendancy. Combés describes their mode of life: their food (which is little besides boiled rice), their clothing, their houses and furniture; and their usages and laws regarding conduct, crimes, and penalties. He regrets the prevalence of slavery, which profanes all social relations, and even destroys all kindness and charity. There is no class of freemen; all are either chiefs or slaves. All offenses are atoned for by the payment of money, save certain unnatural crimes, which they punish with death. Among the Moros is practiced the ordeal by fire, and the burial of the living for certain crimes; but some escape from these in safety, through their power as sorcerers. The authority and government of the chiefs is described; they are tyrannical and rapacious, and treat as slaves even chiefs who are subject to them. Combés makes special mention of some customs peculiar to the Subanos, or river-people. They are exceedingly rude and barbarous, without any government; and a perpetual petty warfare is waged among them. Their women, however, are more chaste than those of other tribes, and Lutao girls of rank are reared, for their own safety, among the Subanos. Among these people is a class of men who dress and act like women, and practice strict celibacy; one of them is baptized by Combés. A chapter is devoted to their burials and marriages. In the burial of the dead they spend lavishly, clothing the corpse in rich and costly garments; but they have ceased, under Christian influence, to bury the dead man's treasures with him. Marriages are celebrated with the utmost display, hospitality, and feasting; and with entire propriety and decorum. Another chapter describes the boats and weapons used by the natives.

Next we present the famous letter on this subject by Gaspar de San Agustín (June 8, 1720); our text is collated with other versions, and freely annotated from these, and from comments made by Delgado and Mas on San Agustín's statements. San Agustín, who had spent forty years among the Filipinos, begins by expatiating on the great difficulty of comprehending the native character, which is inscrutable—"not in the individuals, but in the race." They are fickle and false, also of a cold temperament, and malicious, dull, and lazy—due to "the influence of the moon." They are ungrateful, lazy, rude and impertinent, arrogant, and generally disagreeable. San Agustín relates many of their peculiar traits, and incidents showing these, to much disparagement of the natives. He berates their ignorance and superstition, their faults of character, their conduct toward the Spaniards, their lack of religious devotion, etc.—exempting, however, from these censures in the main the Pampangos, who are more noble, brave, and honorable, and are "the Castilians of these same Indians;" and the women, who are devout, modest, and moral (although he ascribes this to the subjection in which they are held by the men, and the necessity for the women to support not only their children but their husbands). After all these complaints, San Agustín returns to his former position, that it is impossible to understand the nature of the Filipinos; and all that he has related is but approximate and tentative. For this reason, it is necessary (especially for religious) to know how to conduct oneself with them. He therefore makes various suggestions for enabling their spiritual fathers to guide them discreetly and successfully. No less interesting than his account of the people are the comments made thereon by the Jesuit Delgado (himself long a missionary in the islands), and the Spanish official Mas, who spent some time there and visited many of the islands. The former refutes many of San Agustín's statements, sometimes very sharply; the latter often supports them, but sometimes he finds them in contradiction to what he himself has observed. Fray Gaspar's letter impresses the reader, at first, as being the complaint of an irritable and querulous old man (he wrote it at the age of seventy); but another cause for his mental attitude may be found toward the end of his letter, where he argues against the proposed ordination of Filipino natives as priests—a plan which aroused great opposition from the religious orders. The MS. which we use contains a sort of appendix to San Agustín's letter in the shape of citations from the noted Jesuit writer Murillo Velarde. These are evidently adduced in support of San Agustin's position, and disparage the character of the Indians in vigorous terms. Finally, we present a chapter from Delgado's Historia de Filipinas making further comment on San Agustín's letter, and defending the natives from the latter's aspersions; he refutes many of these, and censures Fray Gaspar severely. He also regards Murillo Velarde's description of the native character as hasty, superficial, and exaggerated. Besides, Delgado reminds his readers of the great services rendered to the Spaniards by the Indians—who alone carry on the agriculture, stock-raising, trade, and navigation on which the support of the Spaniards (who, "when they arrive at Manila, are all gentlemen") absolutely depends—and declares that the Spaniards themselves are arrogant and tyrannical toward the Indians.

Additional information regarding the native peoples is afforded by the Franciscan writer Juan Francisco de San Antonio, in his Crónicas (Manila, 1738–44). He begins with a dissertation on the origin of the Filipino Indians, in examining which he finds many difficulties. He notes several of the mixtures of different races which have produced distinct types; among these he is inclined to class the half-civilized mountain-dwellers in the larger islands—who, as he thinks, spring from either civilized Indians who have retreated to the hill-country, or from the intercourse of native Filipinos with Japanese, Chinese, and other foreigners. The Chinese and Japanese who live in and near Manila, and some Malabar mestizos, are desirable elements of the population. The Negritos are the aboriginal inhabitants; in former times they harassed the Indian natives with frequent raids, and killed all who ventured into the mountain region. In the time of San Antonio, the Indians secretly pay them tribute, in order to avoid their raids. He describes their physical aspect, costume, and mode of life; he conjectures that they came to the Philippines originally from New Guinea. The civilized peoples may all be reduced to the Tagálogs, Pampangos, Visayans, and Mindanaos; all are of Malay stock. Of these, the first probably came from Malacca, as traders, remaining in Luzón as conquerors; the Pampangos, from Sumatra. The Visayans may have come from the Solomon Islands, but this is not certain. In Mindanao, as in Luzón, the black aborigines were driven into the interior by the Malay traders who came there. These latter show much tribal variation, but all must have come from the near-by islands of Borneo, Macasar, or the Moluccas. San Antonio characterizes these Mindanao peoples separately. The coast tribes are partly Mahometan, partly christianized; the missions among them are those of the Recollects and Jesuits. The mountain tribes are apparently the aboriginal natives—also Malayan, according to some, but it may be from Celebes or other islands. All these our author presents as conjectures only; "God is the only one who knows the truth." He proceeds to describe the characteristics and disposition of the Filipino natives, which is full of contradictions. They are hospitable, but neglect their parents; and are deceitful and ungrateful. They are exceedingly clever and imitative, and even show much ability in many occupations and mental exercises; but they are apt to be superficial, incorrect, indifferent to results, slothful and lacking in concentration of mind. "Their understandings are fastened with pins, and attached always to material things." Our writer then describes the languages, mode of writing, manners and names, that are current among these peoples; also their physical features, clothing, and adornments. Curiously enough, San Antonio states that the Visayans have—(in his day) given up the practice of tattooing their bodies. He proceeds to recount the religious beliefs and superstitions of the Filipinos, much as Colin and other early writers have done, but with somewhat more detail in certain matters, especially in regard to the omens and superstitions of the people. Their government and social conditions (especially the former practice of enslavement) are described in detail; also their customs in regard to marriages and dowries, transaction of business, weights and measures, inheritances, etc.

The Editors
June, 1906.

Document of 1691

Source: This document is obtained from the Ventura del Arco MSS. (Ayer library), iv, pp. 53–67.

Translation: This is made by Emma Helen Blair.

Events at Manila, 1690–91

Relation of what occurred in Manila from June 24, 1690 to the present month of June in this year, 1691.

The tragedy which for years has been enacted in this city of Manila has had some variation this year, from the time when the galleon "Santo Cristo de Burgos" set sail for Nueva España up to the present month of July, in which the galleon called "Nuestra Señora del Rosario, San Francisco Javier y Santa Rosa" has been fitted up for the said navigation. By it is [sent] this written relation, which will contain the most notable events which have occurred in Manila, omitting many others, on account of not having secured information of them because they occurred outside of Manila.

I have already written, last year, of the condition in which the affairs of the bishop of Troya remained; to wit, that the necessary decrees were issued by the royal Audiencia that the bishop should restore the [ecclesiastical] government to the cabildo, to whom it belonged, as appears from the acts which the cabildo had presented in the Audiencia—not only by way of appeal from fuerza, but also on behalf of the right of the royal patronage, which resided in that body, since the said Audiencia was exercising the civil government in these islands. These efforts were hindered by the efforts of the auditor Don Alonso, former commander of the troops, and Don Tomas de Endaya, master-of-camp of the army in Manila for which I refer to the account which was given to his Majesty.

This, then, by way of preliminary. When the galleon "Santo Cristo de Burgos" set sail for Nueva España, there was little respite from negotiations of this sort, as we had hoped would be the case until the arrival of the new governor,1 who thought that he would certainly arrive that year. Thus ran the talk of all. But, as the said bishop is so peculiar in his decisions, he made an astonishing resolution; this was, to go in person to the convent of San Agustin, a little after two o'clock in the afternoon, having crossed a great part of the city on foot, accompanied by two clerics (it is evident that they must have been among the most unassuming ones), laden with pistols and other weapons, in order to take away from the said convent the dean, the cantor, and other prebends from the place where they had taken refuge— their safety being, for fear of the bishop, protected by royal decrees.

This performance gave much material for gossip, in which the blame was laid upon the commander of the troops and his favorite Don Tomas, and even on the Augustinian friars themselves, for having all left the city that day in order that thus the bishop could carry out his purpose, without its being easy to secure recourse from the violence which he intended; for the commander of troops had gone to take supper at a country house, the provincial of St. Augustine had betaken himself to a resort on the river, and the prior had left the convent just at two o'clock.

This scheme, if it were one, was not carried out; for the choristers and the vicar of the convent, being informed how the bishop intended to remove thence the persons who were protected by his Majesty and entrusted to their care, made it a point of honor that such an accident should [not] happen, since neither the provincial nor the prior was in the convent; accordingly, by the time the bishop arrived they closed the gates of the convent, not permitting him to enter. Thereupon various colloquies took place between the two parties, making the case more plausible by the detention of the bishop and his satellites at the gate opening into the street. Meanwhile the friars had time to notify the prior and inform the gentlemen of the royal Audiencia.

With the arrival of the prior, entrance into the convent was made easy for his illustrious Lordship, to whom the friars set forth that they could not gratify his wishes without first making the auditors aware of his claims. The bishop agreed to this, but on condition that they notify only Don Alonzo, of whom his illustrious Lordship must have been sure. In short, the fact is that the case first reached the auditors' ears; and they, assembled in session, issued the decrees which, as I mentioned above, they left to the efforts of Señor Fuertes—who in all haste went to the palace, and finding the auditors in the council-chamber, displayed much anger that they should have made such a decision without his presence and counsel.

Since there is no remedy, when a thing has been done, except patience, as the common saying goes, it was now arranged that Señor Fuertes and Señor Ozaeta should go to San Agustín to pacify the bishop, in which task they spent the greater part of the afternoon. The unjust things said by the bishop to Señor Ozaeta, and the uncivil language which he tolerated from the bishop, are not fit to relate. At five o'clock in the afternoon, the bishop went away from San Agustin quite rebuffed but very respectfully treated by the two auditors and their numerous companions. In front of his illustrious Lordship walked his provisor and faithful Achates, Master Don Geronimo Caraballo, bitterly lamenting the miserable condition in which Manila was, since they were hindering their prelate in a resolution so just, since it was to punish those wicked clerics who had taken refuge in San Agustin. It is well to note the pious exclamation of this prebend, for it will be quite important to the case afterward.

This chimerical attempt turned out badly for his illustrious Lordship in the end; and he undertook to be revenged when one was least looking for it. For the news having arrived, on July 30, that one of the two galleons which were expected on the return voyage from Nueva España had reached the Embocadero, and that in it was coming the governor, there was discussion whether his illustrious Lordship was proceeding in the execution of his designs. But it was not thus; for his illustrious Lordship, a few days after this information arrived, posted the auditors as excommunicated, saying that they had incurred this by the bull De cena, forasmuch as they had tried cases which by right belonged to the ecclesiastical jurisdiction, as the law states that these are not separated from that jurisdiction. Notwithstanding the publication of their names, the auditors ignored the censure, as launched a non judice [i.e. "by one who is not a judge"]; but it was not on this account that not only they but the entire city yielded to the pressure of great anxiety. For they feared lest the new governor, whose coming was daily expected, would be tinctured with the same opinions as those held by Don Gabriel, the deceased governor—which were based on the same sort of case as was then occurring. For, they said, since a new governor (who is the only arbiter for all classes in Manila) was at the gates of the city [he might] without searching his own mind, have taken a resolution so unusual that even Don Felipe Pardo had not ventured to execute it against the corporate body of an Audiencia. It is not possible that there should be any secret information. People confirmed it when they learned how Don Tomas de Endaya had sent a despatch to the ship by a person who stood high in his regard, in a very swift champan, so that he could in the name of Don Tomas give his letters and welcome to the governor who was expected, with a valuable present. It was well known that the said champan had been wrecked; but it was also learned that the person who bore that commission had landed, before the wreck of the champan, in one of the provinces there; but it was not known whether the present [that he carried] was landed, and for this reason it was uncertain whether the determinations of the bishop were the results of the assiduity of Don Tomas de Endaya, who was a supporter of the bishop.

The talk went further; for inasmuch as the first news which reached these islands that the ship had arrived at the Embocadero was sent to Don Tomas de Endaya by his brother Don Bernardo—whom, they said, he had made alcalde of Catbalongan, which is the first passage and entrance into these islands—[they said that this was done], first, that he might place in safety the thousands of pesos which he expected would be brought to him by the patache which he had sent to Nueva España, laden with goods belonging to himself and Don Gabriel de Curuzealegui, which was coming on its return voyage; and second, that he might gain the good-will of the new governor with gifts and favors. The latter opinion prevailed, and on this ground people considered the action of the bishop of Troya as not so bold. These alone were the topics discussed, proceeding from the beginnings which they fancied to be facts. But after they experienced some of the actions of the new governor, they regarded as certain that which before they had only considered probable. For, the royal Audiencia having decided that Auditor Don Juan de Sierra should go in their name to welcome the governor, the said auditor went up the river to fulfil his commission, and, having met the piragua in which the governor was coming with his family, the auditor went close to it, to present his message; but neither did the governor open the curtain of the pavilion or stern-cabin of the vessel, nor permit the auditor to speak to him, but obliged him to sheer off from the side of the piragua. At this rebuff, the said auditor was obliged to join the other vessels which accompanied the governor, following the piragua, which was very swift—for from the ranch of Don Tomas de Endaya (where the governor had been entertained as a guest) to Manila is a journey of at least one day, but the piragua made it in much less time. Thus the foresight of Don Tomas gained not only the privilege of entertaining the governor, but the opportunity of becoming his favorite, for which purpose he acted thus.

The governor arrived at Manila about four o'clock in the afternoon; the wind was blowing violently, and the rain fell in torrents, heavier than have been seen for many years in these islands. All these discomforts were overcome by the bold and impetuous disposition of our new governor; but I am not surprised at such haste, since he came for more than to obtain a bishopric. He was lodged in the buildings which the city had made ready for him, where he was awaited by Don Tomas de Endaya, with other citizens of his following, and they retired to his room, which had been prepared for him. He shut himself up there with Don Tomas, and gave orders to the guard that no one should be allowed to enter. At the same time the auditor Don Juan de Sierra arrived to acquit himself of his embassy; he had been thoroughly wet on the river, but the captain of the guard detained him, telling him of the order that he had, not to allow any one to enter. The auditor replied that these orders ought not to apply to an auditor who came in the name of the royal Audiencia. The captain of the guard then carried word to the governor, telling him how Auditor Don Juan de Sierra was there, who had come on behalf of the royal Audiencia to welcome his Lordship. The governor answered that he had come there fatigued, and that he was not ready for visits; and then he continued to walk up and down, hand in hand with Don Tomas, and shut in his room, until the night had well begun. Then the said [Don Tomas] took his leave, returning to his house within Manila, with much contentment, and explained to several confidants how he had firmly established himself, and that they had formed a close alliance; but that it would be more veiled than that which had existed between the said Don Tomas and Don Gabriel—the new governor promising to favor his affairs in every way. Such was the judgment formed at the time, and that opinion is further strengthened every day.

On the following day, early in the forenoon, Don Alonso—who is the person charged with the direction of military affairs—went to visit the new governor, by whom he was very kindly and graciously received. They spent several hours in conversation, alone or in company with the said Don Tomas; and Don Alonso informed him of all the troubles that he and his associates had experienced in regard to matters connected with the bishop of Troya; for this was the principal design which both sides had—the friendly reception of the new governor. The Audiencia did not go to visit the governor until they ascertained whether he would receive them, fearing, on account of the reasons which have been mentioned, that the excommunication which the bishop had made known to them had been imposed through the influence of the governor. But this turned out better than they expected, for he received them with much friendliness; he took a seat below, with them all, trying to treat all with kindness, and gratifying not only Don Tomas and his faction but the Audiencia. Various events and circumstances occurred at the time when he was making arrangements for his entry into the city, which tended to persuade all that no one would govern him, and that his proceedings would be those of an upright judge.

He made, then, his entry, and soon displayed the energy of his nature, and a hasty and vehement disposition. One day, when the soldiers in the guard-room of his palace were talking loudly at a gaming-table, he came down in person, and with his blows broke a cane on the men; with this, he gained among the soldiers the surname of "the good sergeant." He issued numberless proclamations, which no one now observes, because the man's disposition has been recognized. He was very solicitous about the night patrols, not only within but without Manila—obliging those within the walls to go about at night with torches; and ordaining to the people outside that after eight o'clock no one should go out of his house, under penalty of two years in the galleys and two hundred lashes. A Dominican religious who did not know of these new orders, going to hear a confession in his ministry outside the walls of Manila, encountered the patrol within his own village—at which he was surprised, as it was not customary for the patrols to enter the villages outside the walls, on account of the knavish acts which the soldiers are wont to commit under pretext of making the rounds. For this reason the said religious ordered them to depart from the said his ministry, and to patrol in their accustomed beat; but, although they did not obey him, they informed the governor next day of the opposition which the religious had made to the patrol. At this the new governor, being angry without good reason, gave orders that if any minister tried to forbid the patrol, they should notify him three times, and, if he persisted in his opposition, they should seize him by the collar and carry him a prisoner to a fort, until they could report to him on the next day. It is to be noted that these patrols, commanders as well as soldiers, are usually native mulattoes, and mestizos from Nueva España.

At the fiesta of the naval battle, at which the governor was present, he showed extreme resentment, and uttered sharp complaints because he who recited the epistle turned his back on the governor's wife—doubtless thinking that he who recited the gospel had his face turned toward her not because the rubrics require that it be read while facing the people, but in order to show her the attention that was due her; and therefore he criticised him who had recited the epistle. Not less absurd was his assuming that he ought to be named in the prayers at mass, after the king, as is done with the viceroy; and as this was not done at a fiesta at which he was present, he was so vexed that there also he chose to display his resentment. It was with some difficulty that the auditors pacified him at the time, and afterward made him understand how unreasonable he was in the matter.

He prides himself on being very learned, and that he needs no advice from any one, holding it as an established maxim that the religious lie to him in whatever they say or propose in favor of the Indians. From this results the extreme contempt in which the religious now find themselves [held by him], and the grievous oppression which the poor Indians experience; for, from the very month in which this governor entered Manila, the Indians have not ceased their labors [on public works] to this day, without any attention being paid to the times when they ought to attend to their farming, or to the inclemency of the rainy seasons—not even in a sort of pestilence which has prevailed in this [province] of Tagalos among the Indians. Sick as they were, [the officials] obliged them with blows to go to their toil in timber-working, where not a few fell dead from the labor and their illness; and all this, only to build one ship (a very small one), on account of the unnecessary destruction of the galleon "Santo Niño," which Don Juan de Bargas had constructed in his term as governor.

1 Domingo Zabálburu de Echevarri (see Vol. XVII, p. 294).

Bibliographical Data

The documents contained in this volume are obtained from the following sources:

1. Events at Manila, 1690–91.—From the Ventura del Arco MSS. (Ayer library), iv, pp. 53–67.

2. Native races and customs.—From Colin's Labor evangélica, book i, chap. iv, xiii–xvi; from a copy of original edition (1663) in possession of Edward E. Ayer, Chicago.

3. Natives of the southern islands.—From Combes's Historia de Mindanao, Ioló, etc. (Retana and Pastells's reprint), chap. ix–xviii.

4. San Agustín's Letter.—From an early MS. copy in possession of Edward E. Ayer.

5. Native peoples and their customs.—From San Antonio's Crónicas, i, pp. 129–172; from a copy in possession of Edward E. Ayer.

Appendix:
Ethnological Description of the Filipinos

1. Native races and their customs. Francisco Colin, S.J.; Madrid, 1663.
2. The natives of the southern islands. Francisco Combés, S.J.; 1667.
3. Letter on the Filipinos. Gaspar de San Agustín, O.S.A.; 1720.
4. The native peoples and their customs. Juan Francisco de San Antonio, O.S.F.; 1738.

Sources: The material for this appendix is obtained from the following works: Colin's *Labor evangélica* (Madrid, 1663), book i, chap. iv, xiii–xvi; from a copy in the possession of Edward E. Ayer, Chicago. Combés's *Hist. de Mindanao, Ioló*, etc. (Madrid, 1667)—reprinted by Retana and Pastells (Madrid, 1897), chap. ix–xviii; from a copy of the latter in the possession of the Editors. San Agustín's letter, from an early MS. copy in the possession of Edward E. Ayer. San Antonio's *Crónicas* (Manila, 1738), i, pp. 129–172; from a copy in the possession of Edward E. Ayer.

Translations: The above matter is compiled and translated by James Alexander Robertson.

Native Races and their Customs

[This so-called ethnological appendix does not presume to present in exact scientific detail the various races and tribes inhabiting the Philippines; but to give in their own words what the earliest writers especially have themselves observed and experienced concerning some of those races and tribes, in so far as such observations have not hitherto appeared in this series. The accounts contain much of value as showing how the Filipino was gradually transformed in many ways by his contact with his conqueror. For early ethnological information of the Philippines, see Vols. V, VII, XII, XIII, and XVI of this series.]

[Colin in his *Labor evangélica* (Madrid, 1663) devotes pp. 15–19 and 53–75 (comprising chapters iv, and xiii–xvi of book i) to the Filipinos. Those chapters here follow.]

Chapter IV

Of the origin of the nations and peoples who inhabit these islands

25. Although these are islands it will not be necessary to fatigue the mind by discussing (as do San Agustin and other authors in respect to other islands and to America) whence and how people and animals came to them. For if some of these islands have been, at any time since the flood, part of a continent, from that time men and animals could remain in them; while if they have always been islands, the nearness of some of them to others, and of some of them to the mainland of Asia, whence began the propagation of the human race and the settlements of the descendants of Noah, is sufficient reason why some of them could come to settle these regions. And that this was really so, and that the principal settler of these archipelagoes was Tharsis, son of Javan, together with his brothers, as were Ophir and Hevilath of India, we see in the tenth chapter of Genesis, which treats of the dispersion of peoples and the settlement of countries, as we establish in another place.

26. Now then, coming to our theme, when the conquistadors and settlers arrived at these islands and subdued that of Manila, they found three varieties or kinds of people in them. Those who held command of it [i.e., the island of Manila], and inhabited the seashore and river-banks and all the best parts round about, were Moro Malays of Borney (according to their own report). That is an island also, and is larger than any of these Filipinas and nearer the mainland of Malaca, where there is a district called Malayo.1 This place is the origin of all the Malays who are scattered throughout the most and best of all these archipelagoes. From that nation of the Malays springs that of the Tagálogs, who are the natives of Manila and its neighborhood. That is proved by the Tagálog language, which resembles the Malay closely; by the color and lines of the whole body; by the clothing and habit that they wore at the arrival of the Spaniards here; and lastly by the customs and ceremonies, all of which were derived from the Malays and other nations of India. The occasion of their coming to these parts might have been either that they were driven by chance through these seas (as we have seen in our days, borne to these islands people from other unknown islands, who spoke a language that no one understood, and who had been driven by the sea); or they could have come hither purposely in the search for new lands on which to settle, because their own were too crowded, or some disaster had overtaken them which caused them to leave their home forever. But it is very likely that greed and commercial interests attracted them, as occurred in the parts of India with regard to the Moros, Persians, and Arabs. The Portuguese say in their histories that when they reached those kingdoms they found the Moros uppermost and masters of all, by

reason of the commerce which they introduced among the heathen kings and rulers, the natives of the country, whose goodwill the Moros contrived to secure with rich and valuable presents. Little by little they continued to remain in the land and pay the royal duties, until they became so powerful that they revolted against the real rulers and deprived them of the best of their lands. Barros2 says that the first Portuguese found that that had happened in those districts of India some hundred and fifty years before their arrival. In the same way one may imagine the passage of the Malays to Borney to have occurred, and of the Borneans to Manila; and that along with the arms and temporal commerce would come some caciques,3 or priests of the cursed Mahometan religion, who introduced that religion into the villages and maritime nations of these parts. As for me I can readily believe that that great island of Borney in past centuries was continued on the northeast by Paragua, and on the south4 by the lands near Mindanao, as is indicated by the shoals and islets of Paragua on the one side, and those called Santa Juana and other islets and shoals which extend toward Jolo and Taguima, opposite the point of La Caldera on the Mindanao shore. If this assumption be true, as is affirmed by aged Indians of those parts, the opportunity for the Borneans to scatter through the Filipinas is very evident.

27. It is probable that the inhabitants would come to Borney immediately from Samatra, which is a very large land quite near the mainland of Malaca and Malayo. In the midst of that great island of Samatra there is a large and extensive lake5 whose marge is settled by many different nations, whence, according to tradition, the people went to settle various islands. A Pampango of sense (one of these nations) finding himself adrift and astray there through various accidents (and from whom I learned it), testified that those people [of Sumatra] spoke excellent Pampango, and wore the oldtime dress of the Pampangos. When he questioned one of their old men, the latter answered: "You [Pampangos] are descendants of the lost people who left here in past times to settle in other lands, and were never heard of again." It can also be believed that the Tagálogs, Pampangos, and other civilized nations, analogous in language, color, clothing, and customs, came from parts of Borney and Samatra, some from certain provinces or neighborhoods and some from others. That is the reason for the difference of the languages, according to the custom of these uncivilized lands, for every province or neighborhood has a different language.

28. The nations of the Bisayas and Pintados, who inhabit the provinces of Camarines in this island of Luzon, and those of Leyte, Samar, Panay, and other neighborhoods, came, I have heard, from the districts of Macasar, where it is said that Indians live who make designs on and tattoo the body, in the manner of our Pintados. Pedro Fernandez de Quiros, in the relation

which he wrote of the discovery of the Salomon Islands in 1595, says that an island called Madalena was found in ten degrees north latitude, at a distance from Pirù of one thousand eight hundred leguas (which is nearly the same latitude and distance as the Filipinas) where Indians of good proportion, but taller than the Spaniards, and all naked and bearing designs on their bodies, legs, arms, and hands (and some on their faces), in the manner of our Visayans, were found. Consequently, it is apparent that there are other nations of Pintados to be discovered. We have as yet not enough data, nor even a well founded conjecture, to say whether ours originated from the latter, or on the contrary both from some mainland. We know well that people who tattoo the body have been seen in Brasil and Florida. Then, too, this custom was formerly seen in some nations of Scythians in Asia and of Britons in Europa. But we cannot yet determine the legitimate origin of our Visayan Pintados. If some of the natives of Mindanao, Jolo, Bool, and part of Cebu, who are lighter-complexioned, braver, and of better proportions than the pure Visayans, are not Borneans, they might be Ternatans—as may be inferred from the neighborhood of the lands and the communication of one with another; and because in what concerns the worship and religion of the cursed Prophet, even today they are governed by Terrenate; and when they find themselves beset by the troops from Filipinas, they make an alliance and help one another.

29. All those whom the first Spaniards found in these islands with the command and lordship over the land are reduced to the first class, the civilized peoples. Another kind, totally opposed to the above, are the Negrillos, who live in the mountains and thick forests which abound in these islands. The latter are a barbarous race who live on the fruits and roots of the forests. They go naked, covering only the privies with some articles called bahaques, made from the bark of trees. They wear no other ornaments than armlets and anklets and bracelets, curiously wrought after their manner from small rattans of various colors, and garlands of branches and flowers on their heads and the fleshy parts of the arm; and at the most some cock or sparrow-hawk feather for a plume. They have no laws or letters, or other government or community than that of kinsfolk, all those of one line of family obeying their leader. In regard to religion and divine worship they have but little or none. The Spaniards call them Negrillos because many of them are as much negroes, as are the Ethiopians themselves, both in their black color and in their kinky hair. There are still a number of those people in the interior in the mountains. In one of the large islands there are so many of them, that it is for that reason called the island of Negros. Those blacks were apparently the first inhabitants of these islands, and they have been deprived of them by the civilized nations who came later by way of

Samatra, the Javas, Borney, Macaçar, and other islands lying toward the west. If one should ask whence could come the Negros to these islands so distant from Africa and Ethiopias, where negroes live, I answer that it was from nearer India, or citra Gangem, which was formerly settled by Ethiopic negroes and was called Etiopia.6 From there, it is more probable, went out the settlers of African Etiopia, as we prove in another place. Moreover, even today does India have nations of the negro race. Also they could easily pass from the districts of the mainland of India to the nearest islands, and could come from one to the other even as far as these Filipinas. In Nueva Guinea, which is quite near Terrenate, the natives are negroes like those of Guinea, and on that account the first explorers gave them that name; and they could also pass from those to these districts.

30. There is another kind of people, neither so civilized as the first, nor so barbarous as the second. They generally live about the sources of the rivers, and on that account are called in some districts, Ilayas. They are the Tingues, and are called Manguianes,7 Zambals, or other names, for each island has a different name for them. They generally trade with the Tagálogs, Visayans, and other civilized nations who are commonly settled near the sea and river mouths. Although those Ilayas or Tingues are not Christians, they pay some sort of recognition or tribute, and have their system of policy or government. It is thought that they are a mixture of the other barbarous and civilized nations, and for that reason they are midway between the other two classes of peoples in color, clothing, and customs.

We do not pretend to deny by the above that some people could have come from other parts and kingdoms of India extra Gangem (such as Sian, Camboja, Cochinchina), and from China itself, and even Japon, to conquer and settle in parts of these islands—especially the Chinese, from whose histories, and their remains found in various parts, it is learned that in former times they were masters of all these archipelagoes.8 If they were the first settlers of the Javas (as is told by Juan de Barros) they could still more easily have settled in some parts of these islands which are nearer to them.

Persons who know the provinces of Ilocos and Cagayan, in the north of this island of Luzon, assert that they have discovered there the graves of people larger than the Indians, and the arms and jewels of Chinese or Japanese, who, it is presumed, conquered and settled in those parts, led on by the desire for gold.9

Chapter XIII

Of the nature, languages, and letters of the Filipinos

In accordance with the origin which we ascribed to the civilized nations of these islands in chapter four, so also are their capacity, languages, and letters. They are descendants of the Malays of the mainland of Malaca, whom they also resemble in their capacity, languages, and letters.

92. From the shape, number, and use of the characters and letters of this nation it is quite evident that they are all taken from the Moro Malays and originated from the Arabs. The vowel letters are only three in number, but they serve for five in their use; for the second and third are indifferently e, i, y, o, and u, according as is required by the meaning or sense of the word which is spoken or written.

The consonants are thirteen in number, and serve (except at the beginning of the phrase or initial letter) as consonant and vowel; for the letter alone, without a dot above or below, is pronounced with "A."

If a dot be placed above, the consonant is pronounced with "e" or "i."

If the dot be placed below, it is pronounced with "o" or "u." Thus the "B" with the dot above is pronounced "bi" or "be," and with the dot below, "bo" or "bu."

For example, in order to say "cama" [*i.e.*, bed] the two letters "C" and "M" are sufficient without a dot.

If a dot be placed above the "C", it will be "quema" [*i.e.*, "fire"].

If dots be placed below each, it will be "como" [*i.e.*, "as"].

The final consonants are supplied in all expressions. Thus in order to say "cantar" [*i.e.*, "to sing"], one writes "cata," only a "C" and a "T." To say "barba" [*i.e.*, "beard"], two "B's" are sufficient.

With all the supplements, he who reads in that language will, if he be skilful, have no trouble in pronouncing the words or phrases correctly by substituting the letters that must be substituted according to the sense. But since that always occasions difficulty, those who know our characters are studying how to write their own language in these. All of them have now adopted our way of writing, with the lines from left to right; for formerly they only wrote vertically down and up, placing the first line to the left and running the others continuously to the right, just opposite to the Chinese and Japanese, who although they write in vertical up and down lines, continue the page from the right to the left. All that points to a great antiquity; for running the line from the right to the left is in accordance with the present and general style of the Hebrews; and the style of running the lines vertically from the top to the bottom, is that of the oldest nation of the Chinese—which doubtless greatly resembles the method of the Hebrews, whose characters have much resemblance to theirs. Those of the Moro Arabs resemble those of the Syrians. Diodorus Siculus,10 who wrote in the time of the emperor

Cæsar Augustus, in making mention of an island which lay in our middle region, or torrid zone (whither Iamblicus11 the Greek went in the course of his adventures), says that they do not write horizontally as we do, but from top to bottom in a straight line; and that they use characters which, although few in number, make up in their use for many, for each one has four different transformations. Consequently, one may see that that method of writing, and the characters of those nations, are very old.12

93. Before they knew anything about paper (and even yet they do in places where they cannot get it), those people wrote on bamboos or on palm-leaves, using as a pen the point of a knife or other bit of iron, with which they engraved the letters on the smooth side of the bamboo. If they write on palm-leaves they fold and then seal the letter when written, in our manner. They all cling fondly to their own method of writing and reading. There is scarcely a man, and still less a woman, who does not know and practice that method, even those who are already Christians in matters of devotion. For from the sermons which they hear, and the histories and lives of the saints, and the prayers and poems on divine matters, composed by themselves (they have also some perfect poets in their manner, who translate elegantly into their language any Spanish comedy), they use small books and prayerbooks in their language, and manuscripts which are in great number; as is affirmed in his manuscript history by Father Pedro Chirino,13 to whom the provisor and vicar-general of this archbishopric entrusted the visit and examination of those books in the year one thousand six hundred and nine, for the purpose of preventing errors. That was a holy proceeding, and one that was very proper among so new Christians.

The Filipinos easily accustom themselves to the Spanish letters and method of writing. They are greatly benefited thereby, for many of them write now just like us, because of their cleverness and quickness in imitating any letter or design, and in the doing of anything with the hands. There are some of them who commonly serve as clerks in the public accountancies and secretaryships of the kingdom. We have known some so capable that they have deserved to become officials in those posts, and perhaps to supply those offices *ad interim*. They also are a great help to students in making clean copies of their rough drafts, not only in Romance but also in Latin, for there are already some of them who have learned that language. Finally, they are the printers in the two printing-houses in this city of Manila; and they are entirely competent in that work, in which their skill and ability are very evident.

94. Coming now to the other point, that of their languages, there are many of these. For in this island of Manila alone there are six of them, which correspond to the number of the provinces or civilized nations;

the Tagálog, Pampanga, Camarines (or Visayan), Cagayan, and those of the Ilocans and Pangasinans. These are the civilized nations. We do not yet know the number of the nations of the Negrillos, Zambals, and other mountain nations. Although the civilized languages are, strictly speaking, dissimilar, they resemble one another, so that in a short time those people can understand one another, and those of the one nation can converse with those of another—in the same way as the Tuscan, Lombard, and Sicilian in Italia; and the Castilian, Portuguese, and language of Valencia in España. The reason why these languages resemble one another so closely is the same as in Italia and España. For as the latter languages originated from the Roman, just so do these originate from the Malay. For proof of that it is necessary to do nothing else than to compare the words and idioms, or the modes of speech, of each one of these languages with the Malay, as will be seen in the following table, in which is made the comparison of the three most important languages, the Tagálog, Visayan, and Pampanga. Since for the sake of brevity the comparison is made in a few words, whoever is interested can with but slight labor extend the comparison through many words.

Spanish	Malay	Tagálog	Pampanga	Visayan
cielo [i. e., sky]	langriet	lañgit	banoa	laguit
sol [i. e., sun]	mata ari	arao	aldao	arlao
luna [i. e., moon]	bulam	Bouan	bulan	bulan

Of these languages the two most general are the Tagálog, which is used through the greater part of the coast and interior of the island of Manila, and the islands of Lubang and Mindoro; and the Visayan, which is spoken throughout all the islands of the Pintados. Of the two without doubt the most courteous, grave, artistic, and elegant is the Tagálog, for it shares in four qualities of the four greatest languages in the world, namely, Hebrew, Greek, Latin, and Spanish: With the Hebrew, besides the resemblance already noted in the manner of its vowels and consonants, it has the roots of the vocables and their hidden and obscure meaning [sus preñezes, y misterios] and some gutturals; with the Greek, the articles in the declension of nouns, and in the conjugations the abundance of voices and moods; with the Latin, the abundance and elegance; with the Spanish, the fine structure, polish, and courtesy. As a proof of this, Father Pedro Chirino has inserted in his printed relation of these islands an example in the prayer of the Ave Maria,14 as a short and clear instance, with his explanation, with notes in the following manner. It should be noted that the father, belonging to a past age, wrote it in the old style, which has changed here somewhat since then, although not substantially.

The Ave Maria in the Tagálog language

Abe	Guingoong	Maria	matoua	ca	na
Ave	Señora	Maria	alegra	tu	ya
Hail	Lady	Mary	be joyful	thou	now
Napopono	ca	nang	gracia		
Llena	tu	de	gracia		
Full	thou	of	grace		

Ang	Pañginoong	Dios	na	saiyo		
El	Señor	Dios	està	contigo		
The	Lord	God	is	with thee		
Bucor	cang	pinagpala	sa	babaying	lahat	
Singular	tu	bendita	entre	mugeres	todas	
especially,	thou	blessed	among	women	all	

Pinagpala	naman	ang	yyong	Anac	si Jesus
Bendito	tambien	el	tu	Hijo	Jesus
blessed	also	he	thy	Son	Jesus
Santa	Mariang	Yna	nang	Dios	
Santa	Maria	Madre	de	Dios	
Holy	Mary,	Mother	of	God,	

Ypanalangin	mo	caming	macasalanan	ng̃ayon
Seamos intercedidos	de ti	nosotros	pecadores	agora
May we be interceded for	by thee	we	sinners	now

At cum	mamatay	cami,	Amen Jesus.
Y cuando	muramos	nosotros.	[Amen Jesus].
And when	shall die	we.	Amen Jesus.15

The first word, "Aba" is a mysterious one in the Tagálog, and has the force of a salutation, as has "Ave" in Latin; and the same is true of "Bucor" which means "diversity," "distinction," and "singularity." The article is [seen in] "si Jesus." Its abundance lies in the fact that it has many synonyms and turns of thought. Consequently, the above prayer, over and above being elegant, could also be expressed in several other ways just as elegant, and the same sense and meaning would be kept. Its polish and courtesy consists in not saying "Ave Maria" as does the Latin—for that would be a lack of courtesy and a barbarism in the Tagálog—but by the interposition of that polite word "Guinoo." The Visayan [version] does not contain that word, as being a less polished language. However, I am not trying to cast a slur on the latter for that reason, for each language has a beauty and elegance for its natives which does not strike the foreigner.

95. Among the uncivilized nations, although the people are fewer, the languages are more; for almost every river has its own language. In Mindoro (and the same will be true of other districts more remote) we saw the barbarous Manguianes assembling from places but little distant from each other, who did not understand one another. They were so barbarous that they had never seen a Spanish face. The things sent them to attract them were hawk's-bells, nails, needles, and other similar things. They thought that the sounds of the harp and guitar were human voices. When a mirror was held up before them, they exhibited singular effects, in one of fear and in another of joy. The lack of civilization and communication is the reason for the multiplicity of languages. For just as in the primitive multiplication of languages which took place in the tower of Babel, the doctors observe that the languages equaled the number of the families of the descendants of Noah, so among the barbarous nations each one lives to itself alone without any recognition of or subjection to public laws. They are always having petty wars and dissensions among themselves; and, since they lack communication, they forget the common language, and each one has so corrupted its own language that it cannot understand the others. We observed in some districts that one language was spoken at the mouth of a river and another one at its source. That is a great hindrance to the conversion and instruction of those peoples.

96. The polish and courtesy, especially of the Tagálogs and those near them, in speech and writing are the same as those of very civilized nations. They never say "tu" [i.e., "thou"] or speak in the second person, singular or plural, but always in the third person: [thus], "The chief would like this or that." Especially a woman when addressing a man, even though they be equal and of the middle class, never say less than "Sir" or "Master," and that after every word: "When I was coming, sir, up the river, I saw, sir, etc." In writing they make constant use of very fine and delicate expressions of regard, and beauties and courtesy. Their manner of salutation when they met one another was the removal of the potong, which is a cloth like a crown, worn as we wear the hat. When an inferior addressed one of higher rank, the courtesy used by him was to incline his body low, and then lift one or both hands to the face, touch the cheeks with it, and at the same time

raise one of the feet in the air by doubling the knee, and then seating oneself. The method of doing it was to fix the sole of the feet firmly, and double both knees, without touching the ground, keeping the body upright and the face raised. They bent in this manner with the head uncovered and the potong thrown over the left shoulder like a towel; they had to wait until they were questioned, for it would be bad breeding to say anything until a question was asked.

97. The method of giving names was the following. As soon as a child was born, it was the mother's business to name it. Generally the occasion or motive of the name was taken from some one of the circumstances which occurred at the time. For example, Maliuag, which means "difficult," because of the difficulty of the birth; Malacas, which signifies "strong," for it is thought that the infant will be strong. This is like the custom of the Hebrews, as appears from Holy Writ. At other times the name was given without any hidden meaning, from the first thing that struck the fancy, as Daan, which signifies "road," and Damo, signifying "grass." They were called by those names, without the use of any surname, until they were married. Then the first son or daughter gave the surname to the parents, as Amani Maliuag, Ynani Malacas, "the father of Maliuag," "the mother of Malacas." The names of women are differentiated from those of men by adding the syllable "in," as Ilog, "river;" Si Ilog, the name of a male; Si Iloguin, the name of a female. They used very tender diminutives for the children, in our manner. Among themselves they had certain domestic and delicate appellations of various sorts for the different degrees of relationship—as that of a child for his father and mother, and vice versa. In the same way [they have appellations] for their ancestors, descendants, and collaterals. This shows the abundance, elegance, and courtesy of this language. It is a general thing in all these nations not to have special family names which are perpetuated to their successors, but each individual has the simple name that is given him at birth. At present this name serves as surname, and the peculiar name is the Christian name of Juan or Pedro which is imposed at baptism. However, there are now mothers so Christian and civilized that they will not assign any secular name to their children until the Christian name has been given in baptism,16 and then the surname is added, although it has already been chosen after consultation with the parents and relatives. In place of our "Don" (which indeed has been assigned to them with as much abuse as among ourselves), in some districts they formerly placed before their names, Lacan or Gat: as the Moluccans use Cachil, the Africans Muley, the Turks Sultan, etc. The "Don" of the women is not Lacan or Gat, but Dayang, Dayang Mati, Dayang Sanguy, i.e., "Doña Mati," "Doña Sanguy."

There is general distaste among our Tagálogs to mention one another among themselves by their own names alone, without adding something which smells of courtesy. When they are asked by the Spaniards "Who is So-and-so?" and they cannot avoid naming him by his own name, they do it with a certain shamefacedness and embarrassment. Inasmuch as the method of naming one is "the father of So-and-so," as soon as he has children, for him who had no children (among persons of influence) his relatives and acquaintances assembled at a banquet, and gave him a new name there, which they designated as Pamagat. That was usually a name of excellence by some circumlocution or metaphor, based on their own old name. Thus if one was called by his own name, Bacal, which signifies "iron," the new name given him would be Dimatanassan, signifying "not to spoil with time." If it were Bayani, which signifies "valiant" and "spirited," he was called Dimalapitan "he to whom no one is bold." It is also the custom among these nations to call one another among themselves, by way of friendship, by certain correlative names based on some special circumstance. Thus if one had given a branch of sweet basil to another, the two among themselves called each other Casolasi, the name of the thing given; or Caytlog, he who ate of an egg with another. This is in the manner of the names of fellow-students or chums as used by us. These are all arguments in favor of the civilization of these Indians.

Chapter XIV

Of the appearance, features, clothing, and other ancient customs
of the natives of these islands

98. The ordinary stature of these Indians is medium, but they are well built and good-looking, both men and women. Their complexion is yellowish brown, like a boiled quince, and the beard is slight. The Tagálogs wear the hair hanging to the shoulders; the Cagayans longer and hanging over the shoulders; the Ilocans shorter, and the Visayans still shorter, for they cut it round in the manner of the oldtime cues of España. The nation called Zambals wear it shaved from the front half of the head, while on the skull they have a great shock of loose hair. The complexion of the women in all the islands differs little from that of the men, except among the Visayans where some of the women are light-complexioned. All of the women wear the hair tied up in a knot on top of the head with a tasteful ribbon. Both men and women, universally, consider it essential that the hair should be very black and well cared for. For that purpose they use lotions made of certain tree-barks and oils, prepared with musk and other perfumes. Their greatest anxiety and care was the mouth, and from infancy they polished and filed the teeth so that they might be even and pretty. They covered them with a coating of black ink or varnish which aided in preserving them. Among

the influential people, especially the women, it was the custom to set some of the teeth most skilfully with gold which could not fall out, and gave a beautiful appearance. The men did not glory in their mustaches or beards, but quite the contrary; and consequently they pulled them out on purpose. And just as it is an amusement or custom of some of us to gnaw our finger-nails, they get amusement in pulling out the hairs of the beard with certain little bits of cleft bamboo [cañuelas hendidas] or with little shells in the form of pincers. All the women, and in some places the men, adorn the ears with large rings or circlets of gold, for that purpose piercing them at an early age. Among the women the more the ears were stretched and opened, so much greater was the beauty. Some had two holes in each ear for two kinds of earrings, some being larger than others.

99. The men adorned the head with only cendal17 or long and narrow thin cloth, with which they bound the forehead and temples, and which they call potong. It was put on in different modes, now in the Moorish manner like a turban without a bonnet, and now twisted and wrapped about the head like the crown of a hat. Those who were esteemed as valiant let the elaborately worked ends of the cloth fall down upon their shoulders, and these were so long that they reached the legs. By the color of the cloth they displayed their rank, and it was the badge of their deeds and exploits; and it was not allowed to anyone to use the red potong until he had at least killed one person. In order to wear it embroidered with certain borders, which were like a crown, they must have killed seven. The personal clothing of those men was a small garment or short loose jacket [chamarreta] of fine linen which barely reached the waist. It had no collar and was fitted formerly with short sleeves. Among the chiefs those jackets were of a scarlet color, and were made of fine Indian muslin. For breeches they wore a richly colored cloth, which was generally edged with gold, about the waist and brought up between the legs, so that the legs were decently covered to the middle of the thigh; from there down feet and legs were bare. The chief adornments consisted of ornaments and jewels of gold and precious stones. They had various kinds of necklaces, and chains; bracelets or wristlets, also of gold and ivory, on the arms as high as the elbow; while some had strings of cornelians, agates, and other stones which are highly esteemed among them. On the legs, instead of garters, they wear some strings of the same stones, and certain cords of many strands, dyed black. The fingers of the hand are covered with many rings of gold and precious stones. The final complement of the gala attire was like our sash, a fine bit of colored cloth crossed over the shoulder, the ends joined under the arm, which they affected greatly. Instead of that the Visayans wore a robe [marlota] or jacket [baquero] made without a collar and reaching quite down to the feet, and

embroidered in colors. The entire dress, in fine, was in the Moorish style, and was truly rich and gay; and even today they affect it.

The dress of the women, besides the small shirt with sleeves already mentioned, which was shorter for them, for their gala dress had little modesty, was a skirt as wide at top as at bottom, which they gathered into folds at the waist, allowing the folds all to drop to one side. This was long enough to cover them even to their feet, and was generally white. When they went outside the house they wore for a cloak certain colored short cloaks, those of the principal women being of crimson silk or other cloths, embroidered with gold and adorned with rich fringe. But their principal gala attire consisted in jewels and ornaments of gold and stones which they wore in their ears, and on the neck, the fingers of the hand and the wrists of the arms. But now they have begun to wear the Spanish clothes and ornaments, namely, chains, necklaces, skirts, shoes, and mantillas, or black veils. The men wear hats, short jackets [ropillas], breeches, and shoes. Consequently, the present dress of the Indians in these regions is now almost Spanish.

110 [i.e., 100]. Besides the exterior clothing and dress, some of these nations wore another inside dress, which could not be removed after it was once put on. These are the tattooings of the body so greatly practiced among the Visayans, whom we call Pintados for that reason. For it was a custom among them, and was a mark of nobility and bravery, to tattoo the whole body from top to toe when they were of an age and strength sufficient to endure the tortures of the tattooing, which was done (after being carefully designed by the artists, and in accordance with the proportion of the parts of the body and the sex) with instruments like brushes or small twigs, with very fine points of bamboo. The body was pricked and marked with them until blood was drawn. Upon that a black powder or soot made from pitch, which never faded, was put on. The whole body was not tattooed at one time, but it was done gradually. In olden times no tattooing was begun until some brave deed had been performed; and after that, for each one of the parts of the body which was tattooed some new deed had to be performed. The men tattooed even their chins and about the eyes so that they appeared to be masked. Children were not tattooed, and the women only on one hand and part of the other. The Ilocans in this island of Manila also tattooed themselves but not to the same extent as the Visayans. The dress of both men and women among the Ilocans is almost alike in that province. Thus far the dress. We shall now say somewhat of the food and their customs in eating.

101. Their usual sustenance is as stated above, rice, well hulled and cleaned, and boiled only with water, which is called morisqueta by the Spaniards, as if to call it "food of the Moors." The meat is that of a small

fish which is lacking in no part. That is also boiled in water, and with the broth from it, they give a flavor to the morisqueta. For lack of rice and fish they use the herbs and many kinds of native potatoes, and fruits, by which they are sustained well enough. At their banquets they add venison, pork, or beef, which they like best when it has begun to spoil, and to smell bad. Their manner of eating is, to be seated on the ground. Their tables are small and low, round or square, and they have no tablecloths or napkins; but the plates with the food are placed on the same tables. They eat in companies of four which is as many as can get around a small table. On the occasion of a wedding or a funeral, or similar feasts, the whole house will be filled with tables and guests. The food is placed all together on various plates. The people do not shun all reaching out to the same plate, or drinking from the same cup. They relish salt, and salty and acid foods. They have no better dainty for the sick than vinegar and green or pickled fruits. They eat sparingly but drink often; and when they are invited to a banquet, they are asked not to eat but to drink. They waste much time in both eating and drinking. When they have enough and are drunk, the tables are taken away and the house is cleared. If the banquet is the occasion of a feast, they sing, play, and dance. They spend a day and a night in this, amid great racket and cries, until they fall with weariness and sleep. But rarely do they become furious or even foolish; on the contrary, after they have taken wine they preserve due respect and discreet behavior. They only wax more cheerful, and converse better and say some witty things; and it is well known that no one of them when he leaves a banquet, although it be at any hour of the night, fails to go straight to his own house. And if he has occasion to buy or sell, and to examine and weigh gold or silver he does it with so great steadiness that the hand does not tremble, nor does he make any error in the weight.

102. The wine commonly used among them is either that made from palms, as it is throughout India, or from sugar-cane, which they call quilang. The latter is made by extracting the sap from the canes, and then bringing it to a boil over the fire, so that it becomes like red wine, although it does not taste so good. The palm wine is made by extracting the sap or liquor from which the fruit was to be formed. For as soon as the palm begins to send out the shoot from the end of the twig, and before the flower is unfolded, that flower-stock is cut, and a bit of bamboo is fastened to it and is tied to the stalk or shoot. Since the sap naturally flows to that part, as in the pruned vine, all the sap that was to be converted into fruit, flows into that bamboo, and passes through it to vessels, where, somewhat sour and steeped with the bark of certain trees which give it color, heat, and bite, they use it as a common drink and call it tuba. But the real and proper palm-wine is made

from the same liquor before it turns sour, by distilling it in an alembic in ovens that they have prepared for it. They give it a greater or less strength, as they please; and they get a brandy as clear as water, although it is not so hot [as our brandy].18 It is of a dry quality, and, when used with moderation, it is considered even outside Filipinas as healthful and medicinal for the stomach and a preventive of watery humors and colds.

The Visayans also make a wine, called pañgasi, from rice. The method of making it is to place in the bottom of a jar of ordinary size (which is generally of two or three arrobas, with them) a quantity of yeast made from rice flour and a certain plant. Atop of that they put clean rice until the jar is half full. Then water is added to it, and, after it has stood for a few days, it is fermented by the force of the yeast, and is converted into the strongest kind of wine, which is not liquid, but thick like gachas.19 In order to drink it they pour water into the jar. It is a cause for surprise that even though water be poured in again and again, the liquor is pure and liquid wine, until the strength vanishes and is lost, and then they leave it for the children. The method of drinking it is with a tube, which they insert clear to the bottom where the yeast is. They use three or four of those tubes, according to the number of the persons who can find room around the vessel. They suck up as much as they wish, and then give place to others.

103. The banquets are interspersed with singing, in which one or two sing and the others respond. The songs20 are usually their old songs and fables, as is usual with other nations. The dances of men and women are generally performed to the sound of bells which are made in their style like basins, large or small, of metal, and the sounds are brought out quickly and uninterruptedly. For the dance is warlike and passionate, but it has steps and measured changes, and interposed are some elevations that really enrapture and surprise. They generally hold in the hands a towel, or a spear and shield, and with one and the other they make their gestures in time, which are full of meaning. At other times with the hands empty they make movements which correspond to the movements of the feet, now slow, now rapid. Now they attack and retire; now they incite; now they pacify; now they come close; now they go away: all the grace and elegance, so much, in fact, that at times they have not been judged unworthy to accompany and solemnize our Christian feasts.21 However, the children and youths now dance, play, and sing in our manner and so well that we cannot do it better.

They had a kind of guitar which was called coryapi, which had two or more copper strings. Although its music is not very artistic or fine, it does not fail to be agreeable, especially to them. They play it with a quill, with great liveliness and skill. It is a fact that, by playing it alone, they carry on a conversation and make understood whatever they wish to say.

104. All of these islanders are extremely fond of the water for bathing purposes, and as a consequence they try to settle on the shores of rivers or creeks, for the more they are in the water the better they like it. They bathe at all times, for pleasure and cleanliness. When an infant is born, it is put into the river and bathed in cold water; and the mother, after having given birth, does not keep away from the water. The manner of bathing is, to stand with the body contracted and almost seated, with the water up to the throat. The most usual and general hour is at sunset, when the people leave work or return from the field, and bathe for rest and coolness. Men and women all swim like fish, and as if born and reared in the water. Each house has a vessel of water at the door. Whenever any one goes up to the house, whether an inmate of it or not, he takes water from that vessel to wash his feet, especially when it is muddy. That is done very easily; one foot is dried with the other, and the water falls down below, for the floor there is like a close grating.

Chapter XV

*Of the false heathen religion, idolatries, superstitions, and other
things, of the Filipinos*

105. It is not found that these nations had anything written about their religion or about their government, or of their old-time history. All that we have been able to learn has been handed down from father to son in tradition, and is preserved in their customs; and in some songs that they retain in their memory and repeat when they go on the sea, sung to the time of their rowing, and in their merrymakings, feasts, and funerals, and even in their work, when many of them work together. In those songs are recounted the fabulous genealogies and vain deeds of their gods. Among their gods is one who is the chief and superior to all the others, whom the Tagálogs call Bathala Meycapal,22 which signifies "God" the "Creator" or "Maker." The Visayans call him Laon, which denotes "antiquity."

They adored (as did the Egyptians) animals and birds; and the sun and moon, as did the Assyrians. They also attributed to the rainbow its kind of divinity. The Tagálogs worshiped a blue bird as large as a turtle-dove, which they called tigmamanuquin, to which they attributed the name of Bathala, which, as above stated, was among them a name for divinity. They worshiped the crow, as the ancients did the god Pan or the goddess Ceres, and called it Meylupa, signifying "master of the earth." They held the crocodile in the greatest veneration, and when they saw it in the water cried out, in all subjection, "Nono," signifying "Grandfather." They asked it pleasantly and tenderly not to harm them, and for that purpose offered it a portion of what they carried in their boat, by throwing it into the water.

There was no old tree to which they did not attribute divine honors, and it was a sacrilege to think of cutting it under any consideration. Even the very rocks, crags, reefs, and points along the seashore and rivers were adored, and an offering made to them on passing, by stopping there and placing the offering upon the rock or reef. The river of Manila had a rock that served as an idol of that wretched people for many years, and its scandal lasted and it gave rise to many evils, until the fathers of St. Augustine, who were near there, broke it, through their holy zeal, into small bits and set up a cross in its place. Today there is an image of St. Nicholas of Tolentino in that place, in a small shrine or chapel. When sailing to the island of Panay, one saw on the point called Nasso, near Potol, a rock upon which were dishes and other pieces of crockery-ware, which were offered to it by those who went on the sea. In the island of Mindanao, between La Caldera and the river, there is a great point of land, on a rough and very high coast. The sea is forever dashing against these headlands, and it is difficult and dangerous to double them. When the people passed by that one, as it was so high, they offered it arrows, which they shot at the cliff itself with so great force that they stuck there, offering them as if in sacrifice so that it would allow them to pass. There were so many of those arrows that, although the Spaniards set fire to them and burned a countless number of them in hatred of so cursed a superstition, many remained there, and the number increased in less than one year to more than four thousand.

106. They also adored private idols, which each one inherited from his ancestors. The Visayans called them divata, and the Tagálogs anito. Of those idols some had jurisdiction over the mountains and open country, and permission was asked from them to go thither. Others had jurisdiction over the sowed fields, and the fields were commended to them so that they might prove fruitful; and besides the sacrifices they placed articles of food in the fields for the anitos to eat, in order to place them under greater obligations. There was an anito of the sea, to whom they commended their fisheries and navigations; an anito of the house, whose favor they implored whenever an infant was born, and when it was suckled and the breast offered to it. They placed their ancestors, the invocation of whom was the first thing in all their work and dangers, among these anitos. In memory of their ancestors they kept certain very small and very badly made idols of stone, wood, gold, or ivory, called licha or laravan. Among their gods they reckoned also all those who perished by the sword, or who were devoured by crocodiles, as well as those killed by lightning. They thought that the souls of such immediately ascended to the blest abode by means of the rainbow, called by them balañgao. Generally, whoever could succeed in it attributed divinity to his aged father at his death. The aged themselves

died in that presumptuous delusion, and during their sickness and at their death guided all their actions with what they imagined a divine gravity and manner. Consequently, they chose as the place for their grave some assigned spot,23 like one old man who lived on the seacoast between Dulac and Abuyog, which is in the island of Leyte. He ordered himself placed there in his coffin (as was done) in a house standing alone and distant from the settlement, in order that he might be recognized as a god of navigators, who were to commend themselves to him. Another had himself buried in certain lands in the mountains of Antipolo, and through reverence to him no one dared to cultivate those lands (for they feared that he who should do so would die), until an evangelical minister removed that fear from them, and now they cultivate them without harm or fear.

107. They mentioned the creation of the world, the beginning of the human race, the flood, glory, punishment, and other invisible things, such as evil spirits and devils. They recognized the latter to be man's enemy, and hence feared them. By the beginning which they assigned to the world and the human race, will be seen the vanity of their belief, and that it is all lies and fables. They say that the world began with only the sky and water, between which was a kite. Tired of flying and not having any place where it could alight, the kite stirred up the water against the sky. The sky, in order to restrain the water and prevent it from mounting to it, burdened it with islands; and also ordered the kite to light and build its nest on them, and leave them in peace. They said that men had come from the stem of a large bamboo (such as one sees in this Orient), which had only two nodules. That bamboo, floating on the water, was carried by the waves to the feet of the kite, which was on the seacoast. The kite, in anger at what had struck its feet, opened the bamboo by picking it with its beak. When it was opened, out of one nodule came man and from the other woman. After various difficulties because of the obstacle of consanguinity in the first degree, one of the gods namely, the earthquake, after consulting with the fish and birds, absolved them, and they married and had many children. From those children came the various kinds and classes of people. For it happened that the parents, angered at having so many children idle and useless in the house, took counsel together; afterward the father one day gave way to his anger, and was desirous of punishing them with a stick which he had in his hand (a thing which they can never do). The children fled, so that some of them took refuge in the chambers and innermost parts of the house, from whom they say came the chiefs; others escaped outside, and from them came the freemen, whom they call timauas; others fled to the kitchen and lower parts, and they are the slaves; others fled to various distant places, and they are the other nations.

108. It is not known whether there was any temple24 in all these islands, or any place assigned in common for worship; or that the people ever assembled for public functions. In private they were wont to have in their own houses (and not outside them in any cave or like place) some kind of altars, on which they placed their idols, and before them a small brasier with burning aromatics. But although they had no temples, they did not lack priests or priestesses for the sacrifices, which each one offered for his own purpose or necessity. The Tagálogs called those cursed ministers catalonan, and the Visayans babaylan. Some were priests by inheritance and relationship; others by the dexterity with which they caused themselves to be instructed and substituted in the office of famous priests by gaining their good-will. Others were deceived by the devil with his wonted wiles, and made a pact with him to assist them, and to hold converse with him through their idols or anitos; and he appeared to them in various forms. The method of making the sacrifices hinged on the different purposes for which they were intended. If it were for a feast of ostentation and vanity that was being made to some chief, they called it "the feast of the great god." The method of celebrating it was near the house of the chief, in a leafy bower which they erected especially for that purpose, hung round about with hangings in their fashion, namely, the Moorish, which were made from odds and ends of pieces, of various colors. The guests assembled there, and the sacrifice having been prepared (on those occasions of a feast usually some good fat pig), the catalona ordered the girl of the best appearance and who was best adorned, to give the spear-thrust to the animal, amid the ceremony of certain dances of theirs. When the animal was dead it was cut into bits and divided among all the people, as is the blessed bread. Although other animals were killed and eaten, and other viands and refreshments peculiar to those people were used, that animal was the one esteemed and was reverently consumed. The chief part of the feast was the drinking, accompanied, as ever, with much music and dancing.

109. If the sacrifice was because of the danger of death in the house of sickness, the minister ordered that a new, large, and capacious house be built at the expense of the sick person, in which to celebrate the feast. That work was performed in a trice, as the materials were at hand and all the neighbors took part in it. When it was finished, the sick person was taken to the new lodging. Then preparing the intended sacrifice—a slave (which was their custom at times), a turtle, a large shellfish, or a hog—without an altar or anything resembling one, they placed it near the sick person, who was stretched out on the floor of the house on a palm mat (which they use as a mattress). They also set many small tables there, laden with various viands. The catalona stepped out, and, dancing to the sound of gongs,

wounded the animal, and anointed with the blood the sick person, as well as some of the bystanders. The animal was then drawn slightly to one side and skinned and cleaned. After that it was taken back to its first location, and the catalona there before them all, spoke some words between her teeth while she opened it, and took out and examined the entrails, in the manner of the ancient soothsayers. Besides that the devil became incarnate in her, or the catalona feigned to be him by grimaces, and shaking of the feet and hands, and foamings at the mouth, acting as if out of her senses. After she had returned to her senses, she prophesied to the sick person what would happen to him. If the prophecy was one of life, the people ate and drank, chanted the histories of the ancestors of the sick person and of the anito to which the sacrifice was being made, and danced until they fell through sheer exhaustion. If the prophecy was one of death, the prophetess bolstered up her bad news with praises of the sick person, for whose virtues and prowess she said the anitos had chosen him to become one of them. From that time she commended herself to him and all his family, begging him to remember her in the other life. She added other flatteries and lies, with which she made the poor sick person swallow his death; and obliged his relatives and friends to treat him from that time as an anito, and make feasts to him. The end was eating and drinking, for that marked the termination of their sacrifices. Each person who attended the sacrifice was obliged to offer something—gold, cotton, birds, or other things—according to his capacity and wish. The offering was given to the priest or priestess who had performed the sacrifice. Consequently, the latter were generally quite rich and well dressed, and had plenty of ornaments made of various kinds of jewels. On that account, however, they were not honored or esteemed; for they were considered as an idle lot, who lived by the sweat of others. After their duty was once performed no further attention was paid to them, unless they united with their office nobility or power.

110. To give a list of the omens and auguries would consume much time and be useless. If the owl lit on the roof at night it was a sign of death. Consequently, when a house was built some sort of scarecrow was set up to keep that bird away, so that the house might not be lost; for a house would under no circumstances be lived in if that happened. The same was true if any serpent was seen in it after it had been newly built. If they came across a serpent in any road they would not proceed farther, even if their business was very pressing. The same was true if they heard any one sneeze, a rat squeal, a dog howl, or a lizard25 sing. Fishermen would not make use of the first cast of the net or a new fish-corral, for they thought that they would get no more fish if they did the opposite. Neither must one talk in the fisherman's house of his new nets, or in that of the hunter of dogs recently

purchased, until they had made a capture or had some good luck; for if they did not observe that, the virtue was taken from the nets and the cunning from the dogs. A pregnant woman could not cut off her hair, under penalty of bearing an infant without hair. Those who journeyed ashore could not mention anything of the sea; and those who voyaged on the sea could not take any land animal with them, or even name it. When a voyage was begun they rocked the boat to and fro, and let it vibrate, and if the vibrations of the right side were more pronounced the voyage would be good, but if bad they were less. They cast lots with some strands of cord, with the tusks of swine, the teeth of crocodiles, and other filthy things, at the ends; and their good or evil fortune would depend on whether or not those ends became tangled.

111. The oaths of these nations were all execrations in the form of awful curses. Matay, "may I die!" Cagtin nang Buaya, "may I be eaten by the crocodile!" Maguin Amo, "may I turn into a monkey!" The one generally used is Matay. When the chiefs of Manila and Tondo swore allegiance to our Catholic sovereigns, in the year one thousand five hundred and seventy-one, they confirmed the peace agreements and the subjection with an oath, asking "the sun to pierce them through the middle, the crocodiles to eat them, and the women not to show them any favor or wish them well, if they broke their word." Sometimes they performed the pasambahan for greater solemnity and confirmation of the oath. That consisted in bringing forward the figure of some monstrous beast asking that they might be broken into pieces by it if they failed in their promise. Others, having placed a lighted candle in front of them, said that as that candle melted and was consumed, so might he who failed in his promise be consumed and destroyed. Such as these were their oaths.

112. It remains for us to speak of their mortuary customs. As soon as the sick person dies, they begin to bewail him with sobs and cries—not only the relatives and friends, but also those who have that as a trade and hire themselves out for that purpose. They put into their song innumerable bits of nonsense in praise of the deceased. To the sound of that sad music, they washed the body. They perfumed it with storax, or benzoin, and other perfumes, obtained from tree-resins which are found throughout these forests. Having done that they shrouded the corpse, wrapping it in a greater or less number of cloths, according to the rank of the deceased. The most powerful were anointed and embalmed according to the manner of the Hebrews, with aromatic liquors which preserve the body from corruption, especially that made from the aloes wood, or as it is called, eagle-wood. That wood is much esteemed and greatly used throughout this India extra Gangem. The sap from the plant called buyo (which is the famous betel of all India) was also used for that purpose. A quantity of that sap

was placed in the mouth so that it would reach the interior. The grave of poor people was a hole in the ground under their own houses. After the rich and powerful were bewailed for three days, they were placed in a box or coffin of incorruptible wood, the body adorned with rich jewels, and with sheets of gold over the mouth and eyes. The box of the coffin was all of one piece, and was generally dug out of the trunk of a large tree, and the lid was so adjusted that no air could enter. By such means some bodies have been found uncorrupted after the lapse of many years. Those coffins were placed in one of three places, according to the inclination and command of the deceased. That place was either in the upper part of the house with the jewels, which are generally kept there; or in the lower part of it, raised up from the ground; or in the ground itself, in an open hole which is surrounded with a small railing, without covering the coffin over with earth. Near it they generally placed another box filled with the best clothing of the deceased, and at suitable times various kinds of food were placed on dishes for them. Beside the men were placed the weapons, and beside the women their looms or other instruments of labor. If they were much beloved by those who bewailed them, they were not permitted to go alone. A good meal was given to some slave, male or female, and one of those most liked by the deceased; and then he was killed, in order that he might accompany the deceased. Shortly before the entrance of the faith into the island of Bool, one of the chiefs of that island had himself buried in a kind of boat, which the natives call barangay, surrounded by seventy slaves with arms, ammunition, and food—just as he was wont to go out upon his raids and robberies when in life; and as if he were to be as great a pirate in the other life as in this. Others buried their dead in the open country, and made fires for many days under the house, and set guards so that the deceased should not return to carry away those who had remained.

113. After the funeral the lamentations ceased, although the eating and drunkenness did not. On the contrary, the latter continued for a greater or less time, according to the rank of the deceased. The widow or widower and the orphans, and other relatives, who were most affected by grief, fasted as a sign of mourning, and abstained from flesh, fish, and other food, eating during those days naught but vegetables, and those only sparingly. That manner of fasting or penitence for the dead is called sipà by the Tagálogs. Mourning among the Tagálogs is black, and among the Visayans white, and in addition the Visayans shave the head and eyebrows. At the death of a chief silence must reign in the village until the interdict was raised; and that lasted a greater or less number of days, according to his rank. During that time no sound or noise was to be heard anywhere, under penalty of infamy. In regard to this even the villages along the river-bank placed a certain signal

aloft, so that no one might sail by that side, or enter or leave the village, under penalty of death. They deprived anyone who broke that silence of his life, with the greatest cruelty and violence. Those who were killed in war were celebrated in their lamentations and in their funeral rites, and much time was spent in offering sacrifices to or for them, accompanied with many banquets and drunken revels. If the death had happened through violence—in war or peace, by treason, or any other manner—the mourning was not laid aside nor the interdict raised until the children, brothers, or relatives, killed an equal number not only of their enemies and the murderers, but also of any strange persons who were not their friends. Like highwaymen and robbers they prowled on land and sea, and went on the hunt for men, killing as many as they could until their fury was appeased. That barbarous kind of vengeance is called balàta and in token of it the neck was girt with a strap which was worn until the number of persons prescribed had been killed. Then a great feast and banquet was made, the interdict was raised, and at its proper time the mourning was removed. In all the above are clearly seen the traces of heathendom and of those ancient rites and customs so celebrated and noised about by good authors, by which many other nations, more civilized, were considered as famous and worthy of history.

Chapter XVI

Of the government and political customs of these peoples

114. There were no kings or rulers worthy of mention, throughout this archipelago; but there were many chiefs who dominated others less powerful. As there were many without much power, there was no security from the continual wars that were waged between them. Manila had two chiefs, uncle and nephew, who had equal power and authority. They were at war with another chief, who was chief alone; and he was so near that they were separated from one another by nothing more than a not very wide river. The same conditions ruled in all the rest of the island, and of even the whole archipelago, until the entrance of the faith, when they were given peace—which they now esteem much more than all that they then obtained from those petty wars and their depredations. They were divided into barangays, as Roma into districts, and our cities into parishes or collations. They are called barangays, which is the name of a boat, preserving the name from the boat in which they came to settle these islands. Since they came subject to one leader in their barangay, who acted as their captain or pilot—who was accompanied by his children, relatives, friends, and comrades—after landing, they kept in company under that leader, who is the dato. Seizing the lands, they began to cultivate them and to make use of them. They seized as much of the sea and near-by rivers as they could preserve and defend from any other barangay, or from many barangays, according

as they had settled near or far from others. Although on all occasions some barangays aided and protected others, yet the slave or even the timaua or freemen could not pass from one barangay to another, especially a married man or a married woman, without paying a certain quantity of gold, and giving a public feast to his whole barangay; where this was not done, it was an occasion for war between the two barangays. If a man of one barangay happened to marry a woman of another, the children had to be divided between the barangays, in the same manner as the slaves.

115. Their laws and policy, which were not very barbarous for barbarians, consisted wholly of traditions and customs, observed with so great exactness that it was not considered possible to break them in any circumstance. One was the respect of parents and elders, carried to so great a degree that not even the name of one's father could pass the lips, in the same way as the Hebrews [regarded] the name of God. The individuals, even the children, must follow the general [custom]. There were other laws also. For the determination of their suits, both civil and criminal, there was no other judge than the said chief, with the assistance of some old men of the same barangay. With them the suit was determined in the following form. They had the opponents summoned, and endeavored to have them come to an agreement. But if they would not agree, then an oath was administered to each one, to the effect that he would abide by what was determined and done. Then they called for witnesses, and examined summarily. If the proof was equal [on both sides], the difference was split; but, if it were unequal, the sentence was given in favor of the one who conquered. If the one who was defeated resisted, the judge made himself a party to the cause, and all of them at once attacked with the armed hand the one defeated, and execution to the required amount was levied upon him. The judge received the larger share of this amount, and some was paid to the witnesses of the one who won the suit, while the poor litigant received the least.

In criminal causes there were wide distinctions made because of the rank of the murderer and the slain; and if the latter were a chief all his kinsmen went to hunt for the murderer and his relatives, and both sides engaged in war, until mediators undertook to declare the quantity of gold due for that murder, in accordance with the appraisals which the old men said ought to be paid according to their custom. One half of that amount belonged to the chiefs, and the other half was divided among the wife, children, and relatives of the deceased. The penalty of death was never imposed by process of law, except when the murderer and his victim were common men and had no gold to satisfy the murder. In such a case, if the man's dato or maginoo (for these are one and the same) did not kill him, the other chiefs did, spearing him after lashing him to a stake.

117. In a matter of theft, if the crime were proved, but not the criminal, and more than one person was suspected, a canonical clearance from guilt had to be made in the following form. First they obliged each person to put in a heap a bundle of cloth, leaves, or anything else that they wished, in which they might discover the article stolen. If the article stolen was found in the heap, at the end of this effort, then the suit ceased; if not, one of three methods was tried. First, they were placed in the part of the river where it is deepest, each one with his wooden spear in his hand. Then at the same time they were all to be plunged under the water, for all are equal in this, and he who came out first was regarded as the criminal. Consequently, many let themselves drown for fear of punishment. The second was to place a stone in a vessel of boiling water, and to order them to take it out. He who refused to put his hand into the water paid the penalty for the theft. Thirdly, each one was given a wax candle of the same wick, and of equal size and weight. The candles were lighted at the same time, and he whose candle first went out was the culprit.

118. There are three kinds and classes of people: the chiefs, whom the Visayans call dato and the Tagálogs maginoo; the timauas, who are the ordinary common people, called maharlicà among the Tagálogs; and the slaves, called oripuen by the Visayans and alipin by the Tagálogs. The last are divided into several kinds, as we shall relate soon. The chiefs attain that position generally through their blood; or, if not that, because of their energy and strength. For even though one may be of low extraction, if he is seen to be careful, and if he gains some wealth by his industry and schemes— whether by farming and stock-raising, or by trading; or by any of the trades among them, such as smith, jeweler, or carpenter; or by robbery and tyranny, which was the most usual method—in that way he gains authority and reputation, and increases it the more he practices tyranny and violence. With these beginnings, he takes the name of dato; and others, whether his relatives or not, come to him, and add credit and esteem to him, and make him a leader. Thus there is no superior who gives him authority or title, beyond his own efforts and power. Consequently, might was proclaimed as right, and he who robbed most and tyrannized most was the most powerful. If his children continued those tyrannies, they conserved that grandeur. If on the contrary, they were men of little ability, who allowed themselves to be subjugated, or were reduced either by misfortunes and disastrous happenings, or by sicknesses and losses, they lost their grandeur with their possessions, as is customary throughout the world; and the fact that they had honored parents or relatives was of no avail to them, or is of no avail to them now. In this way it has happened that the father might be a chief, and the son or brother a slave—and worse, even a slave to his own brother.

119. Their manner of life and ordinary conduct from the days of old is trade, in all sorts of things by wholesale, and more by retail in the products of the earth, in accordance with what is produced in each district. The maritime peoples are great fishers with net, line, and corral. The people who live inland are excellent farmers and hunters. They are always cultivating rice, besides other vegetables and garden products, quite different from those of Europa. The women also are shrewd in trading, especially of their weaving, needlework, and embroideries, which they make very neatly; and there is scarcely one who cannot read and write. Sometimes the husband and wife go together on their trading, and, whether for this or for any other thing, she must always go ahead; for it is not their custom to go together. Even if it be a band wholly made up of men or of women, or of men and women mixed, and even if the road be very wide, they go in single file one after the other.

120. The maritime peoples were accustomed to make many raids, and those of the interior to set ambushes for such depredations, wasting life in this. Their weapons consisted of bow and arrow; a spear with a short handle, and a head shaped in innumerable ways, most often with harpoon points; other spears without any head, with the point made on the shaft itself (which is now of bamboo and now of wood), a vara long, hardened in fire. They had swords; large, sharp daggers, made very beautifully; and slender, long blowpipes [ceruatanas], through which they shot most dangerous poisoned arrows, in the manner of the inhabitants of Samatra. Such are their offensive weapons. Their defensive weapons are wooden shields and rattan or corded breastplates, and other armor helmets of the same material.

121. What justice, what fidelity, what honesty should there be amid so great cruelty and tyranny? Virginity and purity were ignominious, which is the general vice of idolaters. Whether married or single, the woman who had no lover could not be safe; and by regarding that as an honor, they considered it a dishonor to give their persons free. When men children were born in certain provinces, the mothers themselves performed on them a certain form of circumcision, quite different from that of the Jews and Moros, and only in order to render them more skilful in their lewdness. Yet with all this, they abhorred, and chastised, and rigorously punished incest.

122. In the celebration of their marriages, espousals, and divorces, and in the giving and receiving of dowries, they also proceeded according to reason. In the first place, they agreed as to the dowry, which is promised and given even now by the man, in the sum named by the parents. When it is determined the betrothal takes place, generally with a conventional penalty which is rigorously executed. However, neither men nor women take it for an insult or grieve greatly if the betrothal be refused, because

then they benefit by the fine. The truth is, that if those who are bound by the fine were the parents, after their deaths the children are free to break the contract without incurring the penalty, by only the restitution of the amount received as dowry.

Matrimony at present includes, besides the above, the delivery of the person and the dowry. The latter is not received by the woman but by her parents or relatives, as it were selling their girls, in the manner of the Mesopotamians and other nations. The parents convert the dowry into their own estate, and it is distributed with the other property, at their deaths, among all the children equally. But if the son-in-law has been very obedient to his parents-in-law; then the latter generally return the dowry to their children. The other relatives are only depositaries of what they must again deliver to the children. Besides the dowry, the chiefs formerly gave some presents to the parents and relatives, and even to the slaves, to a greater or less amount according to the rank of the bridegroom.

The pagan ceremony and form of marriage had to be authorized by a sacrifice; for after the marriage had been agreed upon and the dowry paid over, the catalona came, and a hog was brought to her. The ceremonies were performed as in other sacrifices. The lovers having seated themselves in their bridal chamber, each in the lap of an old woman who acted as godmother, the latter gave them to eat from one plate and to drink from one cup. The bridegroom said that he took the woman to wife, and, accepting her, the catalona or babaylana immediately gave them a thousand benedictions, saying to them: "May you be well mated. May you beget many children and grandchildren, all rich and brave," and other things of this sort. Thereupon the hog was slain, and the lovers were married; and when the others became tired of dancing and singing, all became intoxicated and went to sleep. If the recently-married couple did not suit each other, another sacrifice was ordered, in which the bridegroom himself danced and slew the victim—the while talking to his anito, and offering himself to it for the sake of peace and harmony with his wife. That having been done, he calmed himself, confident that then and thenceforth the two would live in harmony, and enjoy their married life in peace.

These nations consider it important to take a wife only from their own family, and the nearer the better. Only they except the first grade [of kinship], for they always considered that as a dissolving impediment. But what marriages were those in which the contract was not indissoluble, and could be dissolved by the woman, if she were to blame, merely returning the dowry! If the husband were to blame, it was not returned; and the marriage could be repudiated by themselves, without any solemnity of law. That was done daily for very slight causes, and new marriages were formed with others. Polygamy was not the fashion among the Tagálogs. However, if the wife bore no children, the husband could with his wife's permission have them by his slave women, in accordance with the example of the ancient patriarchs. Among the principal Visayans, the ministers of the gospel found established the custom of having two or more legitimate wives, and large dowries, which was a great obstacle to Christianity.

123. Thus far in regard to marriage. As to the children and their succession and inheritance, if they were legitimate they inherited equally in the property of their parents. For lack of legitimate children the nearest relatives inherited. If there were illegitimate children, who had for example been had by a free woman, they had their share in the inheritance, but not equally with the legitimate children, for the latter received two-thirds, and the illegitimate one-third. But if there were no legitimate children then the illegitimate received all the inheritance. The children of a slave woman who belonged to the man were given some part of the household effects, according to the will of the legitimate children. In addition the mother became free for the very reason that her master had had a child by her.

There were also adopted children, and the practice was that the one adopted bought his adoption. For the natural parent gave a certain sum to the adopted parent in order to have his son or daughter adopted, and thereupon the latter was adopted without any other subtlety of law or of paternal power. It was done only to the end that the adopted child, if he should outlive the one adopting him, should inherit double the sum that had been given for his adoption. Thus, if ten were given, he must inherit twenty. But if the adopted parent outlived the adopted child, the adoption expired as well as the right of inheritance, which was not given to the heirs of the adopted one, either in whole or in part. But if, on the contrary, the parent died while his own child was living, he left him by way of addition to the sum for adoption doubled, some jewel or slave woman, as a reward for his good services. But, on the other hand, if the child was ungrateful and acted badly, the adoptive parent gave him up, by restoring the sum that had been given for his adoption.

Adultery was not punished corporally, but by a pecuniary fine. Therefore the adulterer, by paying to the aggrieved party the sum of gold agreed upon between them, or given by the sentence and judgment of the old men, was pardoned for the injury that he had committed; and the aggrieved party was satisfied, and his honor was not besmirched. Also he continued to live with his wife without anything more being said on the subject. But those children had by a married woman did not succeed to the nobility of the parents or to their privileges; but were always reckoned plebeians, whom those people call timauas. Likewise those children had by a slave woman, although they were free, as was the mother, were always regarded as of low birth. These who succeeded to the nobility were the legitimate children. In the barangay, when the father was lord of it his eldest son inherited that office; but, if he died, then he who came next in order. If there were no male children, then the daughters succeeded in the same order; and for want of either males or females, the succession went to the nearest relative of the last possessor. Thus no will was necessary for all those successions; for wills were never in vogue among these nations in the form and solemnity of such. As for legacies it was sufficient to leave them openly, in writing or entrusted by word of mouth, in the presence of known persons.

125. A great part of the wealth of these Indians consisted in slaves. For, after gold, no property was held in greater esteem, because of the many comforts that were enjoyed for their mode of living through a multitude of slaves. Thus our Spaniards when they entered the islands found so many slaves that there were chiefs who had one, two, and three hundred slaves, and those generally of their own color and nation, and not of other foreign nations. The most general origin of those slaveries were interest and usury. That was so much practiced among them, that no father would aid his son, no son his father, no brother his brother, and much less any relative his relative, even though he were suffering extreme necessity, without an agreement to restore double. If payment was not made when promised, the debtor remained a slave until he paid. That happened often, for the interest or increase continued to accumulate just so long as the payment was deferred. Consequently, the interest exceeded the wealth of the debtor, and therefore the debt was loaded upon his shoulders, and the poor creature became a slave; and from that time his children and descendants were slaves. Other slaveries were due to tyranny and cruelty. For slaves were made either in vengeance on enemies, in the engagements and petty wars that they waged against one another, in which the prisoners made remained slaves, even though they were of the same village and race; or as a punishment which the more powerful inflicted on the weaker ones, even for a matter of little importance, of which they made a matter of insult. For instance if the lesser did not observe the interdict on talking and noise, usual in the time of the burial of the chiefs; if he passed near where the chief's wife was bathing; or if any dust or any other dirt fell from the house of the timaua upon the chief or his wife when passing through the street: then in these and numberless other similar cases the powerful ones deprived the poor wretches of liberty, and tyrannically made them slaves—and not only them but their children, and perhaps the wife and near relatives. The worst thing is that all those who had been made slaves by war, or for punishment of debts, were rigorously regarded as such, as slaves for any kind of service

or slavery, and served inside the house. The same was true of their children, in the manner of our slaveries, and they could be sold at will. However, the masters were not accustomed to sell those born under their roof, for they regarded them in the light of relatives. Those slaves were allowed to keep for themselves a portion of any profit which they made. The Tagálogs called such true slaves sanguiguilir, and the Visayans halon.

Other slaves were called *namamahay*, for they did not serve their master in all capacities, nor inside his house; but in their own houses, and outside that of their masters. They were bound, however, to obey their master's summons either to serve in his house when he had honored guests, or for the erection of his house and its repair, and in the seasons of sowing and harvest. They [had also to respond] to act as his rowers when he went out in his boat, and on other like occasions, in which they were obliged to serve their master without any pay.

126. Among both kinds of slaves, sanguiguilir and namamahay, it happens that there are some who are whole slaves, some who are half slaves, and some one-fourth part slave. For if the father or the mother were free, and had an only son he was half free and half slave. If they had more than one child, these were so divided that the first followed the condition of the father, whether free or slave, and the second that of the mother. So did it happen with successive pairs. But if there were an odd number of children, the last was half free and half slave. Those who descended from them, if they were children of a free father or mother, were slaves only in the fourth part, as they were the children of a free father or mother, and of one half slave. Sometimes, because it happened that two people had agreed to marry and the man had no wealth for the dowry—or rather, nothing with which to buy his wife—he became her slave. In such case the children were divided in the said manner, and the first, third, and fifth, and the remaining ones in the same way were slaves, inasmuch as they belonged to the father, who was also a slave of the mother—and not only slaves to her, but also to her brothers and sisters and relatives, in case of her death and the division of her property. On the contrary the second, fourth, and others in the same way, were according to their custom free, inasmuch as they belonged to their mother who was free; and they were masters and rulers over their own father and brothers and sisters. The same thing happened in the case of interest, a thing of so great importance among them that, as already remarked, the father would not pardon the debt and interest even to the son, nor the son the father, even in case of necessity, until the one had made a slave of the other for it. Consequently, if one brother ransomed another brother, or a son his father, the latter remained a slave, as did his descendants, until the value of the ransom was paid with interest. Consequently, the captive was gainer

only by the change of master. Such as the above are the monstrous things that are seen where the law of God and Christian charity are lacking. In the division made between heirs, when a slave belonged to many, the time of his service was divided and each of the masters had the share that belonged to him and was his in such slave; and the division was made by months, or as was convenient among the masters. When a slave is not a whole slave but only a half or fourth part, he has the right to compel his master to give him his freedom for the just price at which he is appraised, according to the rank of the slavery, sanguiguilir or namamahay. But if he be a whole slave, the master cannot be compelled to ransom him at any price, even though he should have become a slave for debt, if already the day set for the payment of the debt has passed.

127. There was another kind of service which was not of a truth servitude, although it appeared to be such. It was generally seen among certain persons called *cabalangay*. Whenever such persons wanted any small trifle, they begged the head chief of their barangay for it, and he gave it to them. In return, whenever he summoned them they were obliged to go to him to work in his fields or to row in his boats. Whenever a feast or banquet was given, then they all came together and helped furnish the tuba, wine, or quilan, such being their method of service.

128. The ancient custom in manumission was for the whole sanguiguilir slave to pay ten taes of gold, and the namamahay the half; and, in addition to that, he had to give the half of whatever things he owned. For instance, if he owned two large jars he had to give one. In order to make that conveyance, the slave must make a banquet, at which were present masters, relatives, and friends. At the height of the banquet the delivery of the gold and household articles was made, those present being witnesses that the master had received them. The latter was thereupon satisfied, and the slave was set free.

Even today the Tagálogs are wont, at death, to grant freedom to the children of their slaves who are born in their house, no matter how young they be. However, they do not free the parents of those children no matter how old they be, and even if they have been served throughout life by them. That seems absolutely illogical.

129. To what has been said of dowries and marriages, it must be added that in some districts, besides the *bigaycaya* and those presents made to the relatives, there was *panhimuyat*. This was a kind of present that was given to the mother of the bride, merely in return for the bad and watchful nights that she had passed in rearing her. That *panhimuyat* signifies "watchfulness and care." If the dowry was equal to five taes of gold, the *panhimuyat* was

equal to one *tinga*, which was equivalent to one tae, or five pesos. That was a custom which well shows the harshness and greed of these nations, since the mothers wished to be paid even for the rearing of their daughters.

Also, whenever a chief married any daughter of his and asked a large dowry of his son-in-law, as, for instance, eighteen or twenty taes of gold, the father was obliged to give his daughter certain gifts called pasonor, such as a gold chain, or a couple of slaves, or something proportional to the dowry. It was very shameful to ask a large dowry without giving a pasonor. This is still done, resembling the gifts which among us the father presents to his daughter præter dotem,26 which the civil law calls bona paraphernalia.27

1 For description of Borneo, see Vol. XXXIII, p. 353, note 419. Malayo refers to a portion of the Malay Peninsula. For the origin, settlement, and distribution of the native peoples in the Philippines, see Barrows's account in Census of Philippine Islands, i, pp. 411–417, 447–477; cf. Crawfurd's Dictionary of Indian Islands, pp. 249–253.

2 João de Barros, the great Portuguese historian, was born at Vizeu in 1496 and became page to the crown prince (afterward João III), for whose amusement he wrote his three-volume romance, Cronica de Emperador Clarimundo (Coimbra, 1520). João III appointed him captain of the fortress of San Jorge de Mina, governor of the Portuguese possessions in Guinea, and (1533) treasurer and general agent for Portuguese India. An attempt to colonize a grant of land in Brazil (received 1539) failed, and was abandoned. Barros died in 1570. The book referred to in the text was his Decados, a history of Portuguese India, written in fulfilment of a royal commission. The first "decade" was completed in nine years (1552), the second soon after, and the third ten years later. The fourth was left unfinished at his death, but was completed later by Diogo do Conto, who added eight more volumes. A complete edition was printed at Lisbon in twenty-four volumes (1778–88). Barros was a conscientious writer and a good stylist. (New International Encyclopædia.)

3 An apparent error for the word "kasis," and here wrongly used (see Vol. XVI, p. 134, note 161).

4 Thus (sur) in text; but, as a matter of fact, Paragua stretches northeast from the north point of Borneo, and the Sulu archipelago in the same direction from its northeast side.

5 Sumatra is on the whole deficient in lakes. The largest is Lake Singkara, about twenty miles in length by about twelve to fifteen in breadth, with a depth of twenty-four fathoms, and is the source of the Indragiri River. Another lies near the foot of the mountain Mârapi, and is called Danau Sapuluh kota, or "Lake of the ten forts." There are two others in the country of the Korinchi Malays; and

still another in the country of the Lampungs, toward Java, and called the Ranu (Javanese synonym for "water"). It is about sixteen miles long and eight miles wide. Colin evidently refers to either the first or the last of these. See Crawfurd's Dictionary, p. 416.

6 India citra Gangem (if we accept Marco Polo's division) would correspond to Greater India, or the country extending from the Ganges to the Indus. India extra Gangem, or Lesser India, included the territory between the eastern coast of the peninsula of India, and that of Cochinchina or Champa. See Wright's edition of Travels of Marco Polo (London and New York, 1892), p. 435, note. Colin says (p. 1), that India extra Gangem or Farther India included the coasts of the rich kingdoms of Malacca, Sian, Camboja, Champa, Cochinchina, Tunquin, and China, as far as the confines of Oriental Tartary. The allusion to an Asiatic Ethiopia is hopelessly confused, and may have arisen from Marco Polo's second division of India, which includes Abyssinia.

7 Of the Manguianes, or more properly the Mangyan, Pardo de Tavera says in Etimologia de las nombres de razas de Filipinas (Manila, 1901): "In Tagálog, Bícol, and Visaya, manguian signifies 'savage,' 'mountaineer,' 'pagan negroes.' It may be that the use of this word is applicable to a great number of Filipinos, but nevertheless it has been applied only to certain inhabitants of Mindoro. In primitive times, without doubt, the name was even then given to those of that island who to-day bear it, but its employment in three Filipino languages shows that the radical ngian had in all these languages a sense to-day forgotten. In Pampango this radical ending still exists and signifies 'ancient,' from which we can deduce that the name was applied to men considered to be the ancient inhabitants, and that these men were pushed back into the interior by the modern invaders in whose languages they are called the 'ancients.'" They live in the mountains of Mindoro and are probably a mixture of the Negritos with other Filipinos, and possibly in some localities there may be a small infusion of white blood. They are non-Christian, and are very timid. Their dress consists of the "gee" string, with the addition, in the case of the younger girls, of some forty or eighty yards of bejuco (rattan) wrapped around the waist. They are divided into several tribes, chief among which are the "Buquit," "Bangon," and "Batanganes," who roam in bunches or by families, the oldest acting as chief. They are willing workers, and make nearly all the bancas used in the province. They have no knowledge whatever of agriculture, and do not know the value of money. The census of 1903 shows a population of 7,269. See Census of the Philippines, i, pp. 472, 473, 547, and 548; and ii, p. 15.

8 The Chinese carried on a fairly active trade in the Philippines three centuries before Magellan's discovery of the archipelago. The articles traded by them for

the products of the country consisted of pottery, lead, glass beads, iron cooking-pans, and iron needles. Some of them may have gone north above Manila. See Census of Philippines, i, p. 482.

9 See David P. Barrows "History of the Population of the Philippines," published in vol. 1, of Census of Philippines, for valuable material in regard to the peopling of the Philippines. See also Crawfurd's Dictionary.

10 Diodorus, surnamed Siculus, or "the Sicilian," was a Greek historian, a native of Agyrion, Sicily, who lived in the time of Cæsar and Augustus. After long travels in Asia and Europe he wrote his Bibliotheca, a universal history in 40 books, covering a period from the oldest time to 60 B. C. Books 1–5 and 11–20, besides other fragments, are still extant. The early portion of the work is ethnological, but the later is in the annalist style. (Seyffert's Dictionary of Classical Antiquities.)

11 Either Iamblichus the Syrian Greek romance writer, who lived in the second century A. D., or Iamblichus the Greek philosopher from Chalcis in Syria, who was a pupil of Porphyrius, and the founder of the Syrian school of Neo-Platonic philosophy, and who died about 330 A. D. The latter justified Oriental superstition and had the reputation of working miracles. (Seyffert's Dictionary of Classical Antiquities.)

12 See Vol. XVI, p. 117, note 135.

13 Señor Don Antonio Graiño, a bookman in Madrid, Spain, has an unpublished MS. history by Pedro Chirino, probably a copy of the one mentioned by Colin.

14 See Vol. XII, p. 237.

15 This should be compared with the Ave Maria as given by Chirino (see Vol. XII, p. 237). Colin also gives the same in the Visayan tongue, but as it differs so slightly from the version as given by Chirino ("ginoon" in place of "guinoon," line 2, second word; "sancta," in place of "santa," line 5, first word; "Ynahan" in place of "inahan," line 5, third word; "macasala" in place of "macasasala" line 6, fourth word; and "camatay" in place of "camatai," last line, fourth word), it is omitted here (see ut supra, p. 239). The version in the Harayan tongue that is given (ut supra, p. 238) by Chirino, is omitted by Colin. In his text we retain also his Spanish translation of the prayer.

16 Cf. personal names and the ceremonies attendant on bestowing them among the Bornean Malays, in Furness's Home-life of Borneo Head-hunters (Philadelphia, 1902), pp. 16–53; and Ling Roth's Natives of Sarawak, ii, pp. 273–277.

17 Light thin stuff made of silk or thread; crape. See Velázquez's New Dictionary.

18 "Such is the wine from nipa, called Tanduay. The famous chemist (a Chinese mestizo) Anacleto del Rosario, discovered a process by which the disagreeable taste of this brandy disappears; and it becomes equal to that of Spain in color, smell, taste, and strength." (Father Pastells, in his edition of Colin, i, p. 62, note 2.)

19 Gachas: A certain food composed of flour, milk, and water, to which is added honey or sugar, and the consistency of which is midway between starch and flour paste. (Dominguez's Diccionario.)

20 "Their most popular traditional songs are the Cundimán, the Comintán, the Balitao, the Saloma, and the Talindao. Some are only sung; in others, they sing and dance at the same time." (Pastells, in his Colin, i. p. 63, note 1.)

21 "The dance here described by the author is that which is called in Filipinas Moro-Moro." (Pastells, ut supra, p. 63, note 3.)

22 Pastells (ut supra, p. 64, note 1) discusses the meaning of the word Bathala; he thinks that it is ascertained "by resolving the word into its primary elements, Bata and Ala = 'Son God, or Son of God.' This is why the first missionaries did not deprive the natives of this name when they instructed them about the existence of God and the mysteries of the Trinity, the incarnation, and redemption, as states an anonymous but very circumstantial relation written at Manila, on April 20, 1572. This is more evident in the song which the Mandayan baylanas use in their sacrifices, when they chant the Miminsad, saying: [Here follow the words of this song, for which consult our Vol. XII, p. 270, note.] ... The Mandayas believe that Mansilatan is the father of Batla (man being a prefix which indicates paternity, being, or dominion), and the Búsao who takes possession of the baylanas when they tremble, and of the Baganis when they become furious; it is a power which is derived from Mansilatan.... This interpretation of the word Bathala is confirmed by that word of the Visayans, Diuata; we always find here the same idea signified in the words Diwa and uata, differing only in their transposition.... In closing, we may note that Dewa in Malay, Déwa in Javanese, Sunda, Makasar, and Day[ak?], Deva in Maguindanao, and Djebata in Bornean, signify 'the supreme God,' or 'Divinity.'"

23 The caverns were, in especial, formerly the usual sepulchres of the Indians. The anthropologists have profited by this circumstance for their studies, and for furnishing the museums of their respective nations with skeletons of those natives. (Pastells, ut supra, p. 66, note 1.)

24 The Mahometans [Moros] had their mosque, or lañgà ." (Pastells, ut supra, p. 66, note 3.) Legazpi says (Vol. III, p. 60): "The heathens have no [religious] law at all; they have neither temples nor idols, nor do they offer any sacrifices."

25 A reference to the common little house or chirping lizard, which is often seen and heard on the walls of the houses. See Census of Philippines, i, p. 74.

Arthur Stanley Riggs says in a note in a forthcoming volume, The Filipino Drama: "The common or house lizard in the Philippines has a pretty, chirping note. When one hears a lizard 'sing,' as the Spaniards call the cry, it means, among the Ilocanos, an important visit of some kind. If hunting at the time one hears several lizards sing, he must turn back immediately, as disaster will inevitably follow further progress. Other curious and interesting superstitions obtain in like manner in other parts of the islands."

26 i.e., "over and above the dowry."

27 i.e., "Property which was given to women over and above the dowry, and remained at their own disposition."

The Natives of the Southern Islands

[Francisco Combés, S.J.,1 in his Historia de las islas de Mindanao, Iolo, y sus adjacentes (Madrid, 1667), devotes a number of pages to the peoples of Mindanao and other islands. This matter we translate from the reprint issued (Madrid, 1887) by Pablo Pastells, S.J., and W. E. Retana, book i, chapters ix–xviii.]

Chapter IX

Of the nations of these islands and those adjacent to them

Four nations have renown in this island, the Caragas,2 Mindanaos,3 Lutaos,4 and Subanos.5 That of most renown is the nation of Caraga, which, although it is the smallest numerically, has been the greatest in deeds. In times past that nation was the scourge of the islands, as is today proclaimed by the depredations that still are fresh in memory in the islands of Pintados—especially so in that of Leyte, where there is scarce a village which has not bewailed its ruin. A good part of this ruin extended to Ours, the pirates having pillaged our town of Palo and destroyed all the villages of the coast, taking prisoner the father ransomer,6 who exercised that office for all the jurisdiction, and obliging those who lived in the villages to retire into the mountains. Those nations maintained themselves by their own valor, without protection of the pagan kings; they were bold against all, and no one dared to do anything to them. They are a brave nation on sea and land, and on land they are the first nation of the islands; and by their aid great exploits have been accomplished, as was seen in the conquest of the lake of Malanao, and in all others that have occurred since they were subdued by the gospel and the Catholic arms.

The second nation in estimation is the Mindanao, which includes the kingdoms of Buhayen; for in olden times they were all one nation, and today, although various petty rulers govern them, they are one in customs and language. They are a nation of some valor, and with their policy of being subject to kings they have acquired esteem among the other nations, whom they have united under one political government for achievements that are too great for their own courage. They are treacherous and of little faith, as they are now swayed by the impious worship of Mahomet.

The third nation is the Lutaya. It is a nation common to these islands of Mindanao, Jolo, and Basilan. In all these islands it preserves the name of Lutao, for since that is their vocation it well explains their nature. For Lutao means, in those languages, "he who swims and goes floating over the water." Such is the nature of these people that they know no other house than the ship. In the villages which they have formed they well show the inclination with which they were born; for they are so fond of living on the sea that their houses are built in it, in places which the low tide leaves exposed. In that way they can set upright the trunks of the trees with which they must form their houses, driving them down according to the load which they have to sustain. When it is high tide the houses are very far from the shore, and the water in between is so deep that brigs and craft of heavier tonnage can sail there. These people hate the land so thoroughly that they do not trouble themselves at all about its cultivation, nor get any benefit from it. All their labor lies in fishing, and they get from that the means of barter for whatever they need, even for the wood that they burn and the logs from which they build their houses and craft. Since they are so slightly attached to the land, they easily move to other parts, and know no fixed abode except the sea; for although they recognize villages, in which they assemble, they seldom live in these, for they are scattered through the bays and beaches suitable for their fishing. They live under the kings of Mindanao and Jolo, and the chiefs of the same, and those of the island of Basilan; today with some, tomorrow with others, according to the district in which they are. Those of this island are scattered along all the coast which extends from Samboangan to the river of Mindanao, and have no fixed dwelling in any other part—except some of them who have settled in the city of Cebú and a few others in the village of Dapitan. They are equally esteemed in all parts as being the sinews for the wars of these regions (their campaign field being the sea), and also for their skill in constructing vessels fit for the wars of these regions, and their skill in managing them.

By their constant communication with,all the nations (as they go to all parts for their advantage), and because of their method of living— which is so in the manner of traders, enjoying the fruits of the land—and by the alertness of their intelligence, they are the most capable, the most clear-sighted, and the most crafty people of these islands. Therefore, they maintain the supremacy in everything, and, although they are the smallest in number, and everywhere the most foreign [of all these peoples], they are today the kings, and hold the rulers as their slaves; for now by loans, now by violence, and now by private vengeance, they have established the entire slavery of these islands.

As their work causes but little exertion, naturally they grow up lazy, and only shake off their laziness for the gains and advantages of an industry like trading and sea piracy. And since the gains derived from that source are sure, both because the cunning employed by them is that of finished robbers, and because their wings are those of royal falcons, they are most eager for that exercise, as they are assured by these advantages from all danger; for, whether it be because of the swiftness of their ships or because of their skill in rowing them, no ship of ours has ever been able to overtake them. Assured on that point, they have pillaged whatever their greed has dictated to them. Their method of attack is for all of them to land at once with a terrifying and barbaric cry, the awfulness of which strikes terror to the people as they are caught defenseless and separated and thus incapable of resistance.

They are more circumspect on the sea, when danger does not oblige them to make resistance. For since these natives do not fight for reputation, but only for gain, they seek to assure that, and not to buy it too dear with their blood. Therefore, when they meet a ship which they think cannot make any resistance they go to it in certainty of making it a prize, and that they will catch it a half-legua from shore. However small it be, they do not care to seize it if there is any danger. They continue to row about it, until they cause it to waste its powder in spectacular warfare, and then, when they see it weakening, they attack it with great valor throwing by hand so many missile weapons that no man can [safely] show his face; and when they get within range there is rarely a man who is not wounded, for they hurl these missiles in showers. No matter how well equipped a boat may be, if once it gets within their range it has to surrender; for then their men, both sailors and soldiers hurl their arrows with both hands, so that they confuse those who uncover themselves for the fight. But by startling them from a distance, that danger is not imminent, and less resistance suffices. In order that this may be better understood, I shall relate some attested incidents of such encounters. One happened to an inhabitant of Dapitan, with whom I sailed for many days. He, when going toward his village in a small boat, met the fleet of the Joloans. A ship with one piece immediately left the fleet to pursue him. The Indian carried a musket, and after he had discharged it the enemy, recognizing it, moderated their zeal, and coming within range discharged their own piece. Then they backed water in order to load again and repeated the attack, always keeping a close watch on the musket. In this way they made three attacks, until at the third their piece became enraged, and breaking its carriage, fell into the sea. Thereupon the enemy dared attempt nothing more, and retired. The same fortune happened to Father Antonio Abarca,[7] of our Society, of whom we shall make honorable mention later. He, having left me in Dapitan in order to go over to Bohol, on that same day while sailing toward that island, and while still one legua away from it, found three hostile joangas of Joloans at another island, small and uninhabited, called Illaticasa, which attacked him at the same time. There was but one firearm in the ship, and the father was the only one who knew how to manage it. He seeing himself so far from land, and pursued by an enemy so keen and so swift on the sea, availed himself of his courage, which was great, and of his skill, which was remarkable; and, adroitly fighting, he kept firing at the enemy, until he gained shore, being almost all the time in range of them, and so near that they talked to one another. By that means he saved himself and his people—a thing that would have been impossible in any other manner; but his defense was so fiery that in less than half an hour he fired the gun more than thirty times.

These people are the instruments of all the exploits by sea, for of all the other nations no one will embark unless he is forced; and on account of the little effectiveness that is found by experience in all the others, our enemies, who are watchful for their own safety and for fortunate results, are not hindered by those other peoples. Consequently, he who has most men from this nation is considered the most powerful and is the most feared, as they have power to infest the seas and coasts, making captives and pillaging, and making themselves masters of the crossings and passages necessary for communication with the other islands.

For that same reason the Mindanao has become so feared in these latter years that although he of Buhayen is the true and legitimate king, he is coming to be less esteemed; for since the Mindanao king has many Lutaos, he has also power to make war. And although the king of Buhayen has twenty-fold more vassals, he can make no one uneasy because he has no subjects of this nation; consequently, he has no weight in these islands. For the wars of these nations, now because of their little permanence, now because of the natural ruggedness of their settled parts, are but seldom offensive by land; for the enemy are immediately perceived, and the less powerful avail themselves of the shelter of the mountains. Since the people are of little endurance and less subordination they cannot sustain long campaigns. Therefore, at most the valiant ones set an ambush, and according to the way it falls out the campaign is finished without the spoils being surrendered; for their articles of value, as there is so little good faith among them, are always kept buried, or are so light that they are carried along with them. On that account he alone is judged powerful who has people to make war by sea. In ancient times this power caused all this island to pay tribute to the king of Mindanao in order to be free from his attacks. In the time of Buisan, the father of Corralat, they had hopes of rendering all the islands of Pintados tributary; and, though the island of Burney is so out of the way, more than twenty thousand vassals pay tribute to him in the villages called Suaco. For the same reason, although the Joloan nation is so small, it has become the most distinguished in these islands; for on sea it equals the strength of the Mindanaos, as they have as many or more vassals of the Lutao nation.

The fourth nation is the Subano. They are the settlers along the rivers. To them is due the name suba, which is the equivalent of "river" in the general language of these nations. It is the nation of least esteem, both because of their natural barbarousness, for they live in the plains with as little association with one another as have brutes (one house being located a legua's distance from another, according to where each one wishes to build his hut); and because of their poverty, which is dire. For since they have no other intelligence than [what is required for] their work, their slothfulness reduces their efforts to what necessity [only] requires, so that what is abundant for a laborious life is always lacking with them. They are deficient in civilized ways, along with human intercourse, as they are born so hostile and so averse to communication [with others] that they grow old in their rude settlements without curiosity drawing them from their place of residence, or without their seeing the sea, although some of them live where they hear news of the horror of its tumults and movements. If either necessity or gain has made them give a glance at their rivers, they are satisfied with that, and do not seek a better fortune with its dangers. This inertia forbids them, incapable of giving force to their ambition, from following its impulses with [favoring] winds.

They are as cowardly as treacherous, the one being the consequence of the other. He who better plans a bit of treachery and comes out most safely is considered the most valiant. As they all know one another, they look out for one another, and build their houses so high up that a pike cannot reach and wound them. Their usual practice is to seek a very high tree, where they can build their nests safely; and, their houses being so unostentatious in size and furnishing, a tree holds them easily. The ladder by which they ascend is a log, some grooves that they cut in it serving as steps. On the coming of night they draw this ladder up and thus sleep secure. They teach us the little with which life is satisfied, and the fatigues which our ambition and pride give us; for in order to satisfy our ambition and pride we take upon us so many cares, which, so far as life is concerned, are superfluous, and are not the least of the accidents which our life suffers. This nation is almost wholly in vassalage to the Lutaos, and every village recognizes some chief8 of the latter nation to whom they pay tribute; and that chief bears himself as a king among them, and makes and unmakes at his will. In the beginning, this authority entered under color of protection and support against the king of

Mindanao, and remained in enthroned tyranny, so that today most of this nation are slaves of the Lutaos—their want of intellect subjecting them to a thousand cheats, and their want of protection to a thousand outrages. For since the Lutaos are so alert a nation, and so sharp in their affairs, they have gradually bought the Subanos by trading with them, becoming masters of their entire freedom.

Chapter X

Of the noble and brave nation of the Dapitans

Of this island, which has given empires to so many kings, without doubt the crown is the village of Dapitan; and, although it is so small at present, it has been one of the most densely populated in the past, the one most respected for its power, and in our times the whole, both of these conquests and of their Christian churches. In a small number, reduced to one single village, there is inclosed a nation9 apart from all the others, and superior to all those discovered in nobility, valor, fidelity, and Catholicism. They are descended from the island of Bool, where they anciently occupied the strait made by that island and the island of Panglao, which remains dry at low tide, but at high tide allows a galliot to pass. Therefore many brazas in the sea stand, even today, certain columns of upright wood, as honorable witnesses of the location so gloriously occupied by this nation, and today the venerable ruins of poor although adequate buildings which they sustained. They occupied both shores and the entire island of Panglao. There they conquered the famous people of Bohol; for as their nation was the less numerous in that island, they were obliged to sustain their name by their deeds. The Boholans, conquered and put to flight, abandoned the site which they occupied from the shore of the strait to the coast of Baclayon and took refuge on the river of Loboc, where their name is still preserved in a few families descended from that stock which conquered that island, and only the valor of the Dapitans subdued.10 According to the ancient law of the land the Dapitans can call the Boholans their slaves since less title was sufficient for that in the days of their antiquity, and the most authoritative reason was always that of war.

War exiled the Dapitans from their country, a proof of their valor and the unforeseen accidents of their misfortunes; for they were the only people of all the archipelago who were renowned among foreign princes for their exploits, and to them alone were embassies made. It happened then that in an embassy sent by the king of Terrenate, the most warlike and powerful king known, his ambassador lost [due] respect for the house of the Dapitan princes—then represented by Dailisan and Pagbuaya, who were brothers—by making advances to a concubine. They punished the crime more by the laws of offended and irritated fury than by those of reason, with hideous and indeed cruel demonstrations of contempt, by cutting off the noses and ears of the ambassador and his men. When they had returned to Terrenate, the horrid aspect of his subjects aroused the wrath of the king. He armed all his power in twenty joangas to oppose the Dapitans. His general, doubtful of the outcome, as he knew the valor of those with whom he had to do, made use of a trick by which he assured a deceitful victory. He sent his joangas in, one by one, giving out that they were traders, and under the security of friendship—excusing the above occurrence, in order to divert the attention [of the Dapitans], with the laws of punishment, deserved because of the boldness of their men. The Dapitans, seeing that the Ternatans were attending only to the sale of their goods, lost their caution, and came up with the same confidence as ever. When the Ternatans had all their fleet together, and saw that of the Dapitans, they closed with them. Although the latter placed themselves in a position of defense, they retreated before that multitude, and the terror of arms to which they were unaccustomed; for the Ternatans already had muskets and arquebuses, the use of which they had before other nations, because of their trade with the Portuguese.11 The frightful effects of these, as terrible by their ruin as by their novelty, worked on the minds of the Dapitans. Dailisan was killed in that fray, and his brother Pagbuaya was left the reigning prince. He, seeing how he was involved with the Ternatans, and how much at the mercy of their new [arms]12 was the place occupied by the Dapitans—where the Ternatan ships could succeed in anchoring under the houses of the Dapitans, and using their arms, fight them in safety—resolved to seek another place, better defended. He also thus resolved because these nations regard as unlucky the place where fortune has once shown itself hostile to them, and immediately abandon it as accursed. Even today, in these islands, it is a fact that the house where a chief dies is abandoned by his people and it remains alone, waiting its ruin.13 He sought then a place where, their valor and its ruggedness joining hands, they could make up, aided by the strength of the site, for the small number of their nation. As there were no hills on their coasts, and they were unable to restrain their noble and warlike nature to the confinement and gloomy prison of the retired mountains, where they would be deprived of the trade and benefits of the sea, they crossed to the island of Mindanao, a crossing of fifteen leguas, and twenty from their village, and seized a small rugged hill, which would allow itself to be monopolized by their valor.

The people who elected to follow Pagbuaya numbered one thousand families of freemen, his subjects, without taking into account the unmarried men. In these nations, where there is a law of dowry—or rather a law for the purchase of wives—there are many men who are denied the bonds of matrimony because of their poverty. Neither do we reckon the slaves of the prince, who exceeded five hundred, and many other families of the Lutao nation, who as they now live under the protection of the kings of Mindanao and Jolo, lived then also under the protection of the Dapitan princes.

They had occupied the new site but a short time when their renown caused anxiety to the most remote princes, who were fearful of their power. Consequently, the king of the great island of Burney was the first to send his ambassador with two joangas, soliciting their friendship. While they were yet awaiting the resolution of the Dapitans, the brave Magallanes sighted their coasts with his squadron, as we shall relate in the second book. They immediately made peace with him, being pleased, as brave men, with the valor which they recognized in the unknown people.14 The Borneans were sent away with the message that the Dapitans wished no other friendship than that of their new guests. They have preserved that friendship to this day, as noble people, without any complaint [arising] of their loyalty, even to the lowest slave; and their exploits in favor of our arms have deserved much praise. For the son of that Pagbuaya, called Manooc, following the fidelity of his father, and surpassing it with the good fortune of being a Christian, aided the Spaniards in their first conquests of these islands— especially in the conquest of Manila, the capital of all these islands; and later in the conquest of Camarines, taking at their own expense, in all these feats of arms, their men and the nations subject to them.

That prince, who, as he was the first to become acquainted with the Spaniards (having shared the knowledge of them which his father acquired with the first sight of the squadron of Magallanes), was the first to receive the blessing of acquaintance with our holy faith, giving renown equally to his own banners and to those of our king and sovereign, and receiving the name Don Pedro Manuel Manooc—continued the greatness of his deeds. For besides the services rendered in Manila and the province of Camarines, he sustained war against Mindanao and Jolo, and attacked them with his fleets in their very houses. On one occasion, when among others he went to attack Jolo, he met the king himself, who was also going out with his fleet of twelve joangas. Manooc defeated him and captured his flagship, and, at the cost of many killed, the king escaped as a fugitive, by hastening to the land. He made war on the Caragas, who were the terror of the islands at that time. He subdued the village of Bayug of the Malanao15 nation, who were subject to the Mindanaos, without our arms having any other protection amid so many enemies than that of his valor which made easy so many undertakings. That prince was the father of Doña Maria Uray, who is today living as an example and ornament of these nations because of the perfection of her virtues—which she prefers to a better fortune, for she has spurned marriage with the kings of Jolo in order that she might not subject her faith to the outrages of barbarous and faithless princes. Don Pedro Manuel Manooc left orders that he was to be buried in the city of Cebú, as he had ordered in his will that his bones be taken to that cathedral. His children carried out his orders, thereby showing both their affection to us and their devotion to him.

The women were not inferior in merit. For Doña Madalena Baloyog, the sister of Don Pedro Manuel Manooc, had so great authority among the barbarous Subanos that she alone by her discretion reduced more of them than did the arms of her people by their valor and courage. She obtained the name of pacifier, mistress, and sovereign of the hard hearts of the chiefs of the Subanos. Her authority was so manifest to our men that, the natives of the river of Butuan having rebelled, and killed their alcalde-mayor and their minister, a secular priest, who was then in charge of it,16 it was sufficient for her to assure them of pardon for the deed, and to secure to us their pacification and due obedience forever.

The cousin of Don Pedro Manuel Manooc was Laria, who competed in all things for the greatness of his cousin. He served in the conquest of Maluco with the same nobility and valor, and would receive no pay or rations for his men. In the seven times when the island of Jolo was attacked in war, he took part in all of those conflicts, always showing himself remarkable for his princely actions and soldierly valor.

A son worthy the nobility of such a father was Don Gonçalo Maglenti, the husband of Doña Maria Uray, whom we mentioned above, and the father of Don Pedro Cabelin. The latter is still living and is nowise inferior in his deeds and fidelity to his forbears, as he was reared from childhood with so good merits of nobility and Christian warfare—accompanying his father from the age of seven years, on all occasions of danger; thus he came to despise danger so thoroughly that at the age of thirty (his present age) the enemies of God and of our king whom he has killed in hand-to-hand combats, in various frays, surpass two hundred. Don Gonçalo, then, the father of so illustrious a son, left him enough examples to emulate his valor, for in accordance with his surname (which means "he who hurls down thunderbolts"), his valor hurled them in a constant shower. He opposed the might of the Mindanaos at the time of their greatest arrogance, when they threatened all these islands with their arms. He always went in pursuit of their fleets and of those of the Malanaos which were sent by way of the bay of Pangil17 to aid the Mindanaos, for he was an ally for the defeat of their plans. He subdued from the bay of Pangil to the village of Sidabay, ten leguas from Samboangan, all of the villages scattered through sixty leguas along the coast (formerly many more and superior in number). His care watched perpetually over the islands, and of his own accord he despatched advices to Cebú and Oton at the first rumor of hostile fleets, by means of which the evil designs of the enemies might be frustrated. That care merited for his nation exemption from the tribute and from all personal service, which its natives enjoy today by concession from his Majesty.

In this site the Dapitans—now reduced to the enterprises of his valor to so small a number that they scarce exceed one hundred families—alone and strangers, have defended themselves from the power of all the pirates of these islands, all of whom, pursuing them with their vengeance and injuries, have attempted to extirpate them entirely. And as they have the land so at their mercy, with nations who have inherited so much internal hatred [to the Dapitans] at being subdued by this noble nation, the former have been unable to get one single captive out of their hands, and their sieges are always left crowned with triumphs. For Buhisán, the father of Corralat, and the most warlike of the kings of Mindanao, with one hundred joangas and the incentive of his own person and presence, returned within fifteen months, his haughtiness undeceived. The Joloans, notwithstanding their power, had no better fortune, and left behind seven joangas in the enterprise that they attempted—although the opportunity was so in their favor, when there were scarcely ten men in the stronghold, as the majority had gone to various places for their trade.

Among the Subanos—the ports of their conquest, which surround them on all sides—their valor is so accredited, that a Dapitan has nothing to fear among a hundred of them. For if they see him ready for them, they do not dare to attack him, however thirsty for his blood their hatred makes them; for the Subanos are all the triumphs of the arms of the Dapitans, of which the sound and rigorous execution has drawn the former from their mountains, and made settlements of men from savages scattered among the thickets, who are reduced to more civilized life. Thus has been established a province which, in our time, has been given separate an alcalde-mayor, namely, that of Iligan; and by that province is secured to our arms an opening for the conquest of Mindanao and Jolo, as we have thereby had soldiers, pilots, and most skilful sailors, who are better than all those who sail in these islands. Their village remains as a stronghold opposed to the petty rulers of those peoples.

They are a very prudent race, and are quite Hispanicized in their customs, and by the modesty of their bearing naturally deserved respectable. Thus they do not endure the outrages that the other subdued nations endure, now from the boldness of the soldiers, now from the exigencies of our necessities; for they attend to all things willingly, considering it an honor to satisfy our desires. Consequently, in respect and esteem they are the princes of these islands.

In matters of the Christian faith they yield in no wise to the most pious European nation or to the loyalty of the most distinguished. They are the ones who guard religion. The minister who visits the ports of their coast, with four Dapitans whom he takes as a guard goes as safely as if he were taking an infantry regiment; and no misfortune has ever happened to such an arrangement. For although misfortunes have been experienced in the infidelity of the native Subanos, yet they have been invited by the confidence of the father missionaries, who have gone among them without that valiant guard, as will be seen in the course of this history. Finally, the faith of this island and those near by is owing to the Dapitans; and, to their fidelity and valor, the glorious confidence of our arms.

Chapter XI

The settlers of these islands, and their origin

The owners of these islands are those who people the mountains. They, enamored with their peaceful mode of living, and fed with the happy returns of their cultivation, built their nests there and lost their liking for the coast and love for its occupations. Thereupon, as they were reared in so deep retirement, which is especially great and unconquerable in these natives, because of their slothfulness and because they are so dead to curiosity, by which they have grown old in their gloomy retreats, they gradually became mountaineers; and, their intercourse with other peoples ceasing, they became less alert and more barbarous, allowing the foreign traders to seize the coasts, harbor-bars, and rivers which they found deserted. Since by their trade, and in every way, the latter were making themselves masters of all things, the aborigines, being less valiant, yielded to the foreigners, as these were more civilized. Consequently, on the south coast the rulers of those peoples are the Lutaos, who bear themselves among these nations as princes. In some parts those peoples are called Subanos, as in the jurisdiction of Iligan and Samboangan; in Mindanao, they are called Manobos[18] and Mananapes[19] which is equivalent to "brutes." In Jolo, they are Guinuanos [i.e., Guimbanos], and in Basilan they are called Sameacas,[20] and they are subject in all places equally to the fortune of the Lutaos. No other origin to these peoples can be conjectured than one general to these islands—whose language, since its structure is founded on Malayan roots, shows by its origin the origin of its natives. To this testimony corresponds the arrangement of these islands, which are strung out in a series from Burney and Macaçar, so that there is scarcely any considerable break, and there is no such correspondence in any other part.

The Lutaya nation are new in these islands, and live more on the seas than on their plains. They have no greater stability than is promised by a log in the water where no firm foundation can be laid. They scarcely take their feet from their boats. Their Moorish dress of turban and marlota [i.e., a Moorish robe], their arms and worship, clearly show their origin. With all this agrees their more polished language, which they speak, emulating the grandeur of the princes of these nations who have made an ostentation of speaking it—indeed, because their own especial language approaches more nearly to it than any other, for they owe to it a great number of their words.21 As the Moorish faith [i.e., Mahometanism] is recent in India,22 and thence has steadily spread through these kingdoms it can be understood that this nation [i.e., the Lutaos] occupied these coasts but a short time ago. The Lutaos of this island who are subject to Corralat and the Buhayens (both through commerce and by the submission which they observed toward the king of Ternate) show that they are branches of that stock. They recognize even their protection, which in olden times was the greatest obligation, and give them aid in their wars and protect them from their enemies. By the prowess of the Lutaos those rulers were encouraged to cause grievous depredations among these islands, until the Spaniards established themselves so strongly in Ternate that, checked by that, as a bulwark of the islands, the Moro chiefs did not attempt to pass farther, being content with placing their domestic affairs in safety without risking it for foreign [gains].

There are black negroes in this island, who pay tribute to no one. They resemble those of the island of Negros, and of the uplands about Manila, called Aetas. They live more like brute beasts than like men, and they flee from the sight of all, doing ill to whomever they can. They recognize no village, nor in a land of so many inclemencies do they have any other shelter than that of the trees. They can be seen daily in the bay of Pangil. In the village of Layauan, where I was making the visitation, there appeared to be many of them. They have no other adornments than those which they inherited from nature; and pay so scant respect to decency that they do not secure even what is requisite. Their arms are the bow and arrows dipped in poisons, which they know and with which they prepare the arrows. It appears probable, from what we know of other islands, where these people are found gathered in the most inaccessible mountains, that these are the first ones that occupied all these islands; but, as they are more ancient and are so shut in, nothing more is known of their origin than what is evident from this land, connected by its islands in a chain with those of Burney, Macaçar, and Great Maluco. This nation maintains only one excellence— at the cost, [however,] of its brutal condition and wretched mode of life— namely, its liberty. No power, not even that of our Spaniards, has been able to subjugate them. They are so free in their indomitable barbarism that they will not suffer any subordination among them, not even that which fraternal feeling for their own people might bring about if they recognized dignities or any organized form of social life.23

The Lutaos of Jolo have all their communication with the Borneans, raising the trident of their king24 in the villages of that enormous island. There they are judged to be one people [with the Borneans], and are declared such by the fraternal intercourse that they maintain among themselves — being related by marriage, and conspiring together with their arms for the invasion of these islands, where their squadrons are seen daily under one and the same banner.

But the rulers and nobility of all the islands of Jolo and Basilan recognize as the place of their origin the village of Butuan (which, although it is located in this island, is within the pale of the Visayan nation) on the northern side, in sight of the island of Bool, and but a few leguas away from Leyte and from Bool, islands which are in the same stage of civilization. Therefore, that village can glory at having given kings and nobility to these nations. It is not so long ago since the branches which flourish so well today were lopped from their trunk, that the memory charged with the event that divided them can have forgotten it. The old king of Joló who is now living [i.e., Bongso], saw the one who was dismembered from his people, and whom misfortunes exiled from his fatherland in order to make him venture on another's land, thus giving him the foundation of so warlike a kingdom, which is so feared in these regions. Inasmuch as the tender beginnings of this new kingdom gathered encouragement from the protection of our arms, which it enjoyed for some time as pacific and tributary, it will be well to relate its beginnings before time obscures them.

The dissensions of two brothers obliged the less powerful to seek, by way of exile, a path to liberty which oppression denied him. Those affected to him accompanied him, and with them, seeking a land to his liking, he hit upon the island of Basilan. The one who stirred up that people was named Paguian Tindig,25 then a title of nobility, and today the legacy of kings and princes of the blood royal in the island of Joló. In his company he took his cousin, one Adasaolan, whom his fate gave to him in order to maintain its enmity to him. Some of those in his company allowed themselves to be led away by the fertility and abundance of this island and remained behind, captivated by its advantages. With the rest Tindig went to Joló, whither the report of its wealth, the advantages of its seas and islands, and the fertility of its mountains carried him. They easily conquered the natives, who were barbarians and unaccustomed to the rigors and ambitions of war. They remained as rulers of the island, and their prince was Paguian Tindig, who, as subject to the Spaniards (who had already subdued the river of Butuan), continued in the same allegiance and paid them tribute. His cousin Adasaolan he married to a daughter of Dimasangcay,26 the king of Mindanao named Paguian Goan (a dangerous plan) in order to give himself power in the rivalry [with his brother]. The mother of Corralat, by name Imbog, was a Joloan, and with the communication indispensable to relationship easily infected Adasaolan with the perfidy of Mahomet, and the tyranny and violence of his law; and he, puffed up by the favor of the Mindanao king, and confident of his help, which their relationship promised him, planned to kill his cousin, in order that he might remain absolute master of the island. He blockaded him, unprepared, in his house with four hundred men who had gathered to his standards. But in a happening not expected or feared, love acted, being forewarned, and innocence, being offended. And since there is no confusion that blinds the courage of foresight, he had taken the precaution to pour down along the supports of the house (which are here called arigues, and are of strong wood) a quantity of oil, which rendered the scaling more difficult; and the besiegers, finding more resistance than their presumption imagined, and yielding to so great force, retired. Tindig recognized the difficulty in which he was, and considered war as declared and broken out; and, in order not to stain it with blood at the cost of his men, planned to absent himself and look for aid, respect for which would ensure his condition. He went to Manila for that purpose, having repressed the forefront of his danger, and, as a tributary and subject prince, easily secured the pledge of our arms for his help; and, because he alone could measure the force with the necessity, the means was left to his choice. He thought that two well-armed caracoas would be enough, and, although a powerful fleet was offered him, he refused to accept it; for he considered himself as invincible in his joanga, if reënforced by two Spanish caracoas.

His absence made his rival powerful, for the party without a leader readily unites with that side that has one; and, the cause of the rivalry being wanting, tyranny easily united the forces of the island. Eight well-armed joangas were prepared by Adasaolan, which were given to him by Buhisan, the father of Corralat; and Tindig, having come within sight of Joló, went ahead with a lack of caution, to prepare his people, as he did not believe that the party of his cousin was so in the ascendancy. The enemy who were awaiting him, all ready, as soon as they saw his joanga without the shelter of the caracoas, all surrounded it and boarded it, with the determination to finish the war at one stroke. Ours who were coming behind could not aid him; for he had gone on ahead, as we have said, to advise his men, and to notify his enemies of the war, so that fear could accomplish what he desired without recourse to arms. Overcome by the multitude rather than yielding to force, he was killed. He died unconquerable, his death leaving the tyrant assured of power. The king of Joló, Raya Bongso, who was punished by Governor Don Sebastian Hurtado de Corcuera, in his conquest of Joló, is a good witness of this contest. He, without much questioning, showed even the wounds that he received on that occasion, fighting, although but a lad, at the side of Paguian Tindig, who was his relative.

The Spaniards having arrived, and the cause of their fighting (the protection of him who had fallen) being now removed, and not finding anyone with whom to fight, returned to Manila. The tyrant, flushed with his victory, and being greedy with the hopes that great captures were assured to him in the islands with alliance with the Mindanaos and Borneans, united himself to them; and following their fleets, with so good masters of piracy his people became so great pirates, that they surpassed all in deeds, and by themselves caused so great havoc throughout the islands that they have proved the heaviest scourge that these natives have suffered. And refusing obedience to his Majesty and the tribute which they have always paid, that principality [of Joló] was founded and has less antiquity in these islands than the Spaniards.27

Chapter XII

Beliefs and superstitions of these islands

The general condition of these islands is paganism. From Sangil to Samboangan, the dwellers along the beach follow the law of Mahomet, as well as those of the islands of Basilan and Joló. This last is the metropolis of the false religion, and the Mecca of this archipelago; for there is the tomb of their first master, concerning whom the caciques [i.e., Kasis], for the credit of his deceits, have been establishing innumerable fables, which have already become a lying tradition in this century. One is that he came from Paradise with three others, of whom one went to Java, and another to Burney, and the other two landed at Joló, and thence one went to Mindanao. He of Mindanao was ill received; and because of that, and of having been shipwrecked in the sea by driving on a reef, he went in anger to an island to become a hermit, walking upon the water. But he who was wrecked in a ship could ill keep his footing in the water. Such is the character of lies, that some are quite contrary to others. The outfit that he carried consisted of a net, and it is said that he caught fish on the mountain with it, by dragging it over the ground. But if he found fish on the mountain then the fish surely could not escape him, unless indeed it were a flying-fish. When his followers went to seek him, Satan had already carried him away, and they found only the net—and that stretched out, for it had been placed to dry. From that point they took occasion to discuss so disconnected bits of nonsense as we have mentioned. Thereupon he who remained in Joló obtained the chair of the evil [doctrine], and, as he is accredited with not fewer deceits, he was able to authorize his person and his doctrine with the barbarians; for he also gave them to understand that he could get fresh water from the sea, that he could sail on land, and could establish fisheries on the mountain, as did the other. The use of these errors gave authority for the common people to invent others. They believe that the enchanted boat which they never saw, and whose anchorage they never knew, still exists. The respect that his deceits gained him in life became ignorant and infamous adoration at his death. A sepulcher was erected for him, which became the mausoleum of his memory, and the Mecca of his deceits. They erected it on the famous hill [of Joló], and it was very elegant.28 At its foot they planted the singular fruit which they call the king's fruit,29 which is unique in this archipelago, and of which no one ate except himself, although for devotion the shells were given to the others. As we said, they planted many jasmines, and made their defenses there, so that animals might not defile the mausoleum. As an entrance to it, there was arranged in front of it a little house which was placed at the beginning of the stockade, as if it were an entrance into the well of St. Patrick. There they made their offerings, all of which went to the benefit of the prebendaries of the house, who were generally of the blood of the hypocrite. Thence they took their auguries for the war, for, putting water in a vase, together with some earth from the sepulcher, if it became bitter to the taste the outcome would be bad; but if sweet, it would be happy. It is said that this test was made for the war waged on them by Don Sebastian, in consequence of which the king was always inclined to treat for peace.

By the entrance of our forces upon the hill, that place lost its worship and esteem; for the soldiers turned it all upside down, and dug it up in the hope of finding some treasure, and found no trace of a human body. The Indians were terrified at their boldness, and asked whether those who dared to do so much would not die. Thereupon, those people were left with only the staff [of that teacher], which the Kasis [caciques] keep; for that is the staff of all virtues, and in going out with it (which is at the time of any necessity), all make it great reverence, and attend to all that is asked of them. For if they do not do so, he excommunicates them, with two blows with it which he gives on the house or the boat, and there can be neither health in the one or good luck in the other. All these are the artifices of cupidity, which holds them fast in a deceitful fear by vain terrors.

The other relic is the cap,30 which is the hereditary possession of the kings, and to swear by it is to use the sanction of a great sacrament.

Notwithstanding so many lies that are made up to sustain this deceit, there are but few who esteem it; and in general they are all atheists, and those who have any religion are sorcerers. For as Moros, beyond not eating pork, and practicing circumcision, and [having] a multiplicity of women, they know not anything. They drink wine more than we do, and all their happiness consists in drunken revels—[to them] a positive act of greatness; and thus all their knightly deeds consist in emptying more or fewer jars [of wine], and there is a wedding in which they empty two hundred. All their festivals consist in this. They live in all respects like men without any law who do not know God, and without any mode of worship, and unmindful that there is such in the world. All regard the law as little more or less, and, according to the land they inhabit, follow its customs and laws. Accordingly they are neither Moors, heathen, nor Christians, but barbarous atheists. Corralat, who has civilized his country somewhat, has his mosque, and makes his people attend it. But when they leave their village, each one does as he pleases—except some of the chiefs, who, following the example of the king, have made it a point of honor to appear to be Moors. But the common people, assuredly, lay no stress on that point.

What they believe in thoroughly are omens, which are almost general in all the islands. There are many of them: of birds, like the limocon;31 of insects, like the lizard; of accidental occurrences, like sneezing; of happenings, like deaths or earthquakes; of observances at time of sowing, and of reaping, and of the hunt—all of these have their observances, which they fulfil in order to have luck in the work; for they believe that without these it will be unlucky, and without any profit. Therefore, they do not undertake those things, since in many districts it is considered an omen when anyone asks for a portion of what may be caught (as for instance, of the hunter or fisher), if we say to him when he goes to try his luck: "Divide with me what you shall catch." They consider that as a bad omen, and return to their house, for they believe that they will catch nothing.

Those who are atheists knowingly are the dwellers in mountains; for they have no mosques, or shrines, or any method of praying to God. Those upon whom they call in their illnesses are their ancestors, saying "Alas, my mother!" or "my grandfather." That is rather the natural expression of pain than a prayer in which they experience any efficacy. Where there are some to whom the devil talks (which was more usual in their antiquity), such people offer him their sacrifices,32 and the Indians have recourse to them in their illnesses, so that they could make the same efforts for them. Today the Christian truth has obscured the falsity of hell. At most, the descendants of those ministers of the devil, who were generally women, do what they saw them do without the devil taking any notice of them or talking to them. Others, who lay but small stress on all that, do what they heard said was the custom in the days of their antiquity, let happen what would. But they do it with so little earnestness that it appears to be levity rather than religion. With the same fervor they follow any other rule, so that they always remain without any law, unless it be where the energy and incessant constancy of the missionaries has made them forget their ancient customs, and with continual instruction has made it easy for them to accept the new things of our holy faith.

In Caraga there was a barbarous custom to make their ships lucky, namely, to vow to them the first time upon some name, which was generally the name of one of their captives.

That which has great value in all parts is sorcery; and they hold it in such high esteem that the father hides it from the son, and unless they receive a great profit they refuse to communicate any secret of it. The famous sorcerers are feared, although there is no one who is not ashamed of being called thus, and the word "sorcerer" is one of the insulting words of these natives. My judgment from seeing these [sorceries], so alike, is that they are implicit compacts made with their ancestors. For it also seems impossible that there are herbs of so powerful poison that they can kill so instantly that some persons kill, with only the breath alone by chewing those herbs; and others, by burying those herbs where one has to pass. They also use figures, which they dedicate to him whom they wish to harm, and these accordingly torment him; the figure continues to aggravate the evil upon the sorcerer's enemy. Others work by letters, and that is peculiar to the Moro Kasis [caciques], although the most of all this is fabulous; but as they imagine that it is true, for any accident for which they find no remedy, and of whose cause they are ignorant, they throw the blame on the sorcerer. It is recounted of the king of Burney that, on learning the name of one, he can kill him if he chooses. Sargento-mayor Pedro Duran Monforte having made war in his land, the king was informed of his name, and said that since he knew his name, therefore Monforte could not live much longer, and with that he consoled his people. But thanks to God, the sargento-mayor has been living for three years since that threat. Thus are all their affairs.

He who unites the excellency of a powerful sorcerer to Mahometan ardor is King Corralat. He causes the fish to enter his boat. While one of our fathers was in his boat, a fish leaped in; the king picked it up and, giving it to the father, said: "This is for the father." It is also related that he makes a piece of artillery float on the surface of the water by placing an oar in its mouth. He has a saker, which according to report, when fired, serves him as a good or evil augury. The fact is, that he talks very familiarly with the devil. According to the tale of a Spaniard (and one for which he vouched to me), when he was going from Samboangan on a certain embassy, just as he entered the river the favorite of Corralat told him that, the night previous, his king had asked him whether any ship were to be seen. To his negative answer the king said to him: "Then take note that three ships will arrive tomorrow, and one of them will be Spanish." That was a fact, for two ships from Java entered, and that of the said Spaniard. Thereupon the favorite exclaimed: "Great Saint Corralat, there is no other truth." With such things he has established so much credit that if God do not bury his body in the depths [of the sea], the Mindanaos will worship him and will found another house of Mecca, such as they had in Joló. With that he has become a greater king than any of his forbears; for their fear of him is incredible, as they recognize in him one who has superior power to avenge himself. Consequently, they do not dare undertake anything against his will; for they regard it as certain that they will be unlucky. Since the devil has been so advantaged by that way, he manages to make their fears come out true at times, by which credit for the others is assured.

Chapter XIII

The moderation of their conduct, and the sobriety of their living

Among all the Indians it is a general fact that in what relates to their own persons natural law is more conspicuous, and has a more firmly established empire, than have the nations. Part of that is founded on the slothfulness of their natures, and part on the rudeness of their civilization; the former makes them content with little, and the latter causes them to ignore the niceties of art. Their food proves the first well; and the havoc that they cause, the second. The food is very poor among the wealthy, and requires little labor; for they neither know condiments nor for that purpose are drugs valued among them, of the use of all which they are ignorant. Both slave and ruler, plebeian and prince, eat bread; for, since that consists of a little boiled rice, one cannot eat it more adorned than the other. Since all of them are bakers of this bread, he who wishes to clean it better eats it whiter. He who has no slaves to relieve him from that eats it as he chooses; and, consequently, there is no one who does not know how to cook his food. For they are under the daily necessity, even the richest, of making it; and, as ostentation in ordinary life is so little, it is unavoidable that service is lacking to them on their voyages and navigations, so that they are forced to use their own hands. Those who do not obtain rice—either because the land does not bear it, or because it is limited in any year—eat of many roots, which supply the lack fully, and which require no other preparation than boiling. He who is so well served that he obtains a little fish, venison, or pork, with water and salt alone makes his stew, without the knowledge of other kinds of pottages. In order to give their food a sharp flavor, they are wont to cook it with some herbs of a sour taste. Consequently, in the seasoning of their food they consume nothing, so that they save the cost of butter, oil, vinegar, and all spices. They are accustomed to make their puches [i.e., a sort of pap] and poleadas [i.e., a sort of fritter] from cocoanut milk and the honey made from sugarcane, which are their preserves and royal cakes. But such is at a great wedding or at a feast, where their desire for ostentation arouses their endeavors. Such were presented to me by the king of Joló, Panguian Bachal, while I was visiting at his court. They consisted of a half-dozen small cakes made of rice flour and kneaded with cocoanut-milk, and baked until they turned dark, so that they appeared to be cinnamon to the sight. In fact the color was due to the toasting and to a preserve, like turpentine, made from the fruit of the durion with honey made from sugarcane. This is enough to turn the strongest stomachs—as it were, the chief dainty for the stomach of a bull—oppressive, as it was all night to the Queen mother;33 and we satisfied ourselves with looking at it.

Their clothing is very simple, without stiffening or linings. All are dressed after the same style, and innovations due to curiosity are not allowed. As the country is so hot, they dress very loosely, a fact which makes the cutting out very easy. Each one is the tailor of his own garments. This is the reason why the Indians are so lacking in the communal idea, and are so hostile to assembling and uniting in villages; for since their misery and laziness make them content with the easiest and most natural, which all obtain, they do not need one another. For in each house are found all the trades, and no one makes use of them unless his own necessity compels him. If one goes to fish, he is content with what will satisfy either his appetite or his necessity; and the desire of acquiring does not make him break with his laziness in order to work.

Returning to their clothes, the stuffs worn are generally common to nobles, and plebeians, kings and slaves, and there is no difference between them—except it be in something extraordinary, in which the obligation and ostentation of their chief persons induces them to depart from their accustomed use. At such times they are wont to wear silks and very beautiful stuffs, with buttons and gold lace. Their krises (which are their inseparable weapons) have gilded scabbards and hilts of massy gold. I have seen some of them which were valued at nine slaves each, all covered with precious stones and perhaps encrusted with pearls. But in daily appearance all resemble one another, both in the garments in which they dress and in the fashions that they employ. These clothes consist of breeches and short jacket [ropilla]—or skirt, to be more accurate. That is not worn over a shirt, for with them the first garment is not the shirt, but the skirt, for it is all one. Sometimes they wear a jacket with long skirts cut in the French style; which, although it can be buttoned, is generally worn open, with the breast exposed. In this particular this nation is quite different from the others of this region. They use another style of cut; the skirts and sleeves each ending in a point, and the ends which ought to close over the bosom are brought together in double points, fastened either with a button or with a knot, so that almost all the breast is left open. The breeches are full and white, resembling those which the Spaniards wear for the sake of cleanliness under their black ones. They are girt with a bit of native linen, so long that after having been knotted it hangs from the waist to the knees; and it serves to make their garb more decent than it would be because of the meagerness and thinness of the breeches. Or if they do not have that, then they use two brazas' length of the same cloth or silk, which at its full width they wind about the body, joined in front with one end crossed below the other. In that manner they cover the breeches entirely, and the clothing is much more decent. In this usage, the gala costumes have special elaboration, and it displays their ostentation; for they are wont to wear cloth that is valued at thirty or forty reals of eight. They also wear breeches of the Malay fashion, which are closed like ours, although they are not so tight. It is the rule that they must be of silk with a gold fringe below, or with border and buttons of the same which among these people is always of filigree or of solid gold. In that they consider only ostentation, without any risk of waste.

On the head, in the Moorish style, is worn a turban. Its use throughout the Indias is general, but among these people inviolable. I do not know whether it is because even their hearts are tinged with their cursed worship, or because of hatred to our nation and to our customs, or because of flattery to their natural arrogance—through which they will never, of themselves, come to depreciate their own things. Even yet throughout the islands, those who are esteemed as chiefs are ashamed of appearing without hats.

The clothing of the women is plainer, and such that it becomes indecent; for from the small mantas or textiles of these regions, which are all very thin, they make a sack nine palmos long and open at both ends. They gird this in at the waist as much as may be necessary, so that it falls to the feet; what is left they allow to fall over the legs, and it does not even reach to the knees, or necessarily serve for the decency which modesty requires. They adjust it by drawing it close to one side of the body, and by making folds on the other side of all the extra width in proportion to their body. This sack, which by day is a garment—so shameful to decency, because it so ill satisfies it—serves at night for mattress, sheets, and curtain. For on retiring they ungird the sack, and the part which they doubled about the knees they put up to the head. That is all the opulence and comfort that their beds can boast of, which are made of a thin mat. These are their Holland and Rouen linens, which serve for their opulence and their fastidious cleanliness. That is their whole wealth of quilts and covers, which protect them from the cold and from the mosquitoes. All is so exactly adapted to necessity, that there is no difference between the chief women and the slaves—as I saw in Joló in the queen herself, and in Samboangan in many other women, not inferior to her in vanity. However, the women of highest rank, on retiring let fall a curtain without a covering. And that is all their ostentation and the necessary obligation of modesty for the protection from sight of those who are careless concerning their manner of sleeping, in houses where there is no division of apartments, and where there can be no rooms for the multitude that inhabit them, and where the others throw themselves down pellmell on the floor. At most, the master is protected by that little grandeur. This is in regard to the bed, for in dress no difference is known.

The gala dress of the women of this nation consists wholly of the shirt [sayuelo] which is made in the style usual to the Indians. It is however, drawn close about the breasts, and the sleeves are very long, at times each sleeve taking three or four varas of cloth. The sleeve is gathered at the wrist in a very fine and graceful plait, as the goods that they wear are so delicate. They heighten that gala dress with the wealth of gold, the use of which among these Indias extends to the wrists, which they cover with bracelets, either solid or hollow, and a finger in width. On days of great display they generally wear three or four pairs. The work is beautiful, and these add much to their gay and festive appearance; and they show off the arm loaded with such rich bracelets. For cloaks or mantles they wear textiles of fine silk, and at times of gold [tissue], which they call patolas34 which is a very beautiful and rich kind of goods. Generally, when they leave the house they all wear very long black cloaks; that partly moderates the ugliness and utter indecency of their dress—which of itself is, I know not whether more ugly or more immodest, with its sack above mentioned, which serves them as shirt and petticoat, without its having any distinction either for station, rank, or display.

The houses in which they reside have what is sufficient for their shelter and poor lodging. They have no salons where they can walk, or higher stories where they can amuse themselves, than that which separates them from the ground. This is made with logs, upon which as columns they build their sills, to which they fasten the ends of the beams with their keys. The roof is thatch, which nature furnished, a provision very suitable to the needs of the country—which, as it is so subject to earthquakes, does not allow a greater weight without danger to the buildings. The floor is of bamboos, split or otherwise prepared; for, as these are hollow, they can be split with the same ease, thus avoiding the trouble and niceties of carpentry. Thus the floor is like a grating, and is a necessary precaution of their natural laziness and dirtiness; for by this way of making their floors they avoid having to sweep them, since the houses can so easily be washed and rid of all dirt. They have no benches or chairs, and thus they get rid of the encumbrance of much furniture. They consider a seat on the floor as more secure. They use tables somewhat; these are round and hollowed out in the middle, in the manner of an ordinary brasier, and are built wholly for use rather than for display. In that hollow they put all their dishes, which consist of boiled rice, and fish of the same stew, without there being any danger of the food being spilled out. They use no tablecloths or napkins; and, although they use dishes somewhat, they do not usually feel the lack of these, as the trees with their wide leaves furnish them a cleaner table-service, and the bamboos make them very tasteful jugs and bowls which are formed from their lengths between knots. These also form their jars; for there is a kind of bamboo from which they make jars containing three or four azumbres.35 By cutting four joint-lengths and boring holes in them, they fill a good jar. The cocoanuts yield them cups, for here these are very common.

Chapter XIV

The laws of their private conduct and the general laws of their government

Following are the laws pertaining to them privately as persons. They are as much adapted to the nature of the world (although more clothed with innocence), as they are to their laziness and cupidity which prohibits them from all expense which is not necessary for life, as superfluous. For that I have always said of these natives that they are fine philosophers, adapted to nature. The laws which touch on other matters and have to do with their neighbors are quite at variance with the laws of nature; and these extend to a tyranny so manifestly cruel that at times and in some things it comes to be brutality. I have seen a son who held his father as slave, and, vice versa, a father who held his son as slave; for if one make an outlay for another, they take account of it, as would be done in the case of a stranger. Inasmuch as this son had freed his father by buying him from his master, that man was reckoned as his son's slave, and the same would be true of the son. It may happen that a chief lowers himself [by having intercourse] with his slave-woman, and the son whom she bears may be so cruel that at the death of his father he makes his own mother his slave. Even if, while they are at peace, these points are not cleared up, and the inner tyranny employs external civility, yet, if dissensions alter these relations, and they are divided, the men avail themselves of those rights, and subject their mothers to whatever they choose, and do not allow them to leave their houses. Thus do they come to be served by their mothers at all times. In regard to those who descend from them, there is even less shame; and among another kind of relations is an utter disregard of nature in this respect, for their own nephews are the slaves of their uncles, and, vice versa, uncles are slaves of their nephews.

They do not know what charity is. Consequently, whatever benefits they confer are all placed on account as debts, which their tyranny estimates wholly to their own satisfaction. Unfortunate he whom abandonment or orphanage has flung into the house of another, for now for his sustenance, and again for his rearing, he must become a slave. Kindness is shown at the cost of liberty. Although that was general throughout the islands, in this island it is excessive, as it is a tenet of the perfidious sect of Mahomet; and its cruelty has left no liberty that it has not opposed. Therefore, there is not in this nation the middle class that is found in the others which forms the common people out of the freemen; for there are no freemen, nor any mean between chiefs and slaves. Their community is composed of but two extremes, so far separated. It is a fact that there are many ways by which to reduce men to such a condition, and there is no escape from the injury. For, since self-interest is the advantage of those who are powerful, it unites them against the unfortunate one who dares to proclaim the offense that has been done to him, while his punishment conciliates so many other offenders who might perplex justice; and fear shuts the mouths of those whom the same fortune might gain to his favor in the support of his testimonies. Therefore, when it comes to proof there is always a lack of witnesses for innocence; while on the contrary there is for tyranny an oversupply of ocular witnesses of things that they have never seen or heard. When some stranger goes to a village to trade where he does not have the guaranteed patronage of many powerful relations, in the case of any neglect that is shown him in courtesy or in the laws, they bring such a case against him that to get out of it well he abandons his business and perhaps with his business his freedom. The worst of it is that the punishment is always more than the offense, for the just pay as if they were sinners. Their avarice or tyranny not satisfied with the vengeance taken on the criminal makes the offense related to the very blood, in order to extend their cupidity farther. Hence it is that on account of the crime committed by a single one, they make all the relations slaves. I saw four brothers who were all deprived of their inherited freedom because of the incivility and weakness of one. Finding myself in Iligan—a nation which, as it is so new, is even yet throwing out the sparks of this tyrannical fury it happened that a common woman spoke some insulting words to another woman who had rank; and the latter's husband, coming to me to make a complaint, said to me, exaggerating the offense: "Father, if the Spaniards were not here, and we could rule ourselves by our own laws, we would have made mincemeat [gigote] of that woman with a campilan, and slaves of her brothers and sisters and relatives." Finally, he whom avarice rules with a tyrannical power (for all their laws end in self-interest) gets usury from his offense and employment from his crime.

Avarice rules in all their judgments; and the purse becomes the gallows of all crimes. Money is the vengeance of the aggrieved parties, and the sponge for injuries. When they are paid for, no spot or sign of the offense is left. Although there are crimes which bear especially a capital penalty, yet there is no penalty that cannot be redeemed by money or goods. He who has no possessions at all has still liberty, and can surrender that also. That is the road most traveled by which some come to be the slaves of others; and perhaps the chief, if he be poor, may be the slave of another who is a plebeian. When anyone is caught in adultery, if sudden wrath does not execute him, which is but seldom, the wounds are passed on to his purse, in the endeavor to destroy him, and the husband subjects his own wife to the same harshness and penalty. For here all persons have a separate purse, and the husband is not master of what his wife possesses but only of what pertains to him. Nor, under pretext of managing her possessions, does he have more to do with it than the extent of her permission; and she is always mistress of her own possessions. Thus she pays a fine to her own husband, as if she were a stranger to him. Having received this, the aggrieved party remains as satisfied as when, among the Spaniards, one sword has pinned both guilty ones together. The offender retains a privilege truly insulting and barbarous—that for one year he may have intercourse with the woman without her husband complaining. Then the husband and wife return in all peace to cohabit as before, the offense being again at risk, for another atonement.

They especially abhor theft, and they have assigned an ignominious penalty for the thief, as a warning. This is to cut off the joints of his fingers, more or fewer according to the crime. That perhaps obliges them to pass from the hands to the toes, the penalty being proportioned to the misdeeds of greater atrocity. But that penalty can also be redeemed, as can the others, by money.

Notwithstanding that, some crimes they regard as so capital that they do not respect petitions or allow bribes, and death is the necessary punishment for them. The unnatural crime is one of them, and the severity of the execution well shows their natural horror, for such people are burned, and their houses; and nothing that they possessed is allowed to escape from this rigor, as being contaminated. Or, having caged the offenders, they throw them into the sea, and destroy their houses and fields, by such punishment to make demonstration of their abhorrence.

The most feared crime is that which they call sumban, which is incest in the first degree; for they regard it as assured by long experience and knowledge inherited in tradition from their ancestors, that the land which allows that crime is bound down by wretchedness and misfortunes until its infamy is purged by the rigorous chastisement of the offender. There is no other means which can placate the wrath of heaven. Consequently, when they suffer long droughts, or other general plagues from heaven, they immediately attribute them to this. A case of that nature came to my notice in the year fifty-one, when the drought was general, and so great that even the water of the rivers failed, and that river which had any water that found its way to the sea was rare. The Indians of the village which was in my care on the coast of Siocon came to tell me that it was a punishment from the sky, and that it had been demanded by the awfulness of such crime on the coast of Mindanao, where they said that a mother was living in marriage with her son. They petitioned me to have the offenders punished, and warned me that the punishment should be death without remission, such being their custom, without admitting satisfaction by any other penalty, however excessive it be. The same report was current in the island of Basilan. However, it was without other foundation than that the Indians are gossipy and suspicious, ignorant of the secrets of the sky and ruled by the traditions of the past. They are ruled in that island by greater fear, as they retained more accurately in their memory certain cases that served them as examples and warnings. For, at a certain time, the sky was so leaden that for two years not a drop of rain fell. There was an Indian who violated the respect that he owed to his blood and to nature, with regard to a daughter of his. Although he tried to bury the crime in the depths of his silence, it cried out to the sky as an offense, and was heard distinctly as a sin; for the effect, as ungrateful as evil, always turns against its cause. He was a person of influence, and respect for him did not allow any investigation to be made; but, the villages grieving over the public calamity, and unable to endure their forced famine, men trampled under foot respect and laws, in their judgment that tolerance in so execrable an evil had also vexed and hardened the sky. By common consent they seized father and daughter, and, shutting them up in a cage well weighted with stones, threw them into the sea. In return they experienced from the sky approbation for their avenging zeal, in the heavy rain with which it received them. For at all times God preserves the credit to virtue, and even among barbarians imposed penance on vice, so that those who became familiars of vice could have no excuse.36

The Joloans executed the same punishment with equal severity, but through malicious information. God, who is always the protector of innocence, shielded the wretched; for when they cast two other fathers in the same manner [into the water], he took away the weight of the stones, and gave the men strength to keep afloat, without abandoning them for a whole day, so that, the report of the matter having reached the king, the wonder forced him to seek new information, by which he discovered falsity and recognized innocence. In all the nations innocence considers God as its advocate, and in desperate cases rests secure on His protection.

Judges in suits or causes follow the simple laws of nature, and have no embarrassment of laws and doubts and contrary interpretations. They have no delays by reports or prolixity of writs, for they do not waste a single dedo37 of paper in that. The accusation, the plea, and the evidence are quickly heard—all in the manner of the time of Noah. If there is no testimony, they admit the parties to the oath, which contains terrifying imprecations. With that plea the party is usually content; for the obligation and risk, to which he is exposed by results which are reckoned as punishments of heaven against perjured ones if the rigor of their imprecations is executed, are greatly feared. If perchance the party is satisfied that he has truth on his side, at his petition they do not rest content with that trial, but judgment of red-hot coals or hot iron,38 such as was resorted to in España and other countries, in centuries ruder and more immune from laws by the privilege of their innocence and goodness. If the persons are burned, then their punishment is proceeded with; and if not, the accuser is obliged to make requital. That custom seems to have been communicated by the Moros by way of Terrenate, where it is still observed. However, no one is burned, for since the Ternatans are so skilled in sorcery, they know herbs of such efficacy and bewitchments of such power, that they communicate it to the hands so that they can handle the iron with impunity, as if it were a nosegay of flowers. Also many of those whom they bury alive, that being the punishment of adultery and rape, escape. I say this, for it often occurred that persons escaped from the execution of this test, in the sight of the Spaniards at Ternate, women whose guilt was notorious, but who cleared themselves of suspicion among their people by this proof. I was told many happenings of this sort, during the time that I spent in those islands [i.e., the Moluccas]; and I was assured that it was done by means of an herb, and I was shown some that were famous in its knowledge. These were the ones to whom the accused had recourse in all their exigencies, suborning their expertness with a quantity of money.

Chapter XV

The form of government of these natives

The kings, although so tyrannical in government, and in power so beyond the affliction and trouble which authority and ostentation incur, yet according to the condition of their poverty maintain the form and authority of a court. Peace affairs are in charge of a chief justice or counselor, called zarabandal. That is the greatest court title and he decides the causes and suits, and advises concerning the sentence. In the outside villages where the king does not reside, the chiefs meddle wherever they wish, without other law than their power and will, and their unbridled greed; and the one injured has no recourse, for, in quarrels between the plebeians and chiefs, the king always takes the part of the latter—who are more powerful, and are those who can make trouble for him, and even deprive him of his kingdom. For his principate is founded more on the recognition that they make of his nobility than on any absolute power which secures to him their vassalage; since a slave will say "no" to the king in what does not suit him. That happened in Joló, in the presence of Father Alexandro Lopez. When the father was negotiating through the medium of the king to have the ransom for a Christian put at a humane figure, the other, a Joloan slave by condition, who had the Christian in his power, said to the very face of the king, when the latter asked him to conform to the prices settled upon in the treaty of peace,39 that he would not do it; and that was the end of the matter. That signified that the king's power in execution extended just so far as his vassals wished, and that they would obey him just so far as it pleased them.

They have established orders of nobility, with a distinction of titles which aggrandize it. Some are called *Tuam*, which is the same as "Señor" or the title applied to men in España. Others are given the title of *Orancaya*, which signifies "rich man;" it is the greatest title, and equivalent to grandee of their kingdom. It is equivalent to the same title that España gave to its grandees when his Majesty used more simplicity, and called them Ricos-Homes [*i.e.*, "rich men"]. The rest are called chiefs, and correspond to what we call *caballeros* and *Hijos-dalgo* [*i.e.*, "knights and nobles"]. They have no greater dignity than the honor. Those of the blood royal are called *cachiles* following the custom and style of the kings of Maluco, Terrenate, Tidores, and Xilolos. The same in the peculiar style of Joló are called Paguian.

The Orangcayas or Ricos-Homes become the rulers of vassals, and have some villages in their charge. In those villages, although the king is recognized, and tribute sent to him, in all else those rulers are absolute; and especially in government affairs are they independent. They are the ones who tyrannize most ungovernably over the people; for whatever fine the king imposes upon them, or whatever gift he requests from them, they lay hands upon their subjects, and, as if they were slaves they take away the son from the father in order to sell him. That has been the case so often that, even since they have been made subject to our government, it has been necessary to examine with close attention, whenever they bring any slave to sell, the reason for his slavery; for it has been found that they sell us many slaves without any other right than that of their tyranny, relieving their necessities and making their payments with the first person whom they meet—bringing him, beguiled by some other pretext, to the Spaniards; and the injury was suffered without any complaint, because of the incapacity and dullness of the poor Subanos. The latter, as they are so unused to intercourse with us, and so shut up in their own lives, had no arguments to oppose to what they did not understand; and showed their wonder, surprise, and bashfulness in brute silence. For that reason, where the Orangcayas govern (which are almost all villages of the Subanos or Indians of the mountain), there is scarce one who enjoys liberty. Those chiefs hold them so under their power, that they regard the very leaders and chiefs of the Subano nation as their slaves. That I experienced on a visit which I made on a dangerous occasion, when in order to assure the minds of the people I took with me a Lutao chief who was the absolute master before the Spaniards entered, and to whom they still paid hereditary respect along all the coast of Siocon. Being, then, with all the people and chiefs of the nation assembled together in a village, and I endeavoring to honor them with signs of the greatest affection, the Lutao said: "Do not pay any attention to these people, Father, for they are all my slaves." This he said in a place where we two and the chiefs of the village were alone. I thought that that contempt and arrogance would arouse them; but on the contrary, it softened them, as the affection and presents of a loving prince would his humble vassal. And, although they were not slaves, the respect in which they were born gives the chiefs so much authority, that although we [Spaniards] possess the rule, they, as chiefs, command the people. And, as the latter were reared in that tyranny, their natural disposition made them show respect and natural submission; for, notwithstanding the immunity that our arms give them, they obey those chiefs better than they do us. May that be tempered in part by the Christian government, and the vigilance of our father ministers, and the recourse which they find in the royal officials. For a chief of those natives who was governor of the village of Baluasan, near to Samboangan, when speaking of the wretched subjection in which the Lutaos held them, and the good fortune that had come to them with the entrance of our government, by restraining the Lutao tyranny, and giving arms to persecuted liberty, spoke to me these words: "If you [Spaniards] had not arrived when you did, there would now not be any of us left; for we would already have been finished, and bartered for goods with the people of Macasar." These words consoled me, on account of the fidelity which the interest and recognized advantages of that barbarian guaranteed.40

Such was the government maintained by Corralat. And since he made all of them so powerful, giving them special power by laws, he was very acceptable to the princes of his nation and therefore most secure. These men, then, are the ones who grieve over the losses sustained by the change, who see themselves put under holy laws and just—they who before had no other laws than those of their own will, and their unbridled ambition, laws from which the others suffered as a servile, cowardly, and rude nation.

Chapter XVI

Some peculiarities of the customs of the Subanos

The customs of the Subanos or Indians of the mountains there is no reason for relating; for with more hideous extremes they maintain the evils of the Lutaos, while those peculiar to them are, as it were, the brutal creatures among other citizens. But that even will add praises to the changes that have resulted from the skill of the Omnipotent, and to the zeal of the missionaries, by whose means virtue produced the civilized and Christian conduct which now is theirs. Their dress approaches that of the inhabitants of the beach with whom they have communication. Accordingly, those who traffic with Lutaos or Moros dress in their style; while those familiar with the Visayan nations (such as the peoples of Caraga and the coast of Dapitan), through commerce with them, follow their custom. All their government is confusion, and they wage war, not some nations with others, nor one village with another, but all are, as it were, enemies of the human race. Armed against one another, without subordination or greater subjection than what the might and act of violence of the boldest obtained, they had no other laws in their causes that the might of the one provoked to avenge himself; and his rigor, even in the worst cases, was appeased by gifts. Thus when a Subano came to acquire a poor capital that would enable him to pay for a murder, he committed the murder with the greatest safety, in order that he might be enrolled in the number of valiant and to have authority as such to wear a red turban. Because of that barbaric vanity they would kill their best friend, if they caught him asleep or off his guard; for the barbaric courage of these nations does not consider posts of reputation, but those of security. In Caraga there was a more atrocious custom; for, in order to be able to clothe oneself in the dress of the valiant—namely, a striped turban, and breeches of their peculiar style (which they call baxaque) with similar stripes—one must have killed seven men.41

The peculiarity of this nation, and the thing that gives them some excellence and esteem, is that their women are more chaste and modest. They esteem virginity, and keep it inviolate, even to advanced age, for the vocation of matrimony. It is true that this virtue is aided by their natural disposition, which furnishes for the defense of chastity their native stupidity and shyness; but therewith they succeed in an undertaking which among Lutaos and the other nations of these islands is rare and difficult indeed. This has secured them so much esteem and confidence in this region that the chiefs of high standing among the Lutaos, in order to guard their daughters more safely, have them reared among Subanos; and they do not take them into the dangerous camp of their own nation unless it is to establish them in marriage, and with that station, in safety, as they think. Among this nation there is a class of men who profess celibacy42 and govern themselves by natural law, and they are very punctual and perfect in their observance of it; and such is the feeling of security in regard to them, that they are allowed to go about among the women without any fear or suspicion. Their dress is throughout like that of the women, with skirts of the same fashion. They do not use weapons, or engage in anything else that is peculiar to men, or communicate with them. They weave the mantas that are used here, which is the proper employment of women, and all their conversation is with women. Therefore, the purpose of life which they follow comes to be more extraordinary by its peculiarity and by its perils, considering both the nature of that country, and the little regard that they give to their dangers. So satisfied do they live, either from their own purpose or from their natural disposition, that they have never discredited their position with weaknesses. They were, so to speak, hermits of their religion, and were held in high esteem. And in fact the constancy of their life and modesty of their customs, obliged one to have respect for them. In a nation so barbarous and who knew not God, it appears a prodigy worthy of wonder that one of the special providences of His Divine Majesty, to place such examples of virtue in a country where vice had absolute control, so that the experience of the eyes causes them to esteem what God's love did not obtain. I have known two of these men, and one of them I baptized, to my especial consolation, while visiting the coast of Siocon, which extends for twenty leguas from Samboangan toward Dapitan. His reputation reached me in a different village, for in his own they kept him closely concealed, whether it were for the sake of their ancient observances I do not know. Like a holy man of his law, or because of some fear, he also kept himself hidden; for, as he afterward told me, they had terrified him by telling him that if the Spaniards caught him they would put him in the galleys. By that means, to him whom the pathway of salvation was most easy, they filled it with such difficulties that they made it impossible for him. I knew that they would refuse to let me see him for those same reasons, and therefore made use of a trick and of a dangerous resolution, to catch him. For near the village, which was located on the beach in the shade of trees (the poverty of these barbarians not suffering more shelter), and where in a few hours they would suffer from hunger, having them all before me I told them that if the lavia43 whom they had hidden did not come, then the mass would not begin. Labia is the name they give to those of this profession. The name of this one was Tuto. I added that no one must return to his house until he arrived, and that if he delayed too long, I would go to Samboangan with the chief of the village and the Subanos of importance. That was the same to them as if I were taking them to the galleys; so much does their wretchedness grieve to leave the wretchedness in which they were born, and their lack of intelligence to appear before reasonable people and Spaniards. Without allowing them to talk, or to question whether he was there or not, or where, but assuming that it was a well-known thing, I turned to a relative of the governor, and said to him: "Go for him quickly, for I shall not move from this spot until he comes." He departed without a word, and all of the people remained motionless, staring with fright. When they recovered their equanimity, their whole attempt was to excuse their negligence by empty excuses, which I accepted in order to calm their minds. Inside of an hour I found in my presence him whom I desired so much. He, seeing the love with which I received him, and how differently my purpose was declared from that which his fears gave him to understand, recovered his courage in full, and immediately offered himself for baptism—a matter which I was unwilling to defer, in order that I might leave him with his salvation assured. Consequently, after instructing him briefly, I baptized him, and called him Martin, as that happy lot came to him on that saint's day.44 He satisfied my hopes and hastened to me every time when I afterward visited his village of Malande, very punctually, and always with some special refreshment both for me and for him who in my company had acted as his sponsor.

The other lavia whom I saw was in one of the Joloan islands, called Pangutara.45 Him I found to be already a Christian, whom Father Alexandro Lopez, a great apostle of the Joloans, had reduced and baptized in Samboangan, and called Santiago. This man is naturally very well dispositioned and has no moral defects, and he is a man of a celestial peace and serenity. He is always bubbling with laughter, which is the effect of the security of his soul; for, when the conscience has nothing to fear, the heart has gladness to scatter abroad.

I must not neglect to tell one thing that I noticed in regard to the nature of the people of this profession, from what I could gather from the exterior of those two, which seems to me to be the reason that takes them along the pathway so unusual and difficult in a climate so hot, and lands so dangerous (as he who has had experience in these islands, and who knows the wretchedness of their natives in this region, will know). For the physiognomy of those men is that of eunuchs, and their natural disposition and condition are so cold, that it made me think that they must be so naturally, and that nature kept her virtue under control in this region. But since they behave in all other things with so blameless a life, I shall always consider them as prodigies of the divine Providence in favor of virtue. For no one despises virtue as a thing unknown, since even to barbarians virtue is painted in so natural colors that they respect it naturally, without more external credit than their native security.

This sole spark of good morals have I found among the so great darkness in which the Subanos live. However, they have another custom belonging to the same aspect of their lives, so vile that it is sufficient to obscure greater lights than those of that small spark; for among them is more acceptable the exchange that they make of their women with one another—the husbands mutually agreeing upon this exchange, and celebrating the hideous loan and the vile restitution with dances and drunken revels, according to their custom. Their feasts are like their customs, and one is the manifestation of the other.

Chapter XVII

Burials and marriages of those natives

I have kept these two acts, so contrary in their effects, in order to present them in one place in this chapter, inasmuch as they are of greater display and magnificence, and in them, in spite of the simplicity of those natives, the serious predominates. In the first, which is practiced with their dead, I know not whether to praise more their piety or their generosity and grandeur, or to which of the two virtues recognition is due; for both are carried to the greatest extreme. For their liberality, the obligations of their piety (which declares itself in those attentions a debtor to nature), passes by and tramples under foot the laws of their poverty and the natural simplicity of these Indians, and makes demonstrations superior to their fortune, clothing their dead with the magnificence of princes. In the shroud alone, they clothe the dead person in a hundred brazas of fine muslin, which serves him as a shirt. Over that they place rich patolas, which are pieces of cloth of gold, or of silk alone, worked very beautifully, and of great value, pious generosity endeavoring to give him the best and to clothe him in the finest and most precious garments. It is a law, established by immemorial custom, that the children and near relatives each clothe the deceased in a piece of gauze or of sinampuli (another fabric of equal estimation) arranging it with such loops and knots that they find space for it all. In regard to the dress, this custom is in force even to this day, and no man who respects himself has ever failed in this law. There is no one so poor and so wretched that he does not own a piece [of cloth] eight brazas long, which is reserved for his burial. They have abandoned other demonstrations, or rather, exchanged them for Christian ones, of which we shall speak at the proper place. In that regard they give oldtime Christians much to emulate. For formerly they buried with their dead most of their treasures—gold, bells, and other things, which are highly esteemed among them. Those things were so sacred to reverence that no one, however abandoned and audacious he might be, had the courage to stretch forth his hand to take them—although he could have done so with great safety to himself, as their dead are buried in caves, islets, or solitary mountains, without other guard than their imaginary religion. On the day on which they buried the deceased, about his sepulcher they planted palms, jasmines, and other flowers peculiar to this region. If the deceased was a king, or a prince of equal nobility, they placed a tent above the grave with four white banners at its sides, while inside it they burned perfumes as long as the time of lamentation or memorial lasted, perhaps setting aside some slaves for that employ, in order to make it more lasting.

This heathen display has given way to Christian demonstrations of sumptuous honors and abundant alms which they give for their deceased, as we shall relate in the proper place. But I shall not defer the telling of one which may prove a matter of reprehension to our neglect and forgetfulness, in what is more important to us, namely, that they are wont to have the coffin prepared during the lifetime for their burial. They make those coffins out of one single piece, and from incorruptible woods. They keep them under their houses where they can see them whenever they descend from or ascend to their houses; and they are open to the gaze of all who pass along the street. That is a care that it would be right for them to have learned from the oldtime Christians, whom the faith of what they hope for, ought to arouse with greater demonstrations....

The Subanos follow the Lutaos in some things, their poverty and misery exerting efforts in the worship of their dead, and their barbarism showing itself at the side of their piety, when they throw into the sea, out of grief, the gold of their ornaments, decorations, and their most precious jewels—a custom wellnigh universal in all these islands.46 But in one island their cruelty is shown especially in their alleviation of their grief and their barbaric pity for their calamity, by giving associates to the deceased, and making them companions of their grief, causing the same havoc and loss in others. Because their father, son, near relative, or anyone whom they had loved had died, they would seize their arms in order to kill the first person whom they met, and without other cause for offense than that of their natural disposition and their barbaric ferocity. Thus with the blood of the unfortunate one did they dry the tears of their own ill fortune, finding consolation in the misfortune of others.

The celebration at their marriages is such that in all that has been discovered nothing else can compare with it; and the Spaniards who daily wonder at it as witnesses always do so with new wonder. For if the marriage is of a chief, the celebration begins a week beforehand, and is concluded a week after with dancing to the sound of their bells and drums. There is open table for all who care to go up into the house. The viands consist of wine, for that is the thing in which they are especially solicitous to show display, while they take no account of the food, although it is not lacking. But the deceiving heat of the wine takes away their taste so strongly that they are mindful of nothing. Its heat serves to give spirit and animation to their songs (which are in honor of him who makes the feast), and sprightliness to their dances. The day of the celebration [of the wedding] when the betrothed couple have to appear for the nuptial blessings, the bride, breaking the strict confinement which she keeps all that time, issues forth with a display and gravity superior to her condition; for her relatives and the other Indians of their partisanship are clad in their gala costume, and armed with lance and shield, and escort the bride. The march is to the accompaniment of bells and Moorish dulzainas [i.e., a sort of wind instrument]. The ladies of honor follow in double file, and they generally consist of all the women of the village, who are invited for the sake of greater display of grandeur. Then the girls follow in the same order, while those of greater social standing and higher rank are borne in chairs richly adorned, and carried on the shoulders of four slaves. At the end comes the bride in a certain very spacious chair which allows room for a lady who supports and assists her, and to two or three girls, who serve her with so singular modesty and gravity that it would cause wonder even if she did not affect so great elaborateness; for she scarcely moves an eyelash or must move her hand, those who accompany her substituting themselves for everything. One dries the sweat from her, another fans her, and a third looks after her clothing. Down a different street comes the bridegroom to meet the bride, with a like or even greater retinue in competition with that of the relatives of the bride. The men are in gala costume, and armed; the women are in festal array; and the chief women in chairs. The dress of the bridal pair must be white, until, the [bride's] consent having been given, the bridegroom retires, and exchanges it for a red dress. In this ceremony coquetry displays greater affectations: for the bride takes a half-hour to give her answer, and, after it is given she wastes another long half-hour to reach the lattice of the chapel. And it is necessary to sit down to await the bride for that time, amid the laughter of those who a few days before saw her running and leaping about like a mad she-goat, while on this day she deports herself with so great a demonstration of sedateness and virginal modesty. The precision of her steps, they say, is a necessity, because she is coming bound even to the feet. That is the ceremony that they practice for the reception of the husband who is the one who must come to take those bonds and shackles from her.

On that day the house is all hung with a canopy that covers everything, so that neither walls nor ceiling are seen. The bridal-chamber is open to the sight and richly adorned, for on that day everything gleams with splendor and adornment. The bride is seated on a cushion, near a seat made for the groom from cushions in the Moorish style, with embroidery and strips of silk with a quantity of lace. She is served with the same ostentation as in the street, and displays no more animation than a statue. I was present at one of so great display that, besides the display which the Lutaos showed in their weddings, there came at two o'clock of the same day, marching in a company formed of their men, lancers and arquebusiers, an assembly of men who taking position in the plaza de armas, invited the governor and all the Spanish artillery for that afternoon; and for the following day all the paid soldiers—Pampangos and Cagayanes—giving food to all and serving the Spaniards quite in the Spanish fashion, both in the cuisine and in the courtesies. It is an event of so great preëminence that the governor and all his captains and best soldiers go to it, in order to honor and conciliate those people. And any prince can well go to see those ceremonies, for neither actions nor words show that they are barbarians; but [they appear as] the most modest nation in the world, which is celebrating its marriage without any idea of the [carnal] delights of it. They are so moderate in showing their affection that during three days they do not avail themselves of the license of their estate. Such is the way in which they act that the fathers worthily honor it with their presence, and on that day go to their houses, for they are unaccustomed to the modesty and caution unless it is when they confess and anoint them. Everything is dispensed with on that day because of its gravity. We all, then, went on that day with the superior, and the governor and captains. I was very glad to be a witness of so great splendor, modesty, and gravity in natives who are in other things so simple and unceremonious; and to see a sacrament so hazardous treated with so much devotion, in the respect shown to the ministers of it. That chief spent at that feast more than four hundred arrobas of wine, and more than one thousand birds. Although they are poor, in order to meet the obligations of that day satisfactorily they strip themselves, showing an equally generous spirit in such action with the living as is displayed in the fatherland with the dead; for the greatest displays of their grandeur are the funerals and weddings.

Chapter XVIII

Boats and weapons of these natives

The craft used by the Lutaos for war are, like those of terrible pirates, built with particular attention to speed—both for pursuit, and to seek shelter whenever affairs go wrong with them, or when their undertaking is dangerous to them. For since their wars are always waged for greed, and reputation never induces them, they try to advantage themselves quite at their safety; and they readily abandon any undertaking if they see that it will be costly to them. That care and attention, which govern their boat-building, cause their ships to sail like birds, while ours are like lead in this regard. The planking that they use is very thin, and has no other nails, crotches, or knees than a little rattan. Rattan is the substance which here takes the place of hemp, in tying things together, some planks [in the craft] being tied together with it. For that purpose projecting parts are left at intervals on the inside [of the planks] in which holes are made; and through these the ligament passes, without any harm being done to the plank. Upon so light a foundation they build upper works, as high as they wish, of bamboo upon the cates. The cates are buoys which run on both sides from bow to stern, and they act as outriggers for the ship, which is sustained by these two floats. The ship carries more outside than in. The outside scaffolds allow room for two rows of oars, beside that of the hull. Thus small craft of from seven to twelve brazas (which is the largest size) have a crew of sixty men and upwards. I have seen one that was manned with three hundred hands; for, in order to have the rowing more compressed together they use loose oars, each one handling his own. Those oars are certain round blades, which an Indian manages easily. Therefore, when it is necessary they row exactly to the time of their breathing, by inserting more or less of the oar, according to the force they wish to give. For the rowing is excellent and the oar is put directly into the water, because it is trusted solely to the hands, without being fastened to anything. That is a custom that obliges them to have their craft very flat, and to elevate the sides but little, and they are content to leave but one plank out of the water.

These vessels are crescent-shaped. Consequently, there is but a small keel, or little of it in the water, and that part which they rob from stern and bow is left out of the water—three or four brazas of keel or stem, all of which serves for its speed, and there is little to hold the boat back because of its narrowness. Therefore the helm is not managed like the Spanish helm, by the sweep from the end; accordingly, they use two rudders, one at one side and one at the other, where the flat part of the keel begins. One is usually employed for managing the boat, and both of them when it is stormy. With the second they keep the boat from getting unsteady, which would follow from its lightness, that rudder giving the boat more stiffness and serving as ballast. That is a precaution rendered necessary by its very lightness, the vessels that are lightest being those that require most care by being unsteady. In the middle they have a scaffold, four or six brazas long, which they call burulan or baileo. This consists of a floor raised above the rowers, and has its awning, which is called cayanes. Those awnings are made from the leaves of a small palm which grows in the water. That is the quarters for the fighters and the chiefs, for those vessels do not have any stern-cabin; it is, at the same time, the little castle from which they fight. All that structure finds its support and staunchness in what they call the cates, which are the buoys of which we have spoken. They are made of three or four bamboos as thick as the arm, and even larger, and reach from stem to stern. They are so adjusted that they drag through the water about one and one-half brazas away from the vessel. Consequently, they do not allow it to toss about, however violent the waves, but are the arms that keep the boat safe. They are used in general by all the craft of these islands, and by those of Burney and Maluco; for, since their ships are of no account without this security, they have no safety in the sea nor do the Indians dare to embark. From this circumstance Molina, who represented to the Council that buoys ought to be fastened to the ships so that they could sail or float with a support made of certain bags blown up and thrown alongside, derived his argument. He thought that that would assure the fleets, as they could not then sink, as he had experienced, even if they filled with water. It might have proved successful indeed, and in favor of his discourse, if some heavy sea raised by the hurricanes would not prove sufficient to burst the bags and drag them away from the sides; for hurricanes have more than sufficient violence to break up the stern and destroy the ship. That has been well known by actual experience here; for a few hours of a severe storm are sufficient to destroy the fastenings; and those ships would be wrecked daily if the voyages were not so short, and the vessels of so small burden that they can find shelter in any port. When necessity arises, the men in them beach the vessels themselves, and do so more easily when they go in a fleet, as then they unite their forces. The crossings are so short, because of the multiplicity of islands, that the weather never catches them in such a way that they can not soon escape by drawing near to one land or another. For fair weather this appliance is very useful, so that they take comfort in them freely.

In regard to their weapons, the Lutao nation is the most curious in these islands; for all glory in having the most precious and the finest arms possible. All of them from their earliest age wear their weapons, with so careful a regard to this matter that no one dares to leave his house without his weapons. The wearing of weapons is so much a matter of reputation with them, that they consider it an insult to be obliged to appear without them, regulating their punctiliousness in this region very much according to the laws of España. It casts much shame upon the negligence into which our military force has fallen, by the poor reputation of those here who profess arms, who in the sight of these nations are not ashamed to be seen without swords or daggers; and those which they carry well demonstrate the care with which they serve in their posts, since they necessarily satisfy outward appearance, although they would be useless on occasion. I speak of the simple and common soldiers; and, since this care is lacking in most of them, it ought to be felt more, and with effect, by those who can remedy it. The weapon worn by the natives of the cities is a wavy dagger, which they call a kris. Its blade is engraved with channels and water-lines, which make it very beautiful. The hilt is a small idol, made of ivory for the common man, and of gold for the chiefs, studded with gems which are highly esteemed among them. I saw one worn by the commander Socsocan47—who was the lord of Samboangan when our men conquered it—which was valued at ten slaves. The scabbard was gilded with the same neatness, and at some time had been covered with sheets of gold. I saw a scabbard in Joló, which had a pearl as large as a musket-ball at the end of the chape. The blades are very fine, and, although so small (being scarcely two palmos in length), they are valued at twelve, twenty, or thirty reals of eight.

Such are their arms in peace; those of war, for fighting on the land, are lances and shields. The shield is round among the coast-dwellers of the south, and in the islands of Basilan and Joló. In the rest of this island, the general custom of the long and narrow shield which is used in all the other islands is followed; with these, they shield and protect all the body. From these weapons the kris is inseparable, and they use it at close quarters, and after they have used the lance, which they throw in the usual manner. Their lances show the same care as their krises, and are very much ornamented and engraved, and have their covers gilded. The shaft is of the finest ebony, or of some other beautiful wood; and at intervals they put rings of silver or tin on it. The head is of brass, which is used here, and so highly polished that it vies with gold. It is chased so elaborately that there are lances that are valued at one slave each. At the end they fasten a large hawk's-bell, which they fix upon the shaft in such a manner that it surrounds it; and when they shake the lance it sounds in time with the fierce threats and bravadoes. The valiant use them and as man-slayers, give warning to those who do not know them and those of less valor, so that they may avoid them as they would vipers.

The arms used on sea and land—besides those of the plain, in places where the people fortify themselves with the resolve to defend themselves— in addition to the one mentioned (which are the most deadly), are the bagacayes, which are certain small bamboos as thick as the finger, hardened in the fire and with points sharpened. They throw these with such skill that they never miss when the object is within range; and some men throw them five at a time. Although it is so weak a weapon, it has such violence that it has gone through a boat and has pierced and killed the rower. Brother Diego de Santiago told me, as an eyewitness, that he being seated saw that thing (which appears a prodigy) happen in the same vessel in which he had embarked with a garrison. To me that seemed so incredible that I wished immediately to see it myself; and, cutting a bagacay, I had it thrown at a shield. In Samboanga I saw a bull which was killed immediately by a bagacay which a lad threw at it, which struck it clear to the heart. It is a thing that would cause laughter in Europa, and there would be little esteem for the valor which does not despise such weapons, and they would jest at so frail violence. But it is certain that, at close range, there is no crueler weapon; and it is also certain that, the day on which these Moros have bravery enough to get within range, on that day any ship must yield. For they send in such a shower of these bagacayes that scarce a man is unwounded; while many are stuck like bulls, so that they cannot move for being laden with so many weapons. Then the rowing ceases, and they discharge the missiles with both hands and some from each finger, both rowers and fighters. That throws their opponents into disorder, and they are unable to manage their weapons. There must be many in España who were in the dangerous sieges which Governor Don Sebastian Hurtado de Corcuera undertook against the kings of both Mindanao and Joló—where, in the so great mortality which the glorious boldness and military honor of our men incurred, the most of those who fell, to exalt their fame forever, were slain by arms so weak and apparently contemptible. In the same way they use stakes hardened in the fire which they hurl with accuracy, and which inflict even more damage. The lance is used in the same way, and they hurl it with so extraordinary violence that they pierce a steel-covered shield and transfix the soldier with it, as has been seen often. In an engagement that Captain Gaspar de Morales[48] fought in Joló, his steel-covered shield did not avail him; but the lance passed through it and his arm, and did not fall short of giving him a mortal wound in the breast.

The Negrillos of this island use the bow and arrow, as these are the weapons least difficult to obtain, and more natural [to them], as requiring less skill. They poison arrows, and the wound is consequently always dangerous. The wooden points of the arrows are so hard that those people have no occasion to regret the lack of iron.[49]

The use of the blowpipe [zarbatana], which is one braza long, has extended from the Borneans to the Joloans, and even to the Lutaos of this island. By blowing through it they discharge certain small darts smeared with so deadly a poison that if one single drop of blood is drawn, death is certain to result, if the antidote is not quickly applied. When our soldiers have to make an expedition to Burney, where other weapons are rarely used, they go prepared with the most efficacious antidotes—namely, human excrement, as has always been happily experienced. These blowpipes are sometimes used also as lances, having the iron fastened at one side, so that, if the shot is not accurate, they use it alternately as a lance. Then when the opportunity is offered they make use of their darts. They are so good shots that they can bring down the smallest bird at twenty or thirty paces.

The Joloans who are called Ximbanaos,50 and are more ferocious and of greater determination, are armed from top to toe with helmet, bracelets, coat-of-mail, greaves, with linings of elephant-hide—armor so proof that nothing can make a dint on it except firearms, for the best sword or cutlass is turned. That was an experience acquired by many in the conquest of the Joloans by General Don Pedro de Almonte Verastigui,51 who had brought from Ternate braggarts of that nation, who wielded the campilan or cutlass—a weapon made for cutting off heads, and for splitting the body from top to toe. But they could effect nothing, notwithstanding the heavy blows of those cutlasses; and retired like cowards, giving as an excuse that their weapons would not cut, and that they were only succeeding in ruining them, for they were all nicked by the strong resistance. From the shoulders rise two irons to the height of the helmet and morion by which they protect the head from being cut off. They knot the flaps of their skirts on the breast or coat-of-mail, so that they can bend the knee to the ground, according to their method of fighting, when the case demands it. They wear a plume of feathers above the forehead, such as is seen on mules. They leave nothing unarmed, even to the eyes, which are armed by fierceness—both because of the terrific appearance of their arms, and by the fierceness which they affect. It is the fitting dress, among them, for princes and braggarts. When they put it on they generally take some opium,52 and, rendered furious and insensible [to danger] by it, they enter amid the vessels of a squadron madly, and destroy it with great slaughter. For their arms are lance, kris, or dagger; and with their bounds and leaps, in which they indulge according to their barbarous method of fighting, they appear in many places, always endeavoring to bring down many [of their foes]. Hence, in order that any ball may strike them, it is necessary that it cause disaster in the troop— besides the injuries that their fury has executed in safety, armed so proof against those who dress as lightly as the heat and roughness of the country compel.

The Mindanaos use a weapon quite distinct from that of the Ternatans. It is a campilan or cutlass of one edge, and heavier than the pointless Turkish weapon. It is a very bloody weapon, but, being so heavy, it is a danger for him who handles it, if he is not adroit with it. It has only two forms of use, namely, to wield it by one edge, and to raise it by the other, in order to deal another stroke, its weight allowing time for the spears of the opponents to enter. They do not gird it on, as that would be too much trouble, but carry it on the shoulders, in the fashion of the camarlengos53 who carry the rapiers on their shoulders in public ceremonies in front of their princes. Besides that weapon the Mindanao uses lance, kris, and shield, as do the other nations. Both these and those have begun to use firearms too much, having acquired that from intercourse with our enemies. They manage all sorts of artillery excellently, and in their fleets all their craft carry their own pieces, with ladle, culverins, esmerils, and other small weapons.54

1 Juan Francisco Combés was born at Zaragoza on October 5, 1620. At the age of twelve he entered the Jesuit order as a novice, at Tarragona; after six years of study there, he wished to enter the Philippine missions, and was therefore sent to Mexico to await an opportunity for going to the islands. This did not come until 1643, when Diego de Bobadilla went from Acapulco with forty-seven Jesuit missionaries, of whom Combés was one; five of these died in an epidemic, which carried away one hundred and fifteen of the people on the ship. Combés completed his theological studies at Manila, and was ordained in 1645, being soon afterward sent to Zamboanga. He remained in Mindanao twelve years, often acting as ambassador of the governors to Corralat and other Moro chiefs, and ministering in various places; in 1657 he returned to Manila, where he spent two years, and then three years in Leyte. He was then recalled (1662) to Manila, and tried to induce the authorities there to maintain the forts in the Moro country; but his efforts failed. In 1665 he was sent as procurator for his order to Madrid and Rome; but he died on the voyage, December 29 of that year. (Retana and Pastells's ed. of Hist. de Mindanao, col. vi–xix.)

2 Of the Caragas, Blumentritt says (Tribes of the Philippines, Mason's translation, p. 535): "In older works are so named the warlike and Christian inhabitants of the localities subdued by the Spaniards on the east coast of Mindanao, and, indeed, after their principal city, Caraga. It has been called, if not a peculiar language, a Visaya dialect, while now only Visaya (near Manobo and Mandaya) is spoken, and an especial Caraga nation is no longer known." It is quite probable that the term Caragas was only a local name applied by the people of this district to themselves or applied to them by the Spaniards; and if they ever did exist as a separate people they have been completely absorbed by the surrounding peoples.

3 The Mindanaos (properly Maguindanaos, "people who come from the lake") are mentioned by Pigafetta (Vol. XXXIII, p. 239); they live now, as formerly, principally about the Rio Grande, and they gave name to the island of Mindanao.

They are Mahometan Moros and were the chief obstacle of the Spaniards in Mindanao, but were finally brought under control by General Weyler, and their power and importance is now almost gone. Their political achievements are the only ones of consequence ever made by peoples of the Philippines. See Census of Philippine Islands, i, pp. 466–467.

4 Blumentritt (Tribes of the Philippines) identities the Lutaos with the Mono of the district of Zamboanga, who are frequently called Ilanos, and adds that the name appears to be the Hispanicized form of the Malay Orang-Laút ("Men of the Sea"). The description given by Combes fits rather the Orang-Laút themselves than the Ilanos, who live along the seacoast west of Malabang, and are few in number. The Orang-Laút, called also "Sea Gypsies," "Bajau" and "Sámal-Laút" ("Sámal of the Sea") are found throughout the Malay Archipelago (in the Philippines along southern Mindanao and throughout the Sulu Archipelago), and live for mouths in their small boats. Their original home was Johore and the islands in the strait of Malacca; and they are only imperfectly Mahometanized, some being quite pagans. The Sámal living in towns in Zamboanga and the Sulu Archipelago are probably descendants of the Sámal-Laút who have abandoned their wandering life. See Census of the Philippines, i, pp. 464, 475, 476, 563.

5 The Subanon (Spanish form "Subanos"), or "Men of the Rivers" are an important pagan tribe of western Mindanao, who are found in the mountains of Zamboanga, and extending eastward slightly into Cottabato, Misamis, and Dapitan. For a modern description that agrees essentially with that of Combés, see Census of the Philippines, i, pp. 552–560.

6 Spanish, redentor; in religious orders, the father appointed to attend to the ransoming and return of Christians held captive by Mahometan enemies.

7 Antonio de Abarca, S.J., was born in Villalba in the diocese of Cuenca, September 13, 1610. He entered the Society March 23, 1628, went to the Philippines in 1632, and took his final vows, January 21, 1649. He was a missionary in Mindanao and the Visayan Islands, and rector of Carigara and Cebú. While going to Rome as procurator, he died at sea (January 23, 1660), near Acapulco. (Combés, Pastells and Retana ed., col. 694.)

8 This chief is called timoly by the Subanos; hari-hari by the Mandayas; masali campo, by the Monteses; matado, by the Manobos; bagani, by the Bagobos; and dato and sultán by the Mahometans and Moros. (Pastells and Retana's Combés, col. 655.)

9 The so-called Dapitan nation was a Visayan tribe and lived in Mindanao in the present comandancia of Dapitán in the province of Misámis. Strictly speaking they can be called a distinct tribe with no greater accuracy than can the Caragas.

See Blumentritt's Tribes of the Philippines (Mason's translation); and Pastells and Retana's Combés, col. 779.

10 Baclayón is a village on the extreme southwest coast of Bohol. Loboc is a village of southern Bohol, and two miles inland. (Philippine Gazetteer.)

11 The Portuguese had discovered the Moluccas before Magallanes set out on his memorable voyage in 1519. See Vol. XXXIV, pp. 39, 153.

12 The text which we follow reads "y quan a fauor de sus nueuas." "Nueuas" may possibly be a misprint for "navios," in which case the phrase would read "how much at the mercy of their ships."

13 Even yet infidels abandon a house in which the head of the family has died. Father Pastells says that while crossing the island of Mindanao with Father Heras in 1878, one Sálug died in the house of Silungan, a freedman recently redeemed by the said missionaries. He was baptised before death by Father Pastells. Silungan demanded from the religious the value of the house, which he proposed to abandon. The fathers, however, answered him that since the freedman had died with baptism, the house was purified. This satisfied the heathens, and they did not insist on their demand. (Pastells and Retana's edition of Combés, note 13, col. 655.)

14 This refers to Legazpi's and not Magallanes's expedition. Pagbuaya made friendship with the former, and gave him a pilot to guide him to the inland of Panglao. In book two of Combés's Historia, chapter II, is related rightly the occurrence with regard to the king of Borneo, after the arrival of Legazpi. Combés says that the Dapitans imagined that the Spaniards were eating fire when they smoked, and the hard white sea-biscuits they imagined to be stones. The noise of the artillery they took to be thunder, and the sword with which each one was girt, they thought to be a tail.

15 The term "Malanao" is derived from "ma," "people of" and "lanao," "lake," and has long been used to distinguish the Moros living on the watershed of Lake Lanao. See Census of the Philippines, i, p. 473.

16 In 1596, Fathers Valerio de Ledesma and Manuel Martinez first established the mission of the River of Butuan. That same year, there not being as yet any division into bishoprics, the Manila ecclesiastical cabildo (as the see was vacant), gave Mindanao into the formal possession of the Society of Jesus, an act that was confirmed by Francisco Tello, as viceroyal patron. Later, the question of the jurisdiction about Lake Malanao was argued in court between the Jesuits and Recollects, and was decided in favor of the former by Juan Niño de Tabora, a

sentence confirmed by Corcuera September 5, 1637. (Pastells and Retana's Combés, cols. 655, 656.)

17 The bay of Panguil or Pangil takes its name from a fruit, pangi (Hidnocarpus polyandra—Bl.), which is carried down to the coast by the rivers. (Pastells and Retana's Combés, col. 759.)

18 The Manobos are a Malay head-hunting heathen tribe of northern Mindanao who live in the interior about the watershed of the Agusan River. "Manobo" is a native word, which, in the Bagobo language of the gulf of Dávao, means "man." Blumentritt (with whom Retana agrees) says that the correct form of the name is "Manuba" or "Man-Suba," i.e., "river-people." The term might possibly be extended to the mountain people of Misamis province. See Census of the Philippines, i, pp. 461, 473; Blumentritt's Tribes of the Philippines (Mason's translation); and Pastells and Retana's Combés, col. 780.

19 Blumentritt (Tribes of the Philippines, Mason's translation) says of the Mananapes: "A heathen people alleged to dwell in the interior of Mindanao, possibly a tribe of Buquidnones or Manobos." Retana (Pastells and Retana's Combés, col. 780) says that the appellation is equivalent to "Manap," and is not the name of a tribe, but merely a nickname to indicate that those bearing that name are wild like beasts.

20 Retana (Pastells and Retana's Combés, col. 780), derives "Sameacas" from "Sumasacas," a word which he says is equivalent to the Visayan "tagasaca," "people of the uplands." According to him, they are Malayan Moros, but Montero y Gay (Blumentritt's Tribes of Philippines, Mason's translation) says that they are heathen. It should be observed that Retana is not always a safe guide in etymological and ethnological matters.

21 This entire sentence is, like many others of Combés, of loose and vague construction. Apparently what he means is, that the Lutaos had, like the Javanese, a polite and a vulgar tongue; and that the former more closely resembles the Sanskrit (since he implies that the Lutaos came from India).

22 The Spaniards, mindful of their own struggles with the Moors of Spain (Moros) called all Mahometan peoples Moors.

23 See Vol. XXXVI, p. 174, note 33.

24 A classic allusion, occasioned by the marine life and habits of the Lutaos.

25 Paguian Tindig is equivalent to "just king." In their literal sense, both words signify "he who causes persons and things to pass by the right path." (Pastells and Retana's Combés, col. 727.)

26 Elsewhere written Limansacay; see Vol. IV, pp. 241–278, the account of Gabriel de Ribera's expedition against the Mindanaos in 1579.

27 Such was the first outbreak of hostilities which caused the rebellion of the Moros of Joló against Spain, and originated the piracy of that small archipelago, which wrought so much ruin, and caused so much bloodshed and depopulation among the Visayan and Tagálog islands. (Pastells and Retanas Combés, col. 658.)

28 Regarding the introduction of Mahometanism in those islands, see Vol. IV, pp. 150, 151, 168, 178.

29 A common name for the mangosteen (Garcinia mangostana), a fruit of delicate flavor and highly prized; this tree grows in Joló and Mindanao. (Official Handbook of Philippines, p. 316.)

30 Becoquin: "A sort of cap made with a piece of cloth." When the Joloans made a treaty with the Jesuit Lopez, they ratified it by an oath taken "on the becoquin or cap of Tampan, one of the old-time ministers of their deceit.... When the princes of Joló swear by this becoquin, using this ceremony, it is the strongest oath that they can take, and that which is most respected." (Combés, Hist. de Mindanao, col. 478, 785.)

31 The limocon (Calcophups indica) is a species of turtledove with red feet and beak. It is very beautiful, its plumage being green on a white background. See Delgado's Historia, p. 830.

32 There are offerings and sacrifices among the Mindanao heathen. The first [pagcayog] consist in offering rice, buyo, and money before a small idol of bayog [Pterospermum] wood (placed on a small altar adorned with bamboo and bonga [Areca]), called diuata or Manáug. This idol, which is a poorly-made image, has for eyes the red fruit of the tree called mabugaháy, and is painted with the sap of the narra. The blood sacrifices are of animals, and even of human beings. The first are called talíbong, if the animal sacrificed is a cock, and pag-balílig, if it is a hog. In either case, the priestesses (bailanes) having assembled, to the sound of the agun and guímbao, are clad according to rule; that is, with embroidered handkerchiefs on the head; magnificent red shirts, rich glass beads hanging from the neck; silver medals fastened to the breast; large gold earrings with strings of beads; a jabol or dagmay which serves them as a skirt, and is very skilfully woven and figured with crocodiles and other designs; at the girdle, in the midst of fragrant flowers and hawk's-bells, they carry the balarao or dagger with which the sacrifice of the victim is made; on the arms precious bracelets of ságai-ságai and pamóans; and on the feet hoops and hawk's-bells, which sound in cadence with the dance which legalizes such ceremonies. When the priestesses have taken their places about the altar, upon which the victim is to be sacrificed, they

commence their dances to the sound of the culintangan, some of them playing on the guimbao and the agun. They walk about the altar; they tremble and belch, while singing the "miminsad," until they fall senseless to the ground like those stricken with epileptic fits. Then the spectators go to them, fan them, sprinkle them with water, and the other women bear them up in their arms until they recover consciousness. Then they repeat the ceremony and the chief priestess buries her balarao in the heart of the hog or slits the cock's neck. Thereupon, she sucks up the blood which gushes forth from the victim, partaking thus of the sacrifice. The other bailanes do the same. During the epileptic fit, they assert that Mansilatan has appeared to them and notified them of the good or ill outcome of the war, sickness, harvest, or whatever they have been investigating. Then it all ends in excessive eating and drinking. The human sacrifice is called huaga, and is only practiced among the Bagobos and most barbarous heathen of Mindanao. The victim is offered to the Mandarangan, the god of the mountain or volcano of Apo; this person's value is generally apportioned among those who participate in the sacrifice, and he who pays most is the first to wound the unfortunate victim. The latter is cut into mincemeat in a moment amid the horrifying cries of his infamous executioners. Thanks to the painstaking vigilance of the authorities of that district, and to the incessant care of the missionaries, so impious and criminal a ceremony is almost entirely eradicated, and is only practiced in secret, in the densest woods. In addition to the huaga, there are true cases of cannibalism among the Baganis, who are wont to eat the raw entrails of those who fall before their lances, krises, and balaraos in battle. They do that as a mark of bravery. They have a proverb which says: "I am long accustomed to eat the entrails of men." (Pastells and Retana's Combés, cols. 657, 658.)

33 Referring to Tuambaloca, the queen of Raya Bongso; Bactial (misprinted Bachal in the Combés text) was his bastard son, who for a time ruled Joló, during his father's life.

34 These patolas are mentioned by Pigafetta in his relation. See Vol. XXXIV, p. 59.

35 A measure of capacity equivalent to about one-half an English gallon, or two liters.

36 This last sentence is in the language of the Inquisition, the original being "y aun entre barbaros puso con sambenito al vicioso, para que no tengan escusa los que se le hizieron Familiares." "Sambenito" (translated "penance") is the "garment worn by penitent convicts of the Inquisition;" or "an inscription in churches, containing the name, punishment, and signs of the chastisement of those doing penance."

37 The dedo is a measure equivalent to one forty-eighth of the vara or Spanish yard.

38 Father Pastells has seen the immediate effects of the execution of judgment by boiling water, and cured a young man, who had thrust his hand into boiling water, by sentence of the chiefs, in order to prove his innocence. The judgment of plunging the parties into water is also practiced, and he who remains in the water the shortest time is adjudged the criminal. (Pastells and Retana's Combés, col. 659.)

39 These prices are mentioned in Vol. XLI, appendix.

40 One of the chief causes of the great depopulation of Mindanao and the Visayan Islands was the slavery produced by the piracy of the Lutaos, encouraged by the Moros of Borneo, Célebes, Gilolo, Macazar, Ternate, and the other Moluccas, who brought the slaves in the markets to which they were conveyed. (Pastells and Retana's Combés, col. 659.)

41 The Baganis, who dress in the manner described by the author, generally count the number of their victims, by placing on the edge of the shield as many locks of hair as the assassinations that they have committed. One Macusang gave Father Pastells his shield as a present, as a sign that he would kill no more Christians; and that shield held one hundred and eight locks of hair. (Pastells and Retana's Combés, col. 659.)

42 Now called bido. They dress like women; and some think them hermaphrodites. (Pastells and Retana's Combés, col. 659.)

Henry Ling Roth, in his *Natives of Sarawak and British North Borneo* (London, 1896), i, pp. 270, 271, describes these men in women's attire as found in Borneo, where they are called *Manang bali*. Before such assume women's dress they are unsexed; and thenceforth they endevour to imitate as nearly as possible the women in everything, he who can best do so being regarded as the most successful. Their services are in great demand and they generally grow wealthy, when in order the better to act their assumed character as women, the *manang bali* takes a husband. The latter is despised by the women and disliked by the men of the tribe, and is completely under his so-called "wife's" domination. Men are not brought up in this office as a profession, but one becomes a *manang bali* from pure choice, or by sudden inclination, at a mature age. He is always a person of great consequence in the village, and may become the chief. He has many cares, and acts often as a peacemaker, in which he excels, all little differences being brought to him. His wealth is often at the service of his followers, and he is ready to help in times of trouble and distress. When the *manang bali* marries, he generally adopts some children; and if he has had children before he becomes a *manang bali*, he must give them their portions and start in that career unencumbered.

Cf. the "berdashes" among the North American Indians; see *Jesuit Relations* (Cleveland reissue), lix, pp. 309, 310.

43 Retana (Pastells and Retana's Combés, col. 786) derives "labia" from "labi" and "a" "he who advantages the others." "Tuto" is said by Retana (ut supra, col. 790) to be equivalent to "tuud-tuud" meaning "in real truth."

44 Either the eleventh or twelfth of November. The first date is the day of St. Martin, the blessed confessor; and the second that of St. Martin, pope and martyr, who was martyred in 655.

45 The island of Pañgutarang, of the Sulu group. It is about 11 × 9 miles in extent, and is low, but is densely inhabited and has considerable trade with Joló. It has some settlements of the Sámals, the descendants of the Sámal Laút or "sea gypsies." See U. S. Philippine Gazetteer, and Census of the Philippine Islands, i, p. 464.

46 At present, when anyone dies, those of his house break out into uncontrollable lamentations, and the father or husband becomes so beside himself at times that, seizing his bolo, he slashes right and left whatever he finds, destroying his clothes, furniture, utensils, and even the very floor of the house; and it is necessary to lay hold of him in order to avoid a worse ending to such uncontrolled actions. (Pastells and Retana's Combés, col. 660.)

47 Socsocan (Sofocan, Sogsocan) was a Basilan by birth and one of the most esteemed of Corralat's chiefs. He became friendly to the Spaniards and served them well as commander of the Lutaos. His name is said to signify "he who penetrates the fortresses or the ranks of the enemy." (Pastells and Retana's Combés, col. 735.)

48 Captain Gaspar de Morales was made admiral of the squadron in Joló. He fought bravely in La Sabanilla and in Joló, where he was severely wounded. He became commandant of the stronghold and afterward was governor of the Joloan fort. As governor he was an utter failure; for by his avarice and licentiousness he occasioned the insurrection of Salibansa (whose daughter he had seized), and the loss of the Sulu archipelago for more than two centuries. (Pastells and Retana's Combés, col. 723.)

49 Among woods of extraordinary hardness is the magconó (Xanthostemon verdugonianus naves). This wood is so hard that if a nail be driven into its heart

and it be afterward sawn apart, one does not observe where the saw strikes the nail, and it said that both substances are of equal hardness. Father Pastells asserts that he has seen bits of this wood that have been converted into real flint after only twenty-five years. (Pastells and Retana's Combés, col. 660.)

50 Of these people, properly called Guimbajanos (Guinbajanos, Guimbanos, Guimbas, and Quimpanos), Blumentritt (Tribes of the Philippines, Mason's translation) says: "The historians of the seventeenth century, under this title, designated a wild, heathen people, apparently of Malay origin, living in the interior of Sulu Island. Their name is derived from their war drum (guimba). Later writers are silent concerning them. In modern times the first mention of them is by P. A. de Pazos and by a Manila journal, from which accounts they are still at least in Caroden and in the valley of the Loo; it appears that a considerable portion of them, if not the entire people, have received Islam." Retana (Pastells and Retana's Combés, col. 779) derives the name of these people from guimba, "a mountain." They are not mentioned under this name by the Census of the Philippines.

51 Pedro de Almonte Vérastegui, of Sevilla, was a brave soldier, who served as general and sargento-mayor, and admiral of an expedition against Maluco. He was especially distinguished for his honesty and uprightness. In Sibuguey he attained equal merit with Corcuera, and in 1638 conquered Joló. Diego Fajardo assigned him the encomienda of Lorenzo Cañete, left vacant (July 1, 1645), by the death of the latter's son. (Pastells and Retana's Combés, col. 695.) Almonte Vérastegui has often been mentioned in this series.

52 The Chinese, during the Spanish régime of the Philippines, were allowed to smoke opium under certain rules; but its use was prohibited to the natives, although it was at times used secretly. (Pastells and Retana's Combés, col. 781.)

53 The former officer of the crown of Aragon, who was assigned to duty immediate to the king's person. He enjoyed several privileges, one of them being to hold the royal sword naked in public ceremonies. (Dominguez, Diccionario nacional.)

54 The arms of the natives of Mindanao, like their clothes, are manufactured by themselves. The spears and campilans are said to be finely tempered. They themselves adjust the dies for their pataquias. The sheaths, like the hafts of their krises, are of gold richly engraved. The haft of the kris used by Dato Ayuman of Tabiran was of solid gold, and was engraved with sentences from the Koran in Arabic characters. The usual weapons are: campilans, krises (straight and

wavy), machetes, bolos, ligdaos, súndanes, various kinds of spears, balaraos, and badis. They use coats-of-mail made of brass, tortoise-shell, malibago [-bark], or very thick cloth, or long sashes wound about the breast. Spears and arrows are generally poisoned with the resin of the tree called quemandag or the poison of red ants or scorpions; and the points of their daggers and balaraos are also poisoned. They also use darts made of steel, iron, bone, palm-wood and bamboo. For defense they construct traps, dig pits, and set bamboo points. They use also various kinds of lantacas and other kinds of firearms, with which the Chinese supply them, or which they manufacture themselves. These were considered contraband of war during the Spanish régime. (Pastells and Retana's Combés, col. 782.)

San Agustin's Letter on the Filipinos

[Gaspar de San Agustin, O.S.A., wrote the following letter regarding the Filipinos. This letter has been widely discussed pro and con by various writers, because of the views expressed therein. Many manuscript copies of it exist in various collections, archives, and libraries. The present translation is made from an early manuscript copy, belonging to Mr. E. E. Ayer, of Chicago. In footnotes we give the variant readings of the MS. conserved in the Museo-Biblioteca de Ultramar, Madrid (pressmark "6–5a; caja 17; 21–4a"), that MS. being indicated in our notes by the letter M.; and of the letter as published in Delgado's1 Historia (pp. 273–296, where it shows marks of having been edited by either Delgado or his editor), that publication being indicated by the letter D. Sinibaldo de Mas presents many of the essential parts of the letter in his Informe de las Islas Filipinas en 1842, i, "Poblacion," pp. 63–132. He says: "In order to give an idea of their physical and moral qualities, I am going to insert some paragraphs from a letter of Father Gaspar de San Augustin of the year 1725,2 suppressing many Latin citations from the holy fathers which weigh that letter down, and adding some observations from my own harvest, when I think them opportune." We shall use most of these observations in the annotations herewith presented. Sir John Bowring gives, on pp. 125–139 of his Visit to the Philippine Isles (London, 1859) some excerpts taken from Mas's Informe, but he has sadly mixed San Agustin's and Mas's matter, and has ascribed some of the latter's observations to San Agustin, besides making other errors.3]

Letter from fray Gaspar de San Agustin to a friend in España who asked him as to the nature and characteristics [genio] of the Indian natives of these Philipinas Islands.4

My Dear Sir:

Although your command has so great weight with me, the undertaking of performing it satisfactorily is so difficult that I doubt my ability to fulfil what you ask. It would be more easy for me, I believe, to define the formal object of logic; to give the square of a circle; to find the mathematical [side5] of the double of the cube and sphere, or to find a fixed rule for the measurement of the degrees of longitude of the terrestrial sphere; than to define the nature of the Indians, and their customs and vices. This is a memorandum-book in which I have employed myself for forty years, and I shall only say: Quadraginta annis proximus fui generationi huic, et dixi semper hi errant corde;6 and I believe that Solomon himself would place this point of knowledge after the four things impossible to his understanding which he gives in chapter XXX, verse 18 of Proverbs. Only can they tell the One who knows them by pointing to the sky and saying, Ipse cognovit figmentum nostrum.7 But in order that you may not say to me that I am thus ridding myself of the burden of the difficulty,8 without making any effort or showing any obedience, I shall relate briefly what I have observed, for it would be impossible to write everything, if one were to use all the paper that is found in China.

2. The knowledge of men has been considered by the most erudite persons as a difficult thing. Dificile est, noscere hominem animal varium et versipelle.9 Man is a changeable theater of transformations. The inconstancies of his ages resemble the variation of the year. A great knowledge of man did that blind man of the eighth chapter of St. Mark have who said, with miraculous sight, that he saw men as trees: Video homines velut arbores ambulantes.10 For the tree in the four seasons of the year has its changes as has man in his four ages; and thus said the English poet Oven:

> "Ver viridem flavamque æstas, me fervida canam
>
> Autumnus calvam, frigida fecit hyems."11

"For this is the inconstancy of man in his [various] ages: green in his childhood; fiery in the age of his virility; white in old age; and bald in his decrepitude." But his greatest change is in his customs, for he is a continual Proteus, and an inconstant Vertumnus.12 Thus does Martial paint his friend:

> "Dificilis, facilis, jucundus, acerbus est idem;
>
> Nec tecum possum vivere, nec sine te."13

From this came the proverb "Quot capita, tot sententiæ."14 For in the changeable affection of man are locked up all the meteoric influences of natural transformations.

3. It is a fact that the difficulty of knowing these Indians is not in the individuals, but in the race; for, if one be known, then all are known, without any distinction—so much so that the Greek word monopantos15 fits them, and which another critic gave to another race of people, because they were all homogeneous and uniform among themselves. At the eighth meeting of the last Lateran Council, held in the time of Leo X, the opinion of the Monophysite philosophers16—who give but one single soul to all men, each body having a part of it—was condemned. Doubtless that impious opinion originated from some nation as alike in customs as these Indians;

and it is not the worst thing to have been able to give this humble judgment, although it is defective.17

4. Although we call both the natives of America and those of these Philipinas Islands Indians, it cannot be denied that they are very different; for the inclination of the Asiatics18 is somewhat more docile and more capable of progress through teaching. Accordingly, I shall confine my remarks to the Indians of Philipinas, leaving the definition of the Americans for those who know them; for they have enough chroniclers who have undertaken it, although I doubt that they obtained their desire, such as Father Juan de Torquemada in his Monarchia Indiana,19 Fray Antonio de Remesal,20 and Father Joseph de Acosta.21 For what has been written of them by the bishop of Chiapa, Fray Bernardino de Cassas,22 and by Don Juan de Palafox23 in his treatise on the virtues of the Indians, was written from very remote experience; and they were carried away by the holy zeal of their defense as they were deceived24 by their remote knowledge of the object—as [in viewing] the hills and mountains, which anear are green, but afar are blue. Gold conceals from the sight the degree of its fineness; and one must crush25 the rock himself, and frequently, in order to recognize the truth.

5. The Asiatic Indians of Philipinas, then, are almost the same as those of the other nations of East India, in what regards their genius [genio], temper, and disposition. Consequently, the Malays, Siamese, Mogoles, and Canarines26 are distinguished only by their clothing, languages and ceremonies. I except the Japanese (who are, as Gracian27 learnedly remarked, the Spaniards of Asia) and the Chinese, who, by their culture and civilization, and love of letters, seem to be different—although, touched with the stone of experience, they are the same as the Indians.28 The influence of the stars which rule Assia is common, whence Macrobius and Suetonius complain that the corruption of the good native customs of the Romans proceeded, especially from Persia, whence came great evil both to the Greeks and to the Latins.

6. But leaving this immense sea of peoples and customs, let us return to our natives of these islands, who, besides having been exceedingly barbarous, living without a ruler, and in a confused monarchy,29 have the vices of the islanders; for they are fickle, false, and mendacious, and [that] by the special influence and dominion which the moon exercises upon all the islands, isthmuses, and peninsulas [Chersonesos], of which much will be found in the Theatrum vitæ humanæ of Laurencio Beyerlinch.30

7. The temperament of these Indians, as is proved by their physiognomy, is cold and humid, because of the great influence of the moon. They have but little or no difference among themselves in their temperament, as was remarked by a learned doctor who has had considerable experience in these islands, namely, Doctor Blas Nuñez de Prado. [He observed] that there was no difference, but a great similarity, in the humors of those who had been treated, and a fine natural docility in responding to the medicine; in whatever remedy it was applied to them. For they have not the great rebelliousness and changeableness of the Europeans, because of the infinite combinations made in them by the four humors. The cause of this is the similarity and lack of variety in the food that they use and which their ancestors used, which go to make up a nature different in its root from that of the Europeans, but yet very similar.31

8. This disposition and influence makes them fickle, malicious, untrustworthy, dull, and lazy;32 fond of traveling by river, sea, and lake; fond of fishing, and ichthyophagous33—that is, they sustain themselves best on fish; they have little courage, on account of their cold nature, and are not disposed to work.34 Besides this they have other qualities and vices, of which I do not know the cause, and I do not believe that I can easily know them.35 I shall mention some of them.36

9. First, they are remarkable for their ingratitude; and although ingratitude is an innate vice in all people, through the corruption of original sin in our vitiated nature, it is not corrected in them by the understanding, and they lack magnanimity. Therefore, it is all one to do a good turn to an Indian, and to prepare oneself to receive the blow of his ingratitude. Consequently, if one lend them money, they do not pay it; but instead they run away from the father. Hence there is ground for scruples in regard to lending money to them; for that is a benefit from which evil must result, as they absent themselves and do not come to mass. If others ask them why, they answer that the father37 is angry at them. In them is verified the picture given by the Holy Spirit in chapter xxix, verse[s] 4[–9] of Ecclesiasticus. "Many" (he says) "have thought by artifice to satisfy the thing due, and have given trouble to those who have aided them. So long as they receive, they kiss the hands of him who gives, and humble themselves with promises. But when it comes time to pay, they will beg for time (for they are beggars and not givers); and they will utter tedious and complaining words, and the time is spent in vain. Even though one can pay, he can be got to do so only with great difficulty. For one solidus38 scarcely will he give the half, and that he will think an unjust artifice; and if he cannot pay he will keep the money, and will esteem the debtor as an enemy causelessly, and will return him insults and evil words, and for honor and kindness will

return him dishonor."39 This picture of ingratitude given by Ecclesiasticus fits many, but it fits the Indians better than all other nations, except the Vix solidi reddet dimidium,40 for they pay nothing. This is one of the evil signs that the royal prophet finds in the evil and ingrate in Psalm xxxvi, verse 21: "The sinner shall take the loan, and shall not pay."41 Consequently we find our Indians pagans in this, although they are Christians.42

10. If they borrow anything that is not money, they will never return it until it is requested; and, as an excuse for not having returned it, they say that they have not been asked for it.43

11. Their laziness is such that if they open a door they never close it; and if they take any implement for any use, such as a knife, pair of scissors, hammer, etc., they never return it whence they took it, but drop it there at the foot of the work.44

12. If they are paid anything in advance, they will leave work and keep the pay.45

13. They are naturally rude, and consequently, it is strange to see them, when talking with the father or a Spaniard, first scratch themselves on the temples,46 and, if it be a woman, on the thigh; but the more polished scratch themselves on the head.47

14. It is a thing of great wonder that in everything they make in which there is a right and wrong side, they naturally make it wrong side out. Consequently, they have not thus far been able to give in to difficulty of folding a cloak with its right side in;48 nor [do they understand] it can be that when a shirt or habit is wrong side out, on putting the head in, it is given a turn and remains right side out. Consequently, whenever they see this done, they express more surprise.49 Hence the remark of a discerning man, that all they did was wrong except folding a cloak, because in that operation the wrong side is the face or right side.50

15. When the men walk with their wives, they go in advance, and the wives follow, as that is just the contrary of our custom. This was a bit of carelessness that cost Orpheus the loss of his wife, who was stolen by the prince Auresteo, as we are told in mythology.51

16. They are curious, rude, and impertinent, and accordingly, when they meet the father they generally ask him where he is going and whence he is coming; and innumerable questions, all impertinent and troublesome.52

If any letter is read before them, they will go behind one to see it, although they do [not] know how to read. And if they hear any talking in private, they draw nigh to listen to it, even though it be in a language that they do not understand.

17. They enter, without being summoned, into the convents and the houses of the Spaniards, even into the most secret apartment, but in their own houses they practice many civilities. If the door be locked, they try with might and main to look through the cracks at what is being done, for they wish to know everything.53

They tramp about in the convents and houses of the Spaniards so loudly, that it causes wonder and annoyance; and especially if the father is asleep. In their own houses, on the contrary, they walk about so lightly, that they seem to be walking on eggs.54

18. They are very early risers in their own houses,55 for their poverty and the noise demand that. But if their masters sleep until ten, they must do the same too.

19. They must eat and try all that their masters eat, even though it be something delicious or from Europa; and no Spaniard, and especially the father minister, will have been able to succeed in making them eat out of other dishes than those from which their master eats. I know well that I have been unable to obtain it, notwithstanding my efforts. Neither will they drink out of another and separate jar.56

20. Their manner of sitting is generally on their heels [en cuclillas], and they do that in all places except in the convents, where they break the seats with sitting on them and leaning back in them with out-stretched legs. And they must do this in the balconies, where they can see the women.57

21. They care more for their disheveled hair than they do for their souls; and only they will not imitate the Spaniards if they have the custom of shaving, as is now being introduced with the false hair and perukes.58

22. Their usual habitation and happiness in the convents consists in not leaving the kitchen. There they hold their meetings and feasts, and there is their glory, as is the open country in Castilla. A religious whom I knew, called the kitchen Flos sanctorum,59 because the life of the father and of all the village was discussed there.

23. When they go out alone at night, they must have a blazing torch, and go about waving it like a censer; and then they throw it down wherever they please, and this is usually the cause of great fires.

24. They would rather wear mourning than go about in gala dress, and are accordingly very observant in wearing it during their funerals.60

25. They do not esteem garments or gala dresses given them by their Spanish masters; and accordingly leave such in any place, without perceiving that they are losing them. But any old rag that they wear from their own houses they esteem and value highly.

26. They do not care for any domestic animal—dog, cat, horse, or cow. They only care, and too much so, for the fighting cocks; and every morning, on rising from slumber, the first thing that they do is to go to the roosting-place of their cock—where, squatting down on their heels, in its presence, they stay very quietly for at least a half-hour in contemplation of their cock. This observance is unfailing in them.61

27. They live unwillingly in convents, or in houses where they cannot be at least on the scent of women.

28. It is not known that the Indian has [ever] broken a dish or a crock in his own house, and consequently one will find dishes in them that date from before the arrival of the Spaniards in this country. But in the convents and houses where they serve, they break so many that one would believe that they do it on purpose to do their masters an ill turn.62

29. One may not trust a sword, mirror, glass, musket, clock, or any other rare article to them; or allow them to touch it even with the hands; for immediately, by physical contact alone, they put it out of joint, break it, and harm it. They can only handle bamboo, rattan, nipa, or a bolo, and some few a plow.63

30. They are insolent and free in begging for unjust and foolish things, and this without considering time or season. When I remember the circumstance which happened to Sancho Pancha when he was governor of the island of Barataria, one day after eating64 with an importunate and intrusive farmer, who said that he was from Miguel Turra, I am reminded of the Indians when they beg.65 And we shall say that if they bring four eggs, they think that with justice they ought to be given a price of one hundred pesos. That is so true that when I see an Indian who is bringing something, which is always a thing of no value, or something that is of no use to them, such as ates, mangas, or belinbiles [i.e., balimbing], I repeat those words of Laocoon to the Trojans: Timeo Danaos, [et] dona ferentes (2nd Æneid). An Indian came to beg from the bishop of Troya (as was told me by his illustrious Lordship)—Don Fray Gines Barrientos,66 a specially circumspect prelate—the loan of fifty pesos, for which he took him a couple of guavas. An Indian brought a cock to the Marquis of Villa-sierra, Don Fernando de Valenzuela,67 while he was in the fort of Cavite; and, when that gentleman ordered that he be given more than six times its value, the Indian told him that what he wanted was to be given eighty cavans of rice,68 and that in a time of so great scarcity it was not to be had for two pesos per cavan. But they have this curious peculiarity, that they are just as happy if these things are not given to them as if they had been given. For they have little or no esteem for what the Spaniards give them, and especially the father.

Accordingly, when they sell anything that is worth, say, six,69 they ask thirty, and are satisfied if six be given them.70

They would rather have one real from the hand of the Sangley than one peso from the Spaniard; and the power that the Sangleys have over them is surprising, for they are generally cheated by those people.71

31. They are very fond of play,72 for they believe that it is a restful way in which to gain much, and it is very suitable to their laziness and lack of energy. Therefore, an Indian would rather lie stretched out in his house than gain the greatest wage. On this account, when he gets a peso he stays at home without working, until it is all eaten up or drunk up, for it all amounts to the same thing. This is the reason why they are so poor, in comparison with the Sangleys and mestizos, who live in abundance, for they know how to seek and work.73 Egestatem operata est manus remissa. (Proverbs X, verse 4.)

32. They have contradictory peculiarities, such as being very cowardly, while on some occasions they are rash; for they confess that they would rather suffer a hundred lashes than to have one shout aloud to them—which, they say, penetrates even to the heart, without the cause being known.

33. It is laughable to see them waken another who is sleeping like a stone, when they come up without making any noise and touching him very lightly with the point of the finger, will call him for two hours, until the sleeper finishes his sleep and awakens. The same thing is done when they call anyone downstairs, or when the door is shut; for they remain calling him in a very low tone for two hours, until he casually answers and opens to them.74

34. In another way, they exhibit other rash actions, by which it is seen that their rashness is rather the daughter of ignorance and barbarity than of valor. For it occurs that an Indian, man or woman, may be walking along the road and hear a horse which is coming behind him, running or going at a quick pace; but this Indian never turns his face. If the horse come in front of him, he will not turn out of the road so that he may not be trampled underfoot, if he who comes on horseback does not turn out with greater consideration. The same thing occurs when they see a very large banca coming down upon them with long sweeps of the oars, while they are in a small banquilla; when they will allow themselves to be struck by it, with the danger of being overturned and drowned. It costs much labor to those in the large banca to avoid that, while the others could do it with great ease. This has happened to me on innumerable occasions.75

35. The same thing happens in the rivers where there are crocodiles, although they see them swimming about; for they say the same as do the

Moros [i.e., Mahometans], that if it is from on high it must happen, even though they avoid it. And thus, as says father Fray Gabriel Gomez (History of Argel, book 2, chapter 19), they say in the lengua franca "God is great! Be not led by fancy! The world is just so. If it is written on the forehead that one is to live, then he will live; but if not, then he will die here."76 For their Koran says that each one has his fortune written in the lines of his forehead. These Indians believe the same thing (and they have never seen the Koran), and only because it is great nonsense. They receive no warning from the many misfortunes that happen every day for their sins.77

36. While it is a fact that they are extremely credulous among themselves, they will believe of the Spaniards only what is against them. Therefore, it is evident that the [Christian] faith is a supernatural act, in that they believe the divine mysteries taught by the Spaniards. However, they do not believe some things, or refuse to believe them because they find the contrary profitable. Consequently, there is no one who can persuade them that it is a sin to steal from the religious ministers or the Spaniards. Of this we have such proofs that we have not the slightest doubt that it is so; but, only perceiving it is not being able to remedy it.78

So great is the ease and tenacity with which they believe the greatest nonsense, if this is to the discredit of the Spaniards or against them, that it would be a long undertaking to recount some of it. I have deemed it advisable to mention only two [instances] of it of which I heard79 and of which I was a witness, so that the rest can be inferred from them.

37. While I was in Bisayas in the year 1672, those islands began to be depopulated and the Indians began to take to the mountains from the visitas of Xaro, because a rogue told them a bit of nonsense like the following. He told them that the king of España had gone out fishing, and the Turks had come upon him and made him captive; and that the king had given for his ransom all the Indians of the province of Oton. They believed this so thoroughly that it was with great difficulty that the alcalde Don Sebastian de Villarreal and the father ministers could quiet them, and considerable time passed before they were sure of the whole matter.80

The second: While I was in the village of Lipa, a mine was discovered in that of Tanavan which was said to be of silver. Governor Don Fausto Cruzat y Gongorà sent ministers and officials in order to find out about it and to assay it. These men made their efforts, but the mine only said, Argentum et aurum non est mihi.81 But the devil willed to have some rogue at this time to sow this deceit, namely, that the ministers82 said that the mine would yield no silver until all the old women of Cometan had been caught, and their eyes plucked out and mixed with other ingredients, in order to anoint the vein of the mine with that mixture. This was believed, so that all was confusion and lamentation, and the old women hid in the fields; and it took a long time to quiet them, and cost the ministers great difficulty, as the Indians would not believe them because they were Castilians, until time itself undeceived them.83

38. May God deliver us from any one of those Indians whom they consider as sages, who says any bit of nonsense, even though it be against the faith,84 and they only respond, Vica nong maronong, "Thus say the sages," and it is labor lost to persuade them to the contrary; for the authority that these scholars have over them is incredible.

39. They are extremely arrogant, and hence the son will not obey his father, or the headman, or captain of the village.85 They are only bound in this by fear, and when they have no fear they will not obey. They only recognize the Spaniard to be more than they;86 and this they say only because of an interior impulse, which forces them against their will and without their knowing why. This is the providence of God, so that they can be governed.

40. They are very fond if imitating the Spaniard87 in all his bad traits, such as variety of clothes, cursing, gambling, and the rest that they see the coxcombs88 do. They shun the imitation of the good things in the dealings and civilization of the Spaniards, and in the proper rearing of their children. For in all the rest that treats of trickery, drunken revelries, and ceremonies in their marriages, burials, and tyrannies one against another, they observe exactly what they learned from their ancestors. Thus they unite in one the vices of the Indians and the Spaniards.89

41. Just as the poor are arrogant, so also are the old ones ignorant, and they are not to be distinguished from the youths. Consequently, in their weddings, banquets, and revelries one will see old men with white hair, mixed with the lads; and slouchy old women with their scapularies, clapping their hands and singing nonsensical things with the lasses. Scarcely is there an Indian who knows his age, and many90 do not know the baptismal names of their wives, after they have been baptized for fifty years.91

42. They are so ignorant that they do not have the slightest knowledge concerning the origin of the ancestors from whom they descend, and whence they came to settle these islands. They do not give any information concerning their paganism, which is not the worst; and they only preserve in certain parts some ridiculous abuses, which they observe at births and sicknesses, and the cursed belief that persuades them that the souls of their ancestors or the grandfathers of the families are present in the trees and at the bottom of bamboos, and that they have the power of giving and taking

away health and of giving success or failure to the crops. Therefore, they make their ancestors offerings of food, according to their custom; and what has been preached to them and printed in books avails but little, for the word of any old man regarded as a sage has more weight with them than the word of the whole world.92

43. They act tyrannically one toward another. Consequently, the Indian who has some power from the Spaniard is insolent93 and intolerable among them—so much so that, in the midst of their ingratitude, some of them recognize it, although very few of them. Yet it is a fact that, if the Spaniards had not come to these islands, the Indians would have been destroyed; for, like fish,94 the greater would have swallowed the lesser, in accordance with the tyranny which they exercised in their paganism.95

44. They are wanting in understanding and reflection, so that they do not recognize any means in anything, but go to extremes. Consequently, if one ask them for warm water, they bring it boiling, and then if they are reproached and told that one wishes it more temperate, they go and bring it back as cold as ice.96 In this vicious circle of extremes, they will continue ceaselessly without finding a mean. Consider then, how they will act in prudential matters, where one must seek the mean and not the extremes, as says the poet:97

Es[t] modus in rebus, sunt certi denique fines.

Quos ultra, citraque nequit consistere rectum.98

This is the cause of great anxiety to us, and with them a cause of great happiness to see us grow impatient, even though it cost them some blows, which they take very willingly because they make us impatient. They celebrate this in a lively manner in the kitchen. There is nothing that the Indian regrets more than to see the Spaniard or the father calm, and that he patiently and with forbearance restrains his hand from them when it is necessary; for but rarely do they do anything willingly, and hence the most prudent among them are wont to say that "the rattan grows where the Indian is born."99 Virga in dorso ejus, qui indiget corde (Proverbs x, 13).

They resemble in this a mischievous lad who served a good cleric. One day his master sent him to buy a hen, and he stole and hid a leg.100 His master was silent, and overlooked the incident. It came to pass that the master and the lad walked into a field, where they came upon some cranes, all of them with one foot lifted high in the air. Thereupon the lad said to his master, "Sir, the hen was like these birds which have but one foot." The cleric answered, "No, my lad, for these birds have two feet; and if you do not believe it, look." So saying, he threw a stick at the cranes, which flew away in fright, showing the other foot. At this the lad said, "O, sir, had you done the same with me, the hen would also have had two feet." Doubtless, this lad must have been of the same disposition as these good brothers, who do nothing good without a beating. Tu virga percuties eum (Proverbs XXIII, 14).101

It happened that an Augustinian religious—who still lives and is very well known for his great learning—arrived in these islands in the year 1684, and was given, shortly after his arrival, a lad of eight or nine years for his service. The lad was so clever and lively, that he was held in esteem,102 and the said religious was very fond of him because of his great activity. The lad considered that the father was very patient with him, and chid his neglect very mildly. One day he said to the father "Father, you know that you are new. Consider the Indians like myself. You must not overlook anything. If you wish to be well served, you must keep a rattan, and when I commit any fault, you must strike me with it; and then you will see that I shall move as quickly as a sparrowhawk. For you must know, Father, that the rattan grows where the Indian is born. So have I heard said by the old Indians."103 Trouble enough do the poor wretches have, for one may say of them: Oderunt peccare mali formidinæ penæ.104

45. One can give them nothing, even if it be given,105 for if he happen to give one anything in the presence of others, even if it be a needle,106 all will demand that in justice the same be given to them. In this they closely resemble the laborers of the twentieth chapter of St. Matthew, who construed as an injury the favor that the householder showed to their companions. This is covetousness and lack of consideration. So far is this foolishness carried that the Indian will take fifty lashes willingly, if he knows with certainty that all the others are to get as much. Surely they cause great trouble with this wretched habit, and those who might confer some benefit on them often avoid doing so.

46. They are so distrustful that they think that the ground on which they walk and the air which they breathe are about to fail. This does not make them more provident and industrious, but more foolish and dull. Therefore, if there are many to confess they troop together all in a body, each one desirous of being first. This causes extraordinary trouble and impatience to the confessor. But, if there are but few, they come a legua apart; and one must summon them, and they take an hour to come. If the father rises in anger, or because it is late, then they all come together in a crowd, and say "Father, me only." This is a bit of foolishness in which one can trace the great deficiency of their understanding.107

47. As they are so curious, and fond of knowing whatever does not concern them, what occurs when many of them confess together is wondrous

to see. For all of them keep a steadfast gaze on the one who is confessing. One is astonished and amused to see all the women with their faces turned backward108 so that they seem to be biformed Januses, or paid dancers with a mask at the back of the head. In this manner, they remain until the end of the function. The same is true on Ash Wednesday or at the adorations of the cross on Holy Friday, when all of them wish to kiss at one time, or in other similar functions.

48. They are much given to the sin of blasphemy,109 because of their natural vileness, their pride, and their presumption. Hence it is quite usual for them to complain of God, whom they call Paghihinanaquit, asking why He does not give them this or that, and health or wealth, as He does to other creatures. They utter words of nonsense that horrify those who do not know that it proceeds from their great lack of understanding and consideration, and from their very great disability for conforming themselves with the divine will.110 Thus the royal prophet David, when compelled by his superior enthusiasm to touch what he considered inferior matter, and [when he] lifted up his complaints of the divine Providence, was excused by his ignorance, as will be seen in Psalm LXXII, [23], where he humbles himself, saying: Ut jumentum factus sum apud te: et ego semper tecum.111

49. They are very vain,112 and they spend their money never more willingly than in functions of vanity; for they consider themselves highly, and wish to be esteemed without doing anything worthy of esteem. The men especially, even though they do not have anything to eat, must not for that reason fail to have a shirt and a hat, and to dress in style. They give banquets very frequently, for very slight causes; and everything resolves itself into eating, drinking, and great noise. Their vanity is the only thing that causes them to lessen their laziness, in order to get the wherewithal to keep up this esteem, and applause from their compatriots.113

50. They are revengeful to an excessive degree—so much so that they are vile and cowardly, and the ministers have great trouble in reconciling them with their enemies; and although they do it through fear, it is never with the whole heart, for this passion has great influence over them. And since they need magnanimity and manliness to overcome it, and these virtues are foreign to them,114 hate generally forces its roots into them so deeply that it is impossible to eradicate it in a whole lifetime.115

This is the reason why they are so inclined to litigation, and to going before the audiencias and courts with their quarrels,116 in which they willingly spend their possessions for the sole purpose of making others spend theirs and of causing them harm and trouble. For that they are even wont to pledge their sons and daughters.117

51. In order to be contrary in everything to other nations, they have lust but no love. This is in regard to the illicit love; for in the supernatural love which grace causes in the sacrament of marriage (since divine impulse works in this) their evil disposition is conquered and most of them make very good husbands. But in illicit intercourse the men have no other purpose than bodily appetite, and to deprive [of virginity] as many women as they have done, in order to sport with it. For it is a long established custom among them that the women shall give to the men, and the latter shall be the ones served and fêted; while only blows, kicks, and trouble are given to the women. So true is this that one might say that they have an inferno both in this and in the other world. Hence the women are very poorly clad, for the men want everything for themselves.118

52. But in the midst of this, which appears inhuman, one may praise them for having succeeded in treating their wives as they deserve, in order to keep them submissive and happy; for this submission makes them better, and humble, and prudent, and conformable to their sentence of being subject to man. And if the Europeans would learn this useful and prudent management from them, they would live in greater peace and with less expense; and marriage would be more mild and quiet, and well ordered, according to reason, and better directed toward the end for which it was instituted—as we see is the case with these people, with a fertility that causes our wonder.

53. They have another remarkable custom, which has been taught them by the infernal Machiavelian119 Satan, which is good for their bodies, but bad for their souls. This is that they observe very strictly the concealment of one another's faults and wrong-doing. They endeavor to see that no transgression comes to the ear of the father minister, or alcalde, or any Spaniard. They observe this with peculiar secrecy, although they may be at enmity among themselves, and ready to kill as they say. Consequently, the most serious crime that can happen among them is to tell the father or alcalde what is passing in the village.120 They call that mabibig, because it is the most abominable fault and the only sin among them.121

54. This worst of customs is very prejudicial and troublesome to the Spaniards and to the father ministers. For it might happen that one has one servant (or all) who wastes and destroys the property of his master, and there is [no one] who will tell him what is passing.122 But if it happens that the wasteful servant leave, then all the others tell what he did; and, whatever is lacking afterward, they throw the blame on that absent servant. If the Spaniard reprove the servant whom he most esteems and benefits, asking him why he did not tell of the evil that the other servant was doing, he replies with great dudgeon that they must not accuse him of being

mabibig, or talebearer of what happens. This is what takes place, even if the servants know that they are flaying their master. Consequently, the first thing that they do when any new servant comes is, to threaten him if he turn mabibig, and afterwards make him do all the work that belongs to them all, while the old servants are quite free from toil. Hence the fewer servants a Spaniard has, the better served will he be; for only the newcomer works and does everything, and the others not only do nothing, but are all served by him.123

55. They have another peculiarity, which always causes me great wonder. I am trying to discover the cause therefor, but I only find, so far as I can make out, that it is due to their incapacity and ingratitude and their horror of the Spaniards. This is, that while the difference between the poverty, wretchedness, and want of their houses and the anxiety and poverty in which they live, when compared with the abundance, good cheer, good clothes, and comfort which they enjoy in the service of certain Spaniards is almost infinite, if they happen to be discharged, or to leave for some very slight cause occasioned by their pride and vanity, they turn from one extreme to the other, so contented with the present misery that they do not remember or even consider the past abundance. If they be asked in what condition they lived better, they answer that everything is one and the same, and hence we do not get revenge by sending them away in anger [en embiarlos con Dios]. But what great happiness is theirs!124

56. They would rather scorn the goods of the father or of the Spaniards than enjoy them and profit by them. Hence what they lose is greater than what they spend.

57. They are greatly lacking in foresight. Hence the servants and stewards do not advise their master to procure any article until it is completely gone. Therefore when they say that there is no more sugar or no more oil, it is when there is not [oil] enough to whet a knife.125 Consequently, great deficiencies and annoyances are suffered because of this custom.

58. If there are visitors or guests to dine with the master, they do not consider the guests at all, thus causing the poor master of the house great shame;126 and it is necessary for him to excuse himself by the poor instruction that the devil gave them in this matter. No misfortune can be greater to him than to offend against his civility; and in a manner that seems good to them, for doubtless they are so persuaded by the devil. It is also their custom, when there is company, for all to go to the kitchen and leave the master alone.127

59. Their stomachs are like sackbuts, with systole and diastole;128 and thus they contract and expand them in a wonderful manner. For although

they observe parsimony in their own houses, it is a matter for which to praise God to see them gorge themselves and gulp down things at the expense of the Spaniards, as Quevedo said there of Galalon: "Galalon, who eats but little at home, overloads his goodly paunch at another's expense."129

60. But say to them, Buen provecho;130 for usually these losses are well retrieved when they row. They are horrifying and frightful in venting their anger, both against one another, and against the father ministers; and there would be so much to say in this that it would never be finished.131 They are able to make their complaints in such a manner and to such purpose that they persuade those who know most about their falsity and trickery that they are telling the truth. I remember that an alcalde of experience132 was heard to say, when the Indians came to him with complaints: Audivi auditionem tuam, et timui.133 There are usually Indians, both men and women, in the suburbs of Manila, who hire out as mourners in the manner of the mourners of the Hebrews, and such as were in style in Castilla in the time of the Cid. The authors of the quarrel go first into the house of some lawyer134 well known for his cleverness, who is one of those called in law rabulas,135 who do not know which is their right hand. These men keep books of formulas and of petitions directed against all the human race; for example, in this form, "suit against alcalde;" and then follow all the crimes and excesses that can be committed by alcaldes.136 The same thing is true of suits against ministers and curas, and in them is enclosed all possibility of irregular conduct. Then the said "smith of calumny,"137 as the Italian says, takes the names of the plaintiffs and defendants, and a few facts; and then puts it all in the book from beginning to end [de pe á pa], without omitting one iota. And this is not to speak uncertainly; for in the archives of the court will be found the chart which was discovered in the possession of a certain rabula named Silva, who, in addition to this had skill in counterfeiting royal decrees and documents.

61. When the petition has been made, they go with it to the mourners, and they go to press their suit with a lamentation like that of Magedo for King Josias, which would soften stones.138 That has been investigated by several governors in my time. I remember one investigation by Don Juan de Vargas, and another by Don Gabriel de Cruce-laegui; and many who are living remember them. Let them judge, then, the pity that ought to be expressed for the father ministers, whose honor is exposed to so great danger.

62. Their cunning and diabolical cleverness in making an accusation is not the equal [i.e., is more than the equal] of their capacity; and it is known that they have the special suggestion of the father of discord, Satan. I remember that they brought to a certain provincial a complaint against the

father minister, saying that he kept twelve Indians busy in caring for but one horse. The provincial made an investigation and found that the father had but one Indian, and that he used the said horse a great deal, in order to attend to the administration of souls. When the calumniators were chidden for the falsity of their complaint, they explained it by saying, "Father, that Indian is, in truth, but one; but he is changed every month, and at the end of the year there are twelve men." Just see what subtlety, and what confusion in their arithmetic, in order to make their accusation—the Indians maliciously speaking of a year in order to give color to their calumny.139 So many cases of this sort can be stated, that they are unending. And with all this, these natives have such persuasiveness, or powers of enchantment, that they generally deceive and persuade the most experienced with their lies.

63. Inasmuch as any sort of complaint is received, without subjecting the accuser to a penalty in case that he cannot prove his allegations140—as ought to be the case, and according to the orders of the Mexican Council—no one's honor is safe. For, if they prove their accusations, they are the gainers, while if they do not prove them they return home as cool as ever, for they always go to gain and never to lose.141

64. They are very fond of ceremonial acts and festivals where there is some novelty; and fond of long pilgrimages142 to images of some new miracle, while they forget about the old.143

65. They are especially fond of comedies and farces, and therefore, there is no feast of consequence, unless there is a comedy.144 If possible they will lose no rehearsal, and in all they pay attention only to the witty fellow who does innumerable foolish and uncouth things, and at each of his actions they burst into hearty laughter. He who plays this part acceptably receives his diploma as an ingenious fellow, and has permission to go and come anywhere, and even to cajole the women before their husbands; and the latter must laugh, even though they have no wish to do so. It is very necessary that these representations be not harmful, for many of them are printed. Accordingly, they receive considerable benefit from these functions and external acts, such as the descent from the cross, and other representations, which are patterned after those called escuitales145 in Nueba España—in which is verified the truth of the sentence in the Ars Poetica of Horace, verses 18[0–181].146

Segnius irritant animos demisa per aures,

Quam quæ sunt oculis conspecta fidelibus.

66. Consequently, those who have experience are wont to declare that the faith enters into the Indians through the eyes; and hence it seems worthy

of consideration that it was the apostle St. Thomas whom our Lord147 had prepared for the teaching of the Indians—he who desired that the belief in his glorious resurrection might enter through the eyes: Nisi videro ... non credam (John xx, 25).

67. They are extreme in their observance of their usages and customs, which they call ogali. To be found wanting in these is a great infamy; and, consequently, in order not to break them they will trample everything under foot. The ceremonies and abuses practiced in their weddings and funerals are numerous and curious, and no success has been had in suppressing them, notwithstanding all the efforts that have been made; for all they want from the Spaniards is their clothes, and all the evil that they see in them. I believe that these customs will never be suppressed.148

68. Another curious peculiarity is that although there are generally some few who are jealous, if they have any business with the Spaniards, they will not go themselves, but will send their wives or daughters without any fear of danger, in order that their business may be well despatched.149

69. They are very material and literal in their conversations, and one cannot say the slightest word to the women in jest, however slight it be; for the most discreet thing that they will answer to one will be, Tampalasanca, which means, "You are a150 shameless fellow;" and, if not that,151 a tempest of words, that will make him repent having given occasion for them.152 This alone is their custom with the Spaniards.153

70. It is a thing to be wondered at that even the dogs have another disposition, and have a particular aversion toward Spaniards. When they see Spaniards, they choke themselves with barking. And when the children see a father they cry immediately,154 and thus from their cradle they begin to hold every white face in horror.155

71. They are so cowardly that they fear any Indian who becomes a bully among them—so much that, if they only see him with a poor knife, they fear him so greatly that he can do whatever he wishes. All the village together will not be bold enough to arrest him, for they say that he is posong, which is the same as "bold." I have had many examples of this.156

72. The vice of drunkenness is regarded by them as rank in the fourth degree,157 and they have made it a point of nobility; for the chiefest men think that they are the best workmen at this occupation.158 It is a fact that those most given to this vice are the Ilocans, then the Visayans, and then our Tagálogs.159 The Pampangos can be exempted from this rule, for they are very temperate in this wretched habit, as well as in all the other things which we have mentioned. They are very different: for they are truthful, and love their honor; are very brave, and inclined to work; and are more

civil, and of better customs. In regard to the vices here mentioned (for they are, in the last analysis, Indians like the rest), they keep them more out of sight and covered. In all things the Pampangos have a nobleness of mind that makes them the Castilians of these same Indians. Consequently, that people must be distinguished from the rest in its character, in all that we have said.

73. Returning now to the others, in general, they possess vanity without honor; for among them it is no reason for less esteem to be drunkards, robbers, or connivers in evil deeds, or [to practice] other like virtues.160 They lose reputation and honor only if they get the reputation of being sorcerers. Consequently, in the opinion of a very learned minister, there is no case of a restitution of honor, unless some accusation of this infamous sin is imputed to them. In their marriages and among their kindred their disgust is not moved except by this, for the others are excused by self interest, but this fault is not.161

74. All that I have said of the men is very different in the women, saltem quoad modum.162 For they are of better morals, are docile and affable, and show great love to their husbands and to those who are not their husbands. They are really very modest in their actions and conversation, to such a degree that they have a very great horror of obscene words; and if weak nature craves acts, their natural modesty abhors words.163 The notion that I have formed of them is that they are very honorable, and, most of all, the married women. Although beans are boiled, it is not by the kettleful, as in other regions.164 Scarcely will one find a Tagálog or Pampango Indian woman, who will put her person to trade; and they are not so abandoned as we see in the women in other regions. They are very averse toward the Spaniard, and love the equality [in marriage] of their own nation; and, as a foreign religious said, are suited "each man to each woman." They rarely have any love for a Spaniard. They have another peculiarity, which if the Indian women of America had, that land would not be so full of mulattoes, who are a ferocious and wicked race. This is their horror for Cafres and negroes, which is so great that they would sooner suffer themselves to be killed than to receive them. The Visayan women, however, are ready for everything, and are not so fastidious. On the contrary, they are very ready to consent to any temptation.165

75. The women are very devout, and in every way of good habits. The cause for this is that they are kept so subject and so closely occupied; for they do not lift their hands from their work, since in many of the villages they support their husbands and sons, while the latter are busied in nothing else but in walking,166 in gambling, and wearing fine clothes, while the

greatest vanity of the women is in the adornment and demeanor of these gentlemen, for they themselves are very poorly and modestly167 clad.

76. In all that I have said, to this point, concerning the nature and morals of these poor people, I have done no more than to approximate [to the truth], as the mathematicians have done in the squaring of the circle. For an essential, substantial, and exhaustive definition168 is for some other person, to whom divine Providence chooses to communicate this difficult matter.169 Very praiseworthy is Barclayo, for in his Eupormion and his Argenis,170 he succeeded in discerning the natures of nations; as did Juan Rodemborgio,171 and our Gracian in his Criticon.172 But had they treated of the Filipinos, they would not have been so successful.

77. The bishop of La Puebla, Don Juan Palafox,173 wrote a keen treatise on the virtues of the Indians of Nueva España, in which his uncommon intellect and his holy and good intention are displayed more clearly than is the truth of his argument on the subject; for in a curious way he endeavors to make virtues of all their vices and evil inclinations. For in what they merit before God through their wills, they do not merit if it be the impelling force of their natural inclination and manner of living, because absuetiis non fit passio.174 One cannot, indeed, compare the voluntary poverty of St. Francis with that of the Indians, which is born of laziness and full of greed; for theirs is the infamous poverty which Virgil places in hell: et turpis egestas.175 And just as the economy of a poor wretch is not reckoned as fasting, so it will not be proper to say that if St. Antony176 went barefoot, the Indians do the same; and that they live on certain roots, as did the fathers of the Thebaid.177 For the fasting and the austerities of St. Arsenius178 had a different impelling motive—since he left the pleasures and esteem of the court of the emperor Theodosius179—than that which they can have, being so born and reared, and never having seen anything else. Hence, Ovid says of the Getas that they left the delights and comforts of Roma, and returned to seek the poverty and misery to which they were accustomed in Pontus:

Roma quid meltus scyt[h]ico180 quid frigore peius?

Húc tamen ex illa Barbarus urbe fugit.181

78. It is not my intention to include the Sangley mestizos here, as they are a different race. For although they were the children of Indians at the beginning, they have been approaching more and more to the Chinese nation with the lapse of successive generations. Et compositum ex multis atrahit ad se nuturam simplicis dignioris.182 Consequently, I leave their description for whomever wishes to undertake that task; for I fear that I shall succeed but very ill with the task which I have here undertaken, as it is so difficult.

79. Finally, summing up all the above, the inference will be that all the actions of these wretched beings are such as are dictated by nature through the animal, intent solely on its preservation and convenience, without any corrective being applied by reason, respect, and esteem for reputation. Consequently, he who first said of a certain people that if they saw the whole world hanging on one nail and needed that nail in order to hang up their hat, they would fling the world down in order to make room for the hat, would have said it of the Indians had he known them. For they think only of what is agreeable to them, or of what the appetite dictates to them; and this they will put in action, if fear, which also dwells in them, do not dissuade them.183 Hence they will be seen dressed in the shirts and clothes of their masters, for the sole reason184 that because they no sooner enter any house than they become the owners of everything in it. And the worst thing is that, although they are not good and faithful servants, intrant in gaudium domini sui.185

80. They also have other qualities worthy of envy, non quoad causam sed quoad efectum.186 Such is their contentment with their lot, for they believe that there is no people in the whole world better than they, and that if they possess a bamboo hut, a little rice for a few days, a few small fish, and a couple of leaves of tobacco, they do not envy the tables of Xerxes or Eliogabalus,187 and can sing with Lucan:

O tuta potestas Augusti parvique laris.
Prohl munera nondum intellecta Deum quibus hoc
Contingere templis, vel posuit muris nullo
Trepidare tumulto, Cæsarea pulsata manu.188

81. They are also worthy of envy for the calmness and conformity with which they die, with so wonderful peace, as if they were making a journey from one village to another—the Lord working in these creatures as the Lord that He is,189 for in that transit His mercy shines forth more; and thus said David (Psalm, XLVII, 21) Domini, Domini, exitus mortis;190 whence that reduplication which the Hebrew grammar calls ohatsere,191 signifies the superlative in name and action. The same is the declaration of divine wisdom (Proverbs, XX): In viis justitiæ ambulo, in medio semitarum judicii, ut ditem diligentes me.192 The Father celestial summons them for the relief of their burdens, and of the troubles which they have had during life: Venite qui laboratis, et onerati estis, et ego reficiam vos (Matthew xi, 28).193

For it is a fact that if one consider the life and lot of most of them, they resemble that merchant in the gospel of Matthew (chapter 13), who gave all that he had for the precious pearl; for it costs them more than is apparent to become Christians, with so much cutting of timber, and many personal services; and thus God gives them the true rest of death, as to poor and needy ones. Parcet pauperi, et inopi, et animas pauperum salvas faciet (Psalm, xii, 13).194 Exiguo enim conceditur misseracordia (Wisdom, vi, 7).195

82. In all the aforesaid, I find no more than the claw by which this lion can be recognized, because of the difficulty of the matter; therefore I refer the matter to another who has greater talent and experience, who can tell more, since I cannot do everything.196 I remember once to have heard from an inexperienced preacher this ingenious bit of nonsense, that in praising St. John the Baptist he cited that passage of St. Matthew (chapter xi, [7]), cœpit Jesus dicere [ad turbas] de Joanne;

83. And he said that John was so great a saint, that even in the mouth of Christ our Lord it was [only] possible to begin speaking of him, but that no end could be reached. The same I shall say of this matter, in all candor.

84. There is no little to learn and study in the matter, concerning the manner in which one must behave with them—especially we ministers, who come from remote lands in order to assist and teach them; for because of not understanding this aright many have become disconsolate, and have conceived a horror of the Indians, and have returned to España, or they have lived amid great hardship, in a continual combat of impatience and anxiety, thus frustrating the good vocation which brought them to these islands, a vocation so acceptable to God our Lord. For, as says the angelic doctor St. Thomas, 22, book 188, article 4: Deo nullum sacrificium est magis acceptum, quam celus animarum.197 To those who take this charge upon them, the words of the Lord in His revelations to St. Brigida are of great consolation. Among many others, he says (book 2, chapter 6): Vos ergo amici mei qui estis in mundo procedite securi, clamate, et anuntiate voluntatem meam. Ego ero in corde et in ore vestro. Ego ero dux vester in via et consolator in morte. Non relinquam vos, procedite alacriter quia ex labore cresit gloria.198 For it is a fact that all this exhortation is necessary, in order to combat the friction that is caused to the European disposition by dealing with people of customs so different, and which has caused so many to lose their reason.

85. Therefore the compass to which the navigator must always be attentive, in the gulf of the customs of this exasperating race, is patience. For this is the only remedy which Christ our Lord left to His disciples for the attainment of this ministry: (Luke xxi, [19]) In patientia vestra possidebitis animas vestras; and St. Paul, in Hebrews x, 36: patientia est vobis necessaria, ut reportetis, repromissionis.199

86. With this knowledge and without losing200 this strong protection one must continually consider that all these vices and evil traits are dictated and impelled by their nature, at times aided by the suggestion of the common

enemy when he hopes to succeed in causing us impatience. Very worth considering in this are the words of St. Paul (2 Cor., xi, 19, 20): Libenter enim suffertis insipientes cum sitis ipsi sapientes. Sustinetis enim si quis vos in servitutem redigit, si quis devorat, si quis accipit, si quis extollitur, si quis infaciem vos cædit.201 For all these hardships, and greater, must be suffered here among these brothers.202

87. I confess for my part that, at the beginning, I was afflicted and was greatly tormented, until with the lapse of time I came to realize that such was their disposition and nature, and that these trees could give no better fruit. In time it became to me a motive for praising God to see the variety of conditions and203 customs which He has placed in human nature, which is so beautified with variety; and I took particular pleasure in seeing youths and boys doing all things backward—without any malice, and without having prompters, like actors; but moved only by that hidden peculiarity that makes them so different from all other nations, and so uniform among themselves, [a likeness] which is so great that any one who has seen one of these monopantos has seen them all. With these considerations I lived consoled, and succeeded in making of them wax and wick, as the saying is.204

88. First, one must not shout out at them, for that is a matter that frightens and terrifies them greatly, as can be seen if one cries out at them when they are unaware—when the whole body trembles; and they say that a single cry of the Spaniard penetrates quite to their souls.

89. One must not strike them with the hands, for if we are of flesh, they are of iron, and the hand will suffer greatly, for God does not choose that they be corrected so indecently.205

90. All of their faults must not be overlooked, for they will become insolent and worse daily. Consequently, it is necessary for the father ministers to give them some lashes as a father, with great moderation, for it is enough to give lashes for vanity and haughtiness. This must be observed especially in the lads, as is the order of the Holy Spirit (Proverbs, xxiii, 13, 14): Noli subtrahere a puero disciplinam; si enim percussieris eum virga, non morietur. Tu virga percuties eum: et animam ejus de inferno liberabis.206 The command of St. Gregory shall be observed carefully (2 p. pastoral, chapter 6): Curandum quippe est ut rectorem subditis, et matrem, et patrem se exhibeat disciplina.207

91. Nothing must be taken away from them, or received from them, without paying for it; for they are very poor, and the least thing produces a great want with them. It must be considered that their greatest misery arises from their laziness and rude condition, and that that habit keeps them in

its grasp, and they suffer great poverty; for Egestatem operata est manus remissa (Proverbs, x, 4). We must consider also that they support us and that they pay as they are able for our labors. If anything be given to them, let it be purely208 for God's sake and as an alms, for if it be lent it will be entirely lost, both the merit and the patience209—considering their necessity and not their ingratitude, as a thing ordained by God. Propter miseriam asume pauperem, et propter inopiam eius ne dimitas eum vacuum; et cætera (Ecclesiasticus, xxix, 12).210

92. It is better, in selecting servants among the Indians for the inside of the house, to see that they be the sons of caciques or chiefs. They must be shown neither love nor familiarity. They must indeed always be treated well, but with uprightness and seriousness of face. It must be considered that in proportion as they are better caressed and clothed, the worse and more insolent they will become. This is the teaching of the Holy Spirit in Proverbs xxiv, 21: Qui delicate a pueritia nutrit servum suum, postea sentiet eum contumacem. They must be taught their duties, and must always be ordered to perform them with prudence and circumspection, for otherwise they will come gradually to lose respect for their master, and for the character which God presents to them in the Spaniard in order to dominate them; and then will result the same thing that happened to the log which, Æsop says, was placed in the lake by Jupiter to be king of the frogs. But the frogs, seeing after a time that it did not move, made sport of it, and jumped on top of it, etc. Not many things should be ordered of them at one time; for their memories are very poor, and they will only keep the last one in mind. The keys of the pantry or to the money must not be entrusted to them, for that would be placing opportunity and temptation in their hands, and they never resist it. Good instruction and subjection in the house, and, above all, the good example of life which they see in their masters, instil much into them; and under such conditions they generally become good servants, especially those of the Pampango nation. On the other hand, also, one must not expect a good servant in the house of a bad master.211

93. One must not exhaust them or squeeze them much beyond what they can give of themselves, as we do with the lemon, for all that will be pressed out will be bitter, as says the proverb of the commentary; qui nimis emungit, solet extorquere cruorem.212 Neither is it well or proper to go about visiting the caciques or going up into their houses, except when necessity requires it; for immediately the whole village will be filled with envy and complaint, and the esteem of the father ministers will suffer considerably. Besides, their stench and vice do not render this diversion desirable.213

94. When214 they are sent with a message to any place, one must very patiently await some notable failure caused ordinarily by their natural sloth and laziness.215 Sicut acetum dentibus, et fumus oculis, sic piger his qui miserunt illum (Proverbs, x, 26).216

95. I do not believe that I should omit mention, saltem per transenam,217 of a matter very worthy of consideration—namely, that if God chooses to chastise the flourishing Christianity of these islands for our and their sins, by placing it in the hands of Indians ordained as priests (as appears about to threaten us very soon), if God do not apply a remedy, what abominations will not follow! For to declare that they will change their customs218 and the aforesaid vices is impossible. On the contrary, their arrogance will grow worse with exaltation to so sublime an estate; their cupidity with power will be better fed; their laziness, with the lack of necessity; and their vanity, with the applause that they would wish to have, for they would desire to be served by those whom they would in another estate respect and obey; and the villages would suffer from the curse mentioned in Isaiah xxiv, 2, sicut populus, sic sacerdos. For the Indian who is ordained does not become a priest because it is the calling that conduces to the most perfect estate,219 but because of the great and almost infinite advantage that comes to him with the new estate that he chooses. How much it differs from being a father cura, to be a baguntao or sexton! From paying tribute, to being paid a stipend! From going to the [compulsory] cutting of timber, to being served in it! From rowing in a banca, to be rowed in it! That does not count with a Spaniard, who, if he become a cleric, often gives up an office as alcalde-mayor, captain, or general, with many other comforts in his native place, while his house is exalted above all the nation of the Indians. Let one contrast this with the vanity with which one who has been freed from the oar,220 or from an ax in the cutting of timber, will give his hand to be kissed! What a burden for the village will be the father, and mother, sister and nieces ranked as ladies, when many other better women are pounding rice! For if the Indian is insolent and intolerable with but little power, what will he be with so much superiority! And if the wedge from the same log221 is so powerful, what will it be if driven by so great authority! What plague of locusts can be compared to the destruction that they would cause in the villages?222 What respect will the Indians have for him, seeing that he is of their color and nation—and especially those who consider themselves as good, and even better perhaps, than he who became a cura, while they do not become anything better than bilango or servant? How severely the good cura will chastise them, and for trifling offenses!223 as we see the Indians do when they act as gobernadorcillos of their villages for even a single year—when the first thing that they do, and in which they most delight,

is immediately to place the picota224 in front of their houses, in order to apply lashes with the hangman's strap [penca]. What tyranny will the cura practice on them, such as they are wont to practice if they have any power and authority! How well the wedge of the same wood will force its way, without there being any one to say to him, curita facis? [i.e., "Dost thou play the cura?"]225

96. Therefore, if any insurrection or mutiny should arise, how well could it be arranged and prepared,226 if the cura entered also into the dance, as he is also an Indian and interested? For, in all the insurrections that have occurred in these islands, respect for the father ministers has been of great importance; but the very opposite would have happened if these were Indians. Then in the frequent carousals and feasts of which they are so fond, and on which their vanity and their chieftainship are founded, without any doubt there would be great indecency; for the cura would be very tender of conscience who would not pledge them in their cups. In that and other temptations would happen what Lucian relates in the second of his dialogues.

97. A noble youth had a very beautiful and gentle female kitten, which he esteemed so highly that he begged the goddess Venus to change it into a beautiful maiden, in order that he might marry her. The goddess did so. Thereupon, the youth227 immediately arranged the wedding, to which he invited the best people of the city. While, then, the bride was richly adorned with jewels and surrounded by many other women,228 and the guests, a mouse happened to appear, and began to approach them in order to eat some crumbs of bread which were scattered about. The bride saw it, and, without power to control herself, ran after the mouse throughout the length of the hall, and the guests were unable to restrain her. The groom was ashamed, and said,229 "Gentlemen, your pardon; for this girl was formerly a cat, and will always have the habits and bad traits of that animal."

98. I believe that the same thing would happen with the Indians,230 even when they belong to the caciques or nobility; for it is incredible that they can strip themselves of the peculiarities of their nature. I at least do not believe it at present, although God our Lord can very easily do it, for He is the One who raises up sons of Abraham from the stones. But we must not ask for miracles needlessly, but allow the Indian to remain an Indian, and go to his labor as before. If it is desired to prepare them for the high ministry of the priesthood, it is advisable to test them in the offices of alcaldes-mayor, captains, regidors, and councilors; for it appears to me that there is no one who can say that these said offices are greater and of higher rank and dignity than the priesthood, at least where the Inquisition exists. Then, if they conduct themselves well in the said employments, they can

be given the management of the body and blood of Jesus Christ our Lord; and then one can say with reason: Quia in pauca fuisti fidelis supra multa te constituam.231 For, as the Church teaches us through the mouths of the holy fathers, the dignity of the priesthood is so great that that of the kings or emperors of the world cannot compare with it. Thus says St. Ignatius the Martyr in his epistle to Smyrna, chapter x, Sacerdotium est apex bonorum omnium, quæ sunt in hominibus.232 St. Ambrose, in chapter 2 of his book De dignitate sacerdotum233 says so still more clearly.234 Father Molina235 has considerable to say on this in the first treatise of his Libro de sacerdotes [i.e., "Book of priests"] as has Father Señeri236 in his Cura instruido [i.e., "the cura instructed"].

99. Then is it possible that, even though they are Catholics and faithful sons of the Church, we must exalt to so lofty an estate men against whom there would be so many complaints if they became alférezes of a company in the regiment of Manila? Can the sacred habit of St. Peter, which we religious venerate as that of the greatest dignity, and to which we yield the most honorable place—which, as said the patriarch of Antiochia237 to the emperor of China, is the first rank and order of the Church—be obliged not to experience disgust at such low creatures? I do not know in what it [i.e., the proposal to ordain Indians] can consist, unless it be that in it is realized the vision that the said St. Peter had in Cesarea when the sheet was let down from heaven filled with toads and serpents, and a voice commanded him to eat without disgust—as is read in chapter x of the Acts of the Apostles. For although it signified the calling of heathendom, it must not be understood in moral things of the barbarous and mean nature of some peoples that compose that heathendom, in order to constitute the ecclesiastic hierarchy.238 When I come to discuss this matter, I find no end, and I find that we can only say: Domine adauge [nobis] fidem (Luke [x]vii, [5]).239

100. It is also a fact that the sacred canons do not demand from those who are ordained more than an honorable life and example, and a sufficient knowledge. Then, in order to dispense the spurious and legitimate240 and the mestizos, there is a brief of Gregory XIII which begins "Nuper ad nos relatum est,"241 issued at Roma, January 25, one thousand five hundred and seventy-five. For all that, I regard them [i.e., Indians as priests] as irregular, not only for the reasons given and stated above, but also because they lack the ecclesiastical and priestly mental ability, and the prudence necessary; and without these all the rest serves as almost nothing, as Pedro Urceblo sang with graceful elegance in his "Epigrams:"

> Sis licet ingenuus clarisque parentibus ortus;
>
> Esse tamen vel sic bestia magna potes.

Adde docus patriæ et claros tibi sume propinquos;

Esse tamen vel sic bestia magna potes.

Sint tibi divitæ242 sit larga et munda supellex;

Esse tamen vel sic bestia magna potes.

Denique, quidquid eris, nisi sit prudentia tecum;

Magna quidem dico, bestia semper eris.243

101. May God our Lord preserve your Grace for the many years of my desire. Manila, June 8, one thousand seven hundred and twenty.244 Your humble servant, who kisses your hand,

Fray Gaspar de San Agustin

[On a loose paper inserted in the copy of this letter owned by the Museo-Biblioteca de Ultramar (which as stated above, is unsigned), which was formerly owned by the well known Spanish scholar Pascual de Gayangos, is the following: "According to paragraphs [of this letter] which Paterno inserted in his work *La antigua civilizacion de Filipinos* (Madrid, 1887), p. 241, this letter must have been written by father Fray Gaspar de San Agustín; and according to Sinibaldo Mas, who inserts entire passages from this MS. in his *Informe sobre el estado de Filipinas en 1842,* i, pp. 63–132, and attributes it to Father Gaspar." Paterno has not had access to the document itself, but has used Mas.]

[Subjoined to the letter is the following, the origin of which we cannot account for, but which indicates the wide circulation that the letter must have had.]

Questions of Father Pedro Murillo [Velarde]245 of the Society of Jesus

102. What is the Indian? *Reply*—The lowest degree of rational animal. *Question*—How many and what are his peculiarities? *Reply*—Twenty-one, as follows:

Pride	Without honor.
Friend	Without loyalty.
A drunkard	Without satiety.
Compassionate	Without mercy.
Reserved	Without secrecy.
Long-suffering	Without patience.
Cowardly	Without fear.

Bold	Without resolution.
Obedient	Without submissiveness.
One who practices austerities	Without suffering.
Bashful	Without sense of honor.
Virtuous	Without mortification.
Clever	Without capacity.
Civilized	Without politeness.
Astute	Without sagacity.
Merciful	Without pity.
Modest	Without shame.
Revengeful	Without valor.
Poor	Without corresponding [mode of life].
Rich	Without economy.
Lazy	Without negligence.

Laus Deo.

Résumé of the entire letter by the said
Father Murillo

103. The Filipino Indian is the embryo of nature and the offspring of grossness. He does not feel an insult or show gratitude for a kindness. His continual habitation is the kitchen; and the smoke that harms all of us serves him as the most refreshing breeze. If the Indian has morisqueta and salt, he gives himself no concern, though it rain thunder and lightning, and the sky fall. He is much given to lying, theft, and laziness. In the confessional he is a maze [embolismo] of contradictions, now denying proofs and now affirming impossible things. Now he plays the part of a devout pilgrim over rough roads and through the deepest rivers, in order to hear mass on a workday at a shrine ten or twelve leguas away; while it is necessary to use violence to get him to hear mass on Sunday in his parish church. They are impious in their necessities with the father, but liberal and charitable to their guests, even when they do not know them; and through that they are greatly disappointed. At the same time they are humble and proud; bold and atrocious, but cowardly and pusillanimous; compassionate and

cruel; slothful and lazy, and diligent; careful and negligent in their own affairs; very dull and foolish for good things, but very clever and intelligent in rogueries. He who has most to do with them knows them least. Their greatest diversion is cock-fighting, and they love their cocks more than their wives and children. They are more ready to believe any of their old people than even an apostolic preacher. They resemble mellizas,246 in their vices and opposite virtues. In lying alone, is no contradiction found in them; for one does not know when they are not lying, whether they are telling the truth by mistake. One Indian does not resemble another Indian, or even himself. If they are given one thing, they immediately ask for another.247 They never fail to deceive, unless it crosses their own interest. In their suits, they are like flies on the food, who never quit it, however much they be brushed away. Finally, there is no fixed rule by which to construe them; a new syntax is necessary for each one; and, as they are all anomalous, the most intelligent man would be distracted248 if he tried to define them. Farewell.

[Delgado has the following interesting chapter (pp. 297–302 of his *Historia*) on this letter, which it is judged advisable to present at this place.]

Chapter VII

Some considerations concerning the matter in Father Gaspar de San Agustín's letter

I confess that I read this letter, in which the reverend author criticises the customs and dispositions of the natives of Filipinas, some years ago. But I read it as I am wont to read other letters, for diversion and amusement, without thinking much about its artfulness, and I was delighted with its erudition. However, when I afterward considered its contents with some degree of thought, I saw that it brought forward, in its whole length, no solid proof of what it tries to make one believe; and it appeared to me a hyperbolical criticism from the very beginning. On that account I resolved to make a few brief commentaries on the matter in the letter, both for the consolation of those whom our Lord may call to these missions, and so that it may be understood that at times sadness and melancholy are accustomed to heighten things, making giants out of pygmies—all the more, if a relish for revery and grumbling be joined with a tendency to exaggeration and with figures of speech corresponding thereto. Consequently, I am surprised that the reverend annalist or chronicler [i.e., San Antonio] of the seraphic province of San Gregorio praises this letter, saying that it is worth printing, since its author has penetrated as far as one may penetrate into the characters of the natives of these islands. And yet the author confesses that it is as difficult to define their nature as are the eight impossible things which are recounted there. That seems to me a fine hyperbole.

From the above one can see that, as he commenced this letter by affirming a hyperbole with eight hyperboles, it is not surprising that I called it hyperbolical; and especially if all the hyperboles that it contains from its beginning to its end be enumerated. But ere I begin to express my opinion I would like to sum up two contradictory and opposite expressions that I find in these authors. The reverend father Fray Gaspar says of the Indians, in his letter, that the difficulty of knowing the Indians lies not in the individual but in the race, for, if one be known, all are known.

Father Pedro Murillo says, in his approbation of the Cronicas,249 that "there is no fixed rule by which to construe the Indians; for each one needs a new syntax, all being anomalous. With the Indians the argument does not conclude by induction, since no one is like to himself; for, in the short circuit of a day, he changes into more colors than a chameleon, takes more shapes than a Proteus, and has more movements than a Euripus.250 He who has most to do with them, knows them least. In short, they are an aggregate of contrarieties, and the best logician cannot reconcile them. They are an obscure and confused chaos, in which no species can be perceived and no points of exactness distinguished." All these terms considered one by one, compose a very exaggerated hyperbole, in which this author showed his great erudition and little experience, for he only ministered in a few missions, and for a short time. For during most of the time while he lived in these islands he did not leave the professor's chair, except for a short time; and all that he tells of his journey to and travels among the Visayas was learned in passing and hastily, in company with the provincial who visited those missions. There he obtained very little light on the character and temperament of the Indians, as he had no dealings with them as one settled among them. And, just as in this expression he opposes himself without much reason to the reverend father Fray Gaspar, who after forty years of ministry, affirms that the Indians are well designated by the Greek word monopantas—a term which was given to a certain people by a critic, as they were all similar and homogeneous—so also when he affirms that all are anomalous and heterogeneous because they cannot all be constructed in one and the same syntax, does he go beyond the credence that can be given to his ingenious hyperboles. The experience that the said Father Murillo could have is of the Indians who go about in Manila and its environs, who are interpreters, servants in accounting-rooms and secretarial offices, who are accustomed to deal with Spaniards of all kinds, with creoles, mestizos, Sangleys, and other kinds of people who assemble there for trade. They have learned fraud and deceit, as well as the bad morals and propensities of all and every one of them. As is seen, one cannot judge of a whole nation—and much less of all the nations of the islands, who are diverse and distinct in genius and customs by the cases of these Indians who speak Spanish. And taking into account so great diversity, I affirm that it is impossible to find a definition that admits and includes all of them. For these persons whom I have mentioned, reared among so many classes, and among people so heterogeneous, and who are imbued with customs so diverse, cannot form rules by which to explain their own nation, much less by which to define the other nations.

Now if the statements of authors in regard to physical or moral matters are so at variance that we can say that each author has a different opinion—as says the proverb, Quot capita, tot sententiæ—and if thus far no ground and certain point has been found at which the understanding may stop, how is it strange that they do not find, in order to describe Indians with customs so unusual and artificial as have those of Manila, a compound idea made up of all that they have learned from the Spaniard, both good and evil; all that they have learned from the Guachinango;251 and what they have learned from the mestizo, the Sangley, the Moro, the Malabar, the Cafre, and all the other people with whom they have intercourse and with whom they trade? Granting this to be true, it appears that the definition of Father Murillo fits these Spanish-speaking Indians, but not the others, who have not had any intercourse with diverse classes of people. On this account it seems to me that father Fray Gaspar hit the definition exactly, when he said in his letter that the Asiatic Indians of Filipinas are almost the same as all the people of the nations of Eastern India, in what concerns their genius, disposition, and inclination; and are not distinguished one from another except in their rites, clothing, and languages. I add, in what regards their abilities and capacities—which are so good, and in general so well inclined—that I believe that if children, either boys or girls, were taken from Filipinas to Viscaya or to Castilla, the natives [of those countries] would not distinguish them from the Vizcainos, Castilians, or mountaineers. For their vices are not due so much to their nature, as to their bad rearing and education; and they are easily instructed both in the evil and in the good. And notwithstanding what father Fray Gaspar, Father Murillo, and Fray Juan [Francisco] de San Antonio have said, they would have been more successful had they not said, with exaggeration, that it would be impossible to write everything that they have observed of the Indians, on all the paper that is found in China. That is a hyperbole that transcends all faith. Thus does he continue in all that he says; and he affirms, further, that it surpasses all that we can touch with the hands or see with the eyes. Hence from the beginning we can state those two rules of law: semel malus, semper præsumitur malus; and the other, malum ex quocumque defectu.252...

What mystery is there in the customs and genius of the Indians that should make them so deep and inscrutable that we cannot reach them, sound them, and explain them? since they are Indians like all the rest of the people of Asia, without there being more or less in them. Therefore, "these profundities, this intricate, confused chaos, this aggregate of contrarieties, this maze of contradictions, are a collection of rhetorical locutions or tropes invented in order to exaggerate and to use hyperboles in what of itself has no mystery—these definitions remaining purely in the manner of speech, or of the conception, of their authors; or perhaps in a mere misapprehension formed by a critical, melancholy, or affected genius.

But since in this letter, the evil propensities of the Indians, both men and lads, who act as servants, are set down in detail, let us see on the other hand, somewhat of the good that the Indians possess. For one should not write and consider only the evil, and omit as fitting all the good, in order thereby to make the object more detestable. For, as says a mystical writer, we must not possess the nature of the dung-beetle, which goes always to the dungheap, but that of the bee, which always seeks out the sweet and pleasant. Let us see what Father Murillo says of the good: "They are most clever in any handiwork, not in inventing but in imitating what they see. They are most beautiful writers; and there are many tailors and barbers among them. They are excellent embroiderers, painters, goldsmiths, and engravers, whose burin has not the like in all the Indias (and I was even about to pass farther if shame did not restrain me), as is seen clearly in the many good engravings that they make daily. They are good sculptors, gilders, and carpenters. They make the water craft of these islands, the galleys, pataches, and ships of the Acapulco line. They act as sailors, artillery-men, and divers; for there is scarce an Indian who cannot swim excellently. They are the under-pilots of these seas. They are very expert in making bejuquillos,253 which are gold chains of a very delicate and exquisite workmanship. They make hats, petates or rugs, and mats, from palm-leaves, rattan, and nito,254 which are very beautiful, and embroidered with various kinds of flowers and figures. They are remarkable mechanics and puppet-showmen, and they make complicated mechanisms which, by means of figures, go through various motions with propriety and accuracy. There are some jewelers. They make powder, and cast swivel-guns, cannon, and bells. I have seen them make guns as fine as those of Europa. There are three printing houses in Manila, and all have Indian workmen. They have great ability in music. There is no village however small, that has not its suitable band of musicians for the services of the Church. They have excellent voices—sopranos, contraltos, tenors, and basses. Almost all of them can play the harp, and there are many violinists, rebeck, oboe, and flute players. The most remarkable thing is, that not only do those whose trade it is make those instruments; but various Indians make guitars, flutes, harps, and violins, for pleasure, with their bolos and machetes. And by the mere seeing those instruments played, they learn them almost without any teaching; and the same thing occurs in other things. On this account it is said that the Indians have their understanding in their eyes, since they imitate whatever they see, by another like it." This is what Father Murillo says; but he left the most important things in the inkhorn. I will add them here, as I have heard them affirmed many times by the Spaniards in Cavite, namely: Who are the men who convey and conduct the ships and galleons from Acapulco and other kingdoms? Is it the Spaniards? Ask that of the pilots, masters, and boatswains, and they will all affirm that this great and inestimable good is due to the Indian alone. (Here is indeed where a hyperbole will fit exactly.) Besides this, who are the people who support us in these lands and those who furnish us food? Perhaps the Spaniards dig, harvest, and plant throughout the islands? Of a surety, no; for when they arrive at Manila, they are all gentlemen. The Indians are the ones who plow the lands, who sow the rice, who keep it clear [of weeds], who tend it, who harvest it, who thrash it out with their feet— and not only the rice which is consumed in Manila, but that throughout the Filipinas—and there is no one in all the islands who can deny me that. Besides this, who cares for the cattle-ranches? The Spaniards? Certainly not. The Indians are the ones who care for, and manage and tend the sheep and cattle by which the Spaniards are supported. Who rears the swine? Is it not the same Indians? Who cultivates the fruits—the bananas, cacao, and all the other fruits of the earth? of which there is always abundance in the islands, unless unfavorable weather, locusts, or some other accident cause their loss? Who provide Manila and the Spaniards with oil? Is it not the poor Visayan Indians, who bring it in their vessels annually? Who furnishes so great profit to the Spaniards in Manila with the balate255 and sigay; and who buys these products very cheaply from the wretched Indians, and resell them for double the sum to the pataches of the coast and to the Sangleys? Who guide and convey us to the villages and missions, and serve us as guides, sailors, and pilots? Perhaps it is the Spaniards? No, it is the Indians themselves, with their so exaggerated, magnified, and heightened laziness. Is this the thanks that we give them, when we are conquering them in their own lands, and have made ourselves masters in them, and are served by them almost as by slaves? We ought to give God our Lord many thanks, because He maintains us only through the affection and by the useful labors of the Indians in this land; and He would perhaps have already driven us hence if it were not for this usefulness of theirs, and for the salvation of the Indians. We also owe many thanks to the Indians, since God our Lord sustains us in their lands by their means; and because we would die of starvation if they did not sustain us, provide us with food, serve us, and conduct us through the islands with so much love and security that they would all first perish before the father in whatever perils arise.

These and many other like things were overlooked by Father Murillo, who was enraptured by their music, engraving, and rugs. By the aforesaid, one will see with how little truth the statement is printed that the Indians are the greatest enemies that the father ministers have; for certainly all the above could not be reconciled with such a proposition. On the contrary, it must be said that the Indians are those who defend us from our enemies; for, in the presidios, who are the soldiers, who sail in the war fleets, who are in the vanguard in war? Could the Spaniards, perchance, maintain themselves alone in this country, if the Indians did not aid in everything? Little experience and less reflection would he have who should propose such a thing. Therefore, these two things do not harmonize well, that those who hate us should defend us, and that those who are our greatest enemies should be the ones to maintain and support us. Nor is it to be wondered at that there have been insurrections on several occasions; these, perhaps, have not arisen because the Indians were ill-disposed to the Spaniards; but, on the contrary, we know that many of them have been caused by the cruelty, wickedness, and tyranny of some alcalde-mayor and other Spaniards who, having been elevated from low beginnings, try to become gods and kings in the provinces, tyrannizing over the Indians and their possessions. This is often the cause of the insurrections. Would that I could mention some especial cases in this matter. However, I do not care to dip my pen in blood, and write tragedies instead of history. For, although I could say more, the authority and arrogance that every Spaniard assumes upon his arrival in this country is incredible.

1 Juan José Delgado was a native of Cadiz; the time of his birth is not known. In 1711 he left Spain for Filipinas, and perhaps remained for some time in Mexico: it is probable that he reached Filipinas as early as 1717. He seems to have spent most of his life in the Visayan Islands—Sámar, Cebú, Leyte, etc.—but to have visited most of the peoples in the archipelago at some time or other. His Historia was written during the years 1751–54; the date of his death is not known. See sketch of his life in the Historia (Manila, 1892), pp. x–xi.

2 Mas used the MS. of the Museo-Biblioteca de Ultramar, which is wrongly dated. See post, pp. 278–280. Of the letter itself he says (i, "Poblacion" p. 63): "These paragraphs and other ancient documents will show us ... how little the individuals who now occupy us have changed since that time."

3 For instance, Mas says (p. 63): "Here follows what the author of the celebrated work on the Philippines, called Cronicas franciscanas [referring to San Antonio's Chronicas] says: 'The very reverend father, Fray Gaspar de San Agustin, an Augustinian from Madrid,'" etc. Bowring makes this: "Among the most celebrated books on the Philippines are the 'Cronicas Franciscanas' by Fr. Gaspar de San Agustin, an Augustine monk of Madrid;" and following gives the impression that he makes the selections directly from San Agustin—a ridiculous error.

In regard to the word "monk" used by Bowring, that author is again in error, technically at least, an error that is quite often met with in many works. As pointed out by Rev. T. C. Middleton, O.S.A., in a letter dated December 8, 1902, the only regulars in the Philippines who could rightfully be styled "monks" were the Benedictines. The members of the other orders are "friars," the equivalent of the Spanish "frailes." The monks are strictly cloistered. The friars appeared first in the thirteenth century, and do not live a strictly cloistered life.

4 M. reads on the outside wrapper: "Letter by Fray Gaspar de San Agustin;" and the heading of the letter is as follows: "+ Letter written by an aged religious of Philipinas to a friend in España, who asked him as to the nature and characteristics of the Indian natives of these islands." D. reads: "Letter written by the very reverend father Fray ... giving him an account ..."

5 M. and D. read "mathematical side;" and continuing D. reads "of the double of the cube of the sphere."

6 i.e., "I was with this generation for about forty years, and I said 'These people always err from the heart.'" M. omits the Latin phrase and reads in its place "and I have only learned that they are almost incomprehensible." D. reads as M. and then adds "and therefore I shall only say," followed by the Latin phrase.

7 i.e., "He himself knew our formation." The last word of the Latin phrase is omitted in M.

8 D. reads "excuse myself from the burden and difficulty."

9 i.e., "It is difficult to know man—a changeable and variable animal." M. gives only the first four words of this Latin phrase.

10 i.e., "I see men as trees walking."

11 Not set off into lines in the Ayer MS. A literal translation of the citation, which is rather freely translated in the text, is: "Spring makes me green; burning summer, yellow; autumn, white; and chill winter, bald." M. omits all the quotation after the first three words; D. reads "Glaucumque" instead of "flavamque." The poet mentioned by San Agustin was a Welshman by the name of John Owen, or, according to his Latin name, Joannis Audoenus. He was born about 1560,

at Armon, Wales, and died in London, in 1622. He studied law at Oxford, and afterward became a teacher at various places. He imitated the Epigrams of Martial, and his Epigrammata were published first in three books at London, in 1606, but were later augmented by seven more books. They were reprinted many times in various countries and even translated into other languages—among the latter, into English, French, and Spanish (Madrid, 1674–82). One of the best editions is that printed at Paris in 1774.

12 D. omits this last phrase.

13 M. omits the epigram. It is the forty-seventh epigram of the twelfth book, and is translated thus in Henry G. Bohn's Epigrams of Martial (London, 1877): "You are at once morose and agreeable, pleasing and repulsive. I can neither live with you nor without you." It has been several times translated into English verse.

14 i.e., "As many opinions as persons."

15 From the Greek words μονος, "one," "single," and πας, "all;" thus meaning, "homogeneous."

16 The Monophysites held that there was but one nature in Christ. They were condemned at the fourth general council held at Chalcedon in 451, but the decision of that council was a few years later set aside by an imperial encyclical issued by the emperor Basilicus. During the next century the Monophysites split up into many sects, and fought among themselves. The Monophysites still exist in Armenia, Egypt, Syria, and Mesopotamia; and are represented by the Armenian National church, the Jacobite Christians of Syria and Mesopotamia, the Coptic church, and the Abyssinian church. The schismatic Christians of St. Thomas are now connected with the Jacobites. See Addis and Arnold's Catholic Dictionary, pp. 597, 598.

17 M. greatly abridges this paragraph, among other things omitting all mention of the Monophysites. D. also omits the latter.

18 At this point M. adds "who are the true Indians, so named from the River Indus or from Indostan, for our Indians are so by catachresis or misusage."

19 The title of the Franciscan Juan de Torquemada's book, is as follows: Ia (–IIIa) Parte de los veynte y un libros rituales y monarchia Indiana con el origen y guerras de los Indios occidentales de sus poblaçones, descubrimiento, conquista, conversion y otras cosas maravillosas de la misma tierra (Sevilla, 1615; in three parts).

20 The title of Antonio de Ramesal's book is Historia general de las Indias Ocidentales, y particular, de la governacion de Chiapa, y Guatemala. Escrivese

juntamente los principios de nuestro glorioso Padre Santo Domingo, y de las demas religiones (Madrid, 1620).

Remesal was born in Allariz in Galicia, and took the Dominican habit in Salamanca, where he also became doctor of theology. He was sent to Central America in 1613, and on his return wrote his book. See Moreri's Dictionaire, vii, p. 68; and Hoefer's Nouvelle biographie générale, xli, col. 956.

21 See Vol. VIII, p. 38, note 1.

22 Bartolome (not Bernardino) de las Casas, the great apostle of the Indians. He first went to the New World in 1502 as a planter, became a Dominican religious in 1510, and in 1514 began to preach against the cruelty inflicted on the Indians by the Spaniards, for the purpose of alleviating their misfortunes, making numerous trips to Spain. He finally obtained from Cárlos I the "New Laws," which were so rigorous that an attempt to enforce them resulted in an insurrection in Peru under Gonzalo Pizarro, for an account of which see Pedro Gutiérrez de Santa Clara's Historia de las guerras civiles del Peru, 1544–1548 (Madrid, 1904–05). He finally returned to Spain for the last time, and died after a few years in the Dominican convent of Valladolid. His writings are many, and important. The reference in the text may be to his Brevissima relacion de la destruycion de las Indias (Sevilla, 1552); or to his Historia general de las Indias, which existed only in MS., until 1875.

23 See Vol. XXIX, p. 189, note 42. San Agustin probably refers to his Virtudes del Indio (1650?). Palafox left many writings, a number of which are of a controversial nature.

24 In D., "taught."

25 In D., "collect."

26 M. and D. call these last two peoples the "Mogores" and the "Camarines."

27 Baltasar Gracian was born in Calatayud, Aragon, in 1601, and entered the Society of Jesus in 1619. He taught belles-lettres, philosophy, moral theology, and the Holy Scriptures, and preached for several years. He was rector of the college at Taragona, Catalonia, where he died December 6, 1658. His first book, El Heroë, appeared in 1630. The most famous of his numerous works was his Criticon, which is probably the book referred to in the text. It is a sort of satire on the vices and customs of the times; and in places reminds one of Pilgrim's Progress. It was published in three parts, the first in 1650 at Madrid, and the other two at Huesca, in 1653. Most of his works were published under his brother Lorenzo's name. His talent in writing is vitiated by his affectation and other faults. See Ticknor's History of Spanish Literature (New York, 1854); Sommervogel's Bibliothèque; Moreri's Dictionaire, iv, p. 174; and Hoefer's Nouvelle biographie générale, xxi, cols. 570, 571.

28 M. and D. add "For most of the defects and vices of these Indians are common, on account of the," and continue as above.

29 This passage is badly confused in the three copies. The transcriber of M. has wrongly made the viviendo acephalos of the Ayer copy, bebiendo à sed [i.e., drinking when thirsty?] which hardly makes sense. That MS. continues, "and in confused anarchy," which is better than the Ayer reading. D. reads "Who besides having been living as the greatest barbarians, leaderless, and in confused anarchy."

30 Both M. and D. omit the passage referring to the influence and dominion of the moon. M. gives the names as "Beyerlinhe," and D. as "Bayarlinch."

Laurentius Beyerlinck was a noted Flemish savant and litterateur. He was born at Antwerp in 1578, and, after studying in that city with the Jesuits, went to Louvain, where he enjoyed a benefice until 1605. In that year he was recalled to Antwerp to become head of the seminary, and soon afterward obtained a canonry and then an archdeaconry there. His death occurred in Antwerp June 22, 1627, at the age of forty-nine. Notwithstanding his short life and his religious labors, he wrote a surprising amount. An edition of his Magnum Theatrum Vitæ Humanæ appeared in London, in eight volumes, in 1678. See Moreri's Dictionaire.

31 "When they grow delirious in their sickness, they are never frantic, but calm." (Mas, p. 64.)

32 M. and D. add here "slow."

33 In the Ayer MS. "serithnophagos." D. makes it "ictiófagos," which reading we have adopted; and M. omits the phrase.

34 The abundance of fish is one of the means by which nature aids their necessities. In the rainy season, all the creeks and ravines are full of water and fish. The very rice fields swarm with eels, shrimps, and a species of fish called dalag, which is about two palmos long and more than two inches thick. It is especially interesting for an European to see a crowd of people in the month of October on the high-road, busily fishing in the sowed fields. As the rice is now grown, it is impossible to see the water that bathes and wets its roots, and consequently, when the hooks are drawn out with fish two palmos long on them, it appears to be enchantment, or the inconsequential things of a dream. As the water dries up, the fish, still living, gather down in toward the hollows where there is yet some water; and they are there caught with the hand, or killed with clubs.

"The Indians have three meals [per day]: breakfast, dinner, and supper. These three meals consist of rice boiled in water but dry like the rice cooked in the Valencian style, or like the Turkish pilao. In addition they eat a trifle of fresh or salt fish, some sort of meat stew, camotes, etc.; but rarely do they have more than two different dishes, unless it is the occasion of a banquet. In the dearest provinces, the [expense of] common food cannot be estimated at more than one-half real of silver per day per adult; and since the daily wage that they earn is at least one-half real and their food, it results that this race have great opportunity to save and acquire considerable wealth. But their vices, their few necessities, and their disposition, which is indifferent and lacking in foresight, does not allow them to better the condition of their birth; and they remain in the wake of the mestizos, who are always the wealthy people of the villages." (Mas, pp. 64, 65.)

35 Mas says (p. 65): "It is not easy for anyone to explain them, so long as he tries to consider these men equal to the Europeans."

36 This sentence is omitted in M. and D.

37 All the matter above between the word "father" and this point is lacking in M.

38 The solidus was a coin of the Roman empire, which was at first called "aureus," and worth about twenty-five denarii, but afterward reduced to about one-half that value. It is used in the same manner as "farthing" or "cent" would be in English.

39 These passages are translated as follows in the Douay version of the Bible:

4. Many have looked upon a thing lent as a thing found, and have given trouble to them that helped them.

5. Till they receive, they kiss the hands of the lender, and in promise they humble their voice.

6. But when they should repay, they will ask time, and will return tedious and murmuring words, and will complain of the time:

7. And if he be able to pay, he will stand off, he will scarce pay one-half, and will count it as if he had found it:

8. But if not, he will defraud him of his money, and he shall get him for an enemy without cause:

9. And he will pay him with reproaches and curses, and instead of honour and good turn will repay him injuries.

40 i.e., "Scarce does he return the half."

41 In the Douay version: "The sinner shall borrow and not pay again;" being only one-half the verse. M. omits the reference, but gives the passage.

42 Delgado (Historia, p. 306) commenting on this passage says: "I find noted many actions of the Indian boys who serve in the houses and convents; and all are ridiculous things which we ourselves did in our own country when we were boys like them." He objects to San Agustin's quotation from Scripture on

the ground that it is too general, and that those words were not written merely for them. "If twenty cases have been experienced where the Indian borrower has failed to return what he borrowed, it cannot be said that the entire Tagálog nation are sinners, let alone other nations, which may not have been seen. Such a supposition is illogical."

43 The paragraph structure of M. and D. differs from our text in the above two paragraphs, and in other places throughout this letter; and the paragraphs are also unnumbered in both of these versions. The copy owned by Eduardo Navarro, O.S.A., Valladolid, agrees with the Ayer MS. in having numbered paragraphs, but the numbering is not in all cases the same.

44 At this point the following paragraphs which are not contained in either the Ayer MS. or in D. occur.

"They think that it is a fine thing to meddle and take part in things where they are not invited. Consequently, if any of Ours wishes to attend to any bodily necessity, not fit to mention, even when he least wishes it, there comes an Indian before or behind him even though he leave the banca and seek the most retired spot to do what no other can do for him.

"They cruelly treat the animals that serve them, and the danger of losing them does not move them to the contrary. Thus following the very opposite of St. Paul's command: Non alligavis vos bobi trituranti [i.e., "Thou shalt not muzzle the ox that treadeth out the corn,"—I Tim. v, 18, a quotation from Deut. xxv, 4], they tie the poor cow or carabao to a post after it has worked all day; and, if it is a horse, they feed it without removing bit or bridle. And if they have to look after their carabao it must be on condition of their being atop of it while it moves from place to place; and on the road they make sores on its buttocks."

That the Indian does not shut a door that he has opened, etc.; Delgado says (p. 306): "This is done by boys, and is common in our own country. It is not because of laziness, but perchance, for lack of attention, or the liveliness or mischievousness of boys, in which the aged and prudent Indians cannot be included." He has often seen the carpenters carefully collect their tools and take them away, so that they should not be lost. San Agustin's criticism is too general and has proceeded from what he has experienced in a few foolish lads.

45 "This," says Delgado (p. 307) "is peculiar only to some workmen, and not to all the nations of these islands, and the same thing happens also in our own country among cobblers, tailors, and other deceitful and tricky workmen."

Mas comments as follows (pp. 66, 67): "There is no tailor, cobbler, or workman of any kind, who does not begin by begging money when any work is ordered. If he is a carpenter, he needs the money in order to buy lumber; if a laundryman, to buy soap. This is not for lack of confidence in receiving their pay, for the same thing happens with those who have the best credit, with the cura of the village, and even with the captain-general himself. It consists, firstly, in the fact that the majority have no money, because of their dissipation; and secondly, because they are sure that after they have received a part of their price, their customer will not go to another house, and that he will wait for the workman as long as he wishes (which is usually as long as what he has collected lasts), and that then the customer will have to take the work in the way in which it is delivered to him."

46 M. reads, "in the region of the genitals;" and D., "ears."

47 Delgado says of this: "Let us give thanks to God that our parents reared us in civilized ways; for if they had not, we would do the same. But how many blows and lashes we had to take to become so! And indeed it must be noted that it is not so much because of rudeness that the Indian scratches himself, or does other things somewhat more indecent and coarse, as has happened to me at times when with them; but because of a sort of fear or respect, that so confuses them that they do not know at times what they are doing, or even what they are saying." The criticism, like others of San Agustin, is too sweeping. Delgado has not noticed this among the Visayans, although he has noted it among the Tagálogs. Because some women are coarse, coarseness cannot be charged in general upon all the women of the islands.

48 D. reads "And as yet they have not gotten over the difficulty of folding a cloak with the right side in."

49 M. and D. read "make gestures of wonder."

50 "I have observed that they are very stupid in making anything when one tries to give them instructions, but not when one allows them to work in their own manner. For example, one desires to have the cork which has slipped down into a bottle drawn. The best thing to say then, is 'See here, get this cork out without breaking the bottle. Take care!' Thereupon the Indian goes and fixes it as well as he can. Once I asked an old woman for some fire to light my cigar. There were many live coals on the ground remaining from a fire. She took a handful of earth in her palm, and atop of that placed a coal which she presented to me. In this way they do things that at times show sufficient ingenuity and skill, especially with bamboo and rattan. General Alava declared that their brains were in their hands." (Mas, pp. 67, 68.)

51 These last six words are lacking in M. This refers to the well-known myth of Orpheus and Eurydice. By Auresteo, San Agustin means Aristæus, probably an early Greek poet, but deified as a beneficent god and worshiped in various parts of Greece and other places. He was said to be the son of Apollo and the Thessalian nymph Cyrene, and was reared by Hermes, who made him immortal; although he is also sometimes called the son of Urana and Gæa. His connection with the Orpheus myth was probably an innovation of Virgil (Georgics, iv, ll.

315–558) who tells how he caused the death of Eurydice, who was killed by a serpent while fleeing from his persecutions. See Smith's Dictionary of Greek and Roman Biography and Mythology, and Seyffert's Dictionary of Classical Antiquities (London, 1891).

"It is still the custom in many of the churches for the men to take their positions in the center toward the upper part, and the women in the lower half." (Mas, p. 68.)

52 The last two words are missing in M. and D.

Curiosity, says Delgado (p. 307) and impertinence is a characteristic of all the peoples of Asia.

"They have asked me often as to my employment or occupation, my manner of living, and the amount of my pay. This proceeds from the tolerance and benevolence that they generally find in The Spaniards." (Mas, p. 68.)

53 This argues only their wildness and lack of civilization, says Delgado (pp. 307, 308), and they ought to be taught civilized manners by their masters, or at least by the missionaries. The Spanish houses generally have porters, so that the Indians cannot penetrate into the most retired apartment. It may happen at times in Manila, or in some of the missions; but it is not the custom in the Visayas, or in the province of Tagálos. Delgado has never had such a thing happen to him, for the Indians have always announced their arrival before entering.

54 "This proves the severity with which they are treated by their own people, and the kindness that they experience in us." (Mas, p. 68.)

55 "Thank God," says Delgado (p. 308) "that I find the prognosis above that says 'they are great sleepers' absolutely false."

56 This sentence is lacking in M. and D.

57 In D., "where the women go."

"They do this because they are humored like children in the convents." (Mas, p. 69.)

58 M. and D. omit "and perukes."

59 Literally, "the flower of the saints," perhaps alluding to some book of lives of saints, thus entitled. M. has "the isles of the saints."

60 M. and D. omit the last three words.

61 "Nearly all the villages have theaters for cock-fighting. Before fighting, some very sharp knives are fastened to the spurs so that one or the other is killed at the first meeting. On this account the cockfight does not offer the interest or sport that it does in España and other places, and it occupies the attention of these people solely as a means of winning or losing money. In reality, a cockpit

is a house of play. Before the two fowls are placed in attitude of fight, the bets are placed on two spindles. One of them generally offers a great sum in favor of the black cock, while others bet on the white one, until the sum is matched. The leading cocks are loosed and one of them is killed in less than two minutes. This is in fact a 'monte,' as is playing the races or betting on the jack [at cards]. The Filipinos, by nature idlers and greedy, are passionately fond of play, for they consider it an excellent and unique way of getting money without working; and they gather like flies to these pernicious places, in order to spend what they have and what they can succeed in borrowing or robbing, abandoning their most sacred and peremptory obligations. Furthermore, they pass many hours, both in their houses and in the cockpit, teaching a cock how to fight and to have no fear of the people; and examining the other cocks, in order to ascertain by certain rules and marks which will triumph and which will succumb. There is nothing more commonly seen even in the very streets of Manila itself, than a man squatted down on his heels with one of these fowls, in order that it might become accustomed to the noise, so that it might not grow confused or become frightened in the pit. There are men who take heed of nothing else or have other thought during the day than of their cocks.

"The government authorizes these wretched gatherings, not only on Sundays, but also on Thursdays or fair-days, which are not few, and has rented out the right of opening these theaters. Last year this department produced about 40,000 pesos fuertes. A sad recourse which must have occasioned and will occasion so many tears, crimes, and punishments, since so much vagabondage is thereby caused. There are often serious quarrels, which two judges of the theater end by deciding according to the laws. When any one of the contestants does not conform to the sentence, he has recourse to the alcalde, who takes the evidences in regard to the matter; and these quarrels generally go on appeal to the superintendency and to the upper litigious assembly. These causes are judged according to existing instructions, which were written in America.

"The Indians are also very fond of cards. They play brisca, burro (which is distinct from that of España), and *panguingui*, which is a game played very commonly by the Chinese. In this occupation they often pass all the night until dawn; and the cabezas de barangay lose the tributes of their subjects, and they have to go immediately to jail, or take to the mountain.

"They generally play duplo at their parties—a game consisting in arithmetical combinations—and also our game of forfeits." (Mas, pp. 69–71.)

62 Delgado (p. 308) admits that the youthful servants do break dishes, but they are cheap. "There are Indians in Manila who make and repair watches and other delicate baubles, and do not break them. Consequently, not only can they

handle bamboo, rattan, nipa, and bolos, but also other things; and they make and handle them lovingly."

"This is because they are generally heedless, sometimes through stupidity, and at other times because they are thinking of their sweetheart, or of something else, instead of what they are doing. When the Filipino drops a dish, the Spaniard says nothing, or is satisfied by calling him only a brute, animal, or savage; while in his own home, he would not escape without some buffets, which have more effect on this race than would the Philippics of Cicero." (Mas, p. 71.)

63 "The father must have said this of the country people, or of those who are servants; for among those who devote themselves to the arts there are some who turn out work very delicate and difficult to execute, even in Europa—as, for instance, the textiles and embroidery of piña, and the gold chains or bejuquillos, etc." (Mas, pp. 71, 72.)

64 D. adds "or [rather] not eating." This incident is related in the second part of Don Quixote, chapter xlvii.

65 This sentence is omitted in M. The following is there a question, "And what shall we say if they bring four eggs?"

66 A Dominican and the assistant of Archbishop Pardo, who became acting archbishop after the death of the latter. See Ferrando's Historia de los PP. Dominicos, vi, p. cxlvii; and our Vol. XXXIX, "The Pardo Controversy."

67 Don Fernando Valenzuela, a grandee of Spain, marquis of San Bartolomé de los Pinales and of Villasierra, chief master of the horse, gentleman of the chamber, etc., the favorite of the mother of Carlos II of Spain, Mariana of Austria (with whom his connection was said to be dishonorable), was, as a youth, page to the Duke of Infantado. He went to Rome with the duke, who was appointed ambassador to the papal court. On his return he gained the favor of the queen's confessor the German Jesuit Nitard, who introduced him into court circles. His rise to favor was rapid, for he was talented and handsome. After the downfall of Nitard, he gained entire ascendancy over the weak queen, who showered honors upon him. Finally he was exiled to the Philippines (1670), through the efforts of Don Juan of Austria, uncle of the king, and was imprisoned in the fort of Cavite where he landed March 29, 1679. On the death of Don Juan, the first act of the queen was to have Valenzuela freed from his exile, and a special ship was sent to the Philippines to take him to Spain. It is reported, however, that he died in Mexico, while on his way to Spain, from the kick of a horse. He built the bridge over the Manzanares at Toledo, at the cost of one million ducats. See Harrison's History of Spain (Boston, 1881); Montero y Vidal, i, p. 364; and Concepción, Hist. de Philipinas, vii, pp. 349–364. A document in Ventura del Arco's MS. collection (vol. iii)—which is a compilation from original documents in the Real Academia

de la Historia, Madrid—gives an account of the reception accorded to Valenzuela on his arrival at the Philippines, and some details of his life there.

68 M. reads "rice in the husk."

69 M. and D. add "pesos."

70 Delgado says (p. 308): "If they had as much understanding as the reverend father, they would not do it." The cases cited prove nothing general, since they are only particular cases. "But it must be borne in mind that all the Indians of these islands are very poor, and dress very poorly and live meanly; and when they see that the Spaniards, and especially these bishops and marquises, bear themselves with so great ostentation, and are so free and magnanimous and liberal, as their nobility demands, some Indians of little capacity are emboldened to beg from them things that they ought not; for they think that such men will never remain poor even though they give much." We beg God often for things out of season.

"This is because they know beforehand that they ask nonsense, and assume that their demand will not be granted, but they only are trying to see whether it might be met by any chance; for they are accustomed to the extreme goodness of the Spaniards, and do not fear making them angry by an absurd demand." (*Mas*, pp. 72, 73.)

71 M. and D. read: "Although the Sangleys cheat them, as if they were simpletons, and they are satisfied to be cheated by them."

Delgado says (p. 309): "This I absolutely deny, for I have more than once seen that after the Indians have traversed the whole Parian of the Sangleys to sell their goods, if they are not offered more than four they immediately carry their goods to the Spaniards or to the fathers, in order to get eight for them; and this must be *tongod sa calooy*, that is, for charity, which the Spaniard and the father always practice with them."

"This is a fact, but it needs explanation. The Filipino is by nature phlegmatic, and especially when it is a question of buying or selling anything; for he exerts himself to get the largest profit possible, and the calculation of that costs him much trouble. A countryman comes, for instance, to sell two or three quintals of indigo to a merchant. Thereupon, he does not come alone, but is accompanied by relatives and friends, and sometimes women. Very often the indigo belongs to four or five owners, who all come in the wake of the seller. Each proposition must be communicated to the society that is squatted there in a circle on their heels. The matter is discussed at length, and then it is decided to lower the price one peso per quintal. The buyer claims that the price should be three pesos. Finally this point is settled. Then another discussion begins, namely, that the indigo is damp, and that some pounds must be allowed for waste. In short the transaction is so tiresome and so eternal, that there are very few Spaniards who have the patience to endure so much impertinence and importunity; and they generally end by saying dryly, 'Will you or will you not give it?' And then they order them angrily into the street. The Chinese and mestizos do not hurry them, but on the contrary invite them to eat, and keep them in their houses for three or four hours, and sometimes days. Finally they get the goods for what they wish to give, and more often cheat them like Chinese. For the Filipino is very stupid even in matters of self-interest. Once I was with a Spaniard who was buying indigo. After the trading had cost him more patience than Job must have had, the indigo was weighed before him, the account was reckoned, the money made ready and placed on the table in piles of 20 pesos, while there was one of 7, which was placed separately, and another of reals and copper coins. The man who had been most attentive to everything took the piles of 20's and left the pile of 7. We called him back to tell him to take that money which he had left. Thereupon he took the seven pesos, and it was necessary to call him back the third time to tell him that all the money on the table belonged to him. He himself had determined that the price should be 52 or 53 per quintal, and then he took what was given him. The majority are the same. Then it is learned that a Chinese has bought for 20 the same quantity of indigo for which a Spaniard offered 25. It is said that a Filipino would rather receive one real from a Chinese than one peso from a Spaniard, as we have just seen was written by Father Gaspar." (Mas, pp. 73, 74.)

72 "And tell me, your Paternity," says Delgado (p. 309), "who is not given to this vice in this land?"—an interesting commentary on social conditions.

73 Commenting on this, Delgado (p. 309) says: "Who are the ones who cut the timber, and build the ships, galleys, and galliots, as says Father Murillo, and work in the ships in the port? Then they do this stretched out in their houses, as says our father master? It is true that they are always poor, but the true cause of that is different. Let them not admit into Manila so many heathen Chinese, who possess in themselves all the trades and employments, by which one may seek his livelihood. The Indians would apply themselves to these trades, and would not lie stretched out in their houses, for the Sangleys do not allow them to engage in these or to seek their livelihood."

Mas says (pp. 75–77): "I have never read a single manuscript or printed book about the Filipinos that does not speak of their laziness.

"I, accustomed to hear the term 'lazy' given to Spaniards, and to other men who have been or are idle—rather through the influence of bad laws or because of the lack of laws, than because of the impulses of their physical organization—was ready to believe that the Filipinos would be found to exhibit the same characteristic in regard to this—especially when I remembered the system of delivering the provinces to trading governors and monopolists and the prohibition for so many years of trading with foreign ports, which still exists, with the exception of the city of Manila. But in spite of the fact that these things powerfully influence the obstruction of the founts of wealth and choke incentives to work, I have seen things that have made me change my opinion. For instance, I have desired to send people to get grass for my horses; and, in spite of the facts that it was very abundant and near, and there was not the slightest doubt about the pay, I have been unable to get anyone to go for it. On arriving at a village, I have endeavored to get a guide to accompany me to the next village; and, in spite of the facts that the distance was not more than one hour and the road excellent, I have found it difficult to obtain him. And even I have obtained it by means of the justice, as [a carrier of] baggage; although one pays for this service, according to the schedule, one silver real, with which a Filipino has enough to live on for at least two days. A few weeks before my departure from Filipinas I was at an estate belonging to religious, where there are various individuals who enjoy an annual salary sufficient to support themselves, on condition that they guard the estate against robbers, and that they work whenever necessary, in which case their day's wage is paid them. The question was raised of transferring the rice in the husk from one granary to another, distant about 20 paces, and they were not to work more than the hours usual in that country, which are very few, for which they were to be given one silver real daily, besides their food. All this was in addition to their annual pay. It is to be noted that the season was the dryest and coolest of the whole year, namely, the month of January, and a Filipino's support cost then about five cuartos per diem. However, by no means would they consent to work consecutively all the days, for they said that when night came they were exhausted, and needed rest on the following day. Had I not been present there I would not have believed it. I have been in many Filipino huts where I saw many men and women pass the day without doing anything, while everything was indicative of their poverty. I have examined the condition of the fields, and I have discovered that any man may become wealthy, and yet all live in wretchedness. I have been much surprised to hear that they must be ordered by edict to sow the fields, so that the propitious season may not pass by; and that those who allow their houses to burn are punished. Especially have I noted that the Chinese mestizos, who are partly of the same blood as the most diligent Chinese immigrants, are always comfortable, and some of them have accumulated considerable wealth. This might all be in the hands of the Filipinos, who are the most ancient inhabitants, have enjoyed and enjoy greater protection, and have been owners of all the estates that are now possessed by the mestizos, which the latter have bought by the fruits of their industry and their economy. It is to be noted that all the Chinese who come to Filipinas are very poor, and come from a colder country. Gentil says that the Filipinos have acquired their laziness from the Spaniards; but if they have learned indolence from the Spaniards, why did not the mestizos learn it also, who are on the contrary so active and industrious? Why have they not learned to be diligent from the mestizos, since they have a more continual and intimate intercourse with them than with the Spaniards? I conclude by saying that after examining and weighing everything thoroughly, I am of the opinion that there exists in the nature of the Filipino, quite independent of any accessory and modifying cause, an element of quiet and inertia that is but slightly neutralized by the ambition of acquiring consideration and wealth."

74 Delgado (pp. 309–310) says: "This happens perhaps among the boys who serve in the convents in Tagalos and in no other missions; and I have also seen them awakened in another manner. And although this seems a matter for laughter among us Spaniards, it is not so for them. For they do it in order not to make the other impatient by waking him suddenly, and it serves among them as a kind of prudence and respect. The game thing happens when they call at the door of any house. But generally they enter without the formulas of etiquette."

"This is a hard fact and has been called to my attention often. For in any other matter whatsoever, it is well understood that ignorance makes an unpolished man appear quite distinct from a civilized man. But when it comes to waking one who is sleeping, I cannot conceive that wisdom, or even a knowledge of reading, can have the least influence. But I believe that I have discovered the origin of this peculiarity. The remontados Filipinos of Abra have the greatest respect for a sleeping man. Their deepest curse is 'May I die when asleep.' Their oath, when they come to the province of Ilocos for the election of gobernadorcillos, for causes, etc., is 'May I die when asleep,' 'May a bolt of lightning strike me,' etc. This same fear of dying when asleep exists also in other tribes and in the provinces of Ilocos, and must have been formerly a general idea, since, as we have already observed, the origin of our Christianized Indians and those at present remontados and called infidels was the same. Whether this fear arose from some disease in which the people slept and did not awaken, or whether only from the similitude of sleep to death, it is difficult to ascertain. However, it is always surprising that, since no one now dies or becomes sick because his rest is interrupted, the Indians still constantly preserve this so stupid dread; so that even after a master has ordered his servant to awaken him, the latter has great difficulty in doing it in a quick and positive manner, although he knows that, if he do not execute it, it will put his master out greatly. That shows at least the most powerful influence of habit on the minds of these men. Somewhat similar to this is our custom of saying 'Jesus,' when anyone sneezes—a custom which I have heard expressed by 'God bless you,' 'Á vous souhaits,' 'Salute,' etc., among all the peoples of Europa.... This custom generally allows the man who receives an accident to die without aid, because of not awaking the physician or cura." (Mas, pp. 77, 78.)

75 This is because the Indians do not appreciate the danger, says Delgado (p. 310). This happens often on narrow roads, and not to Indians, but to Spaniards or mulattoes, and neither will yield to the other, whereupon quarrels ensue. But the lesser always yields to the greater. It has happened once or twice to Delgado.

"This is a fact, and a proof of their indifference and stolidity." (Mas, p. 78.)

76 The lengua franca is the trade-jargon of the Orient. The original of the passage above is as follows: "Deó grande nopillar fantacia; mondo cosi cosi; si estar escrito in testa andar andar; sino acá morir." M. reads "an andar andar," and has other slight differences. D. reads "ha (de) andar" and has also other slight differences.

The full name of the author above mentioned is Gabriel Gomez de Losada, and his book is Escuela de trabaios, in quatro libros dividida: Primero, del cautiverio mas cruel.... Segundo, Noticias y govierno de Argel: Tercero, necessidad y conveniencia de la redempcion de Cautivos Christianos: Quarto, el mejor cautivo rescatado.... (Madrid, 1670).

77 M. and D. add (though with a slight difference in wording) "for they will not believe that he who loves danger will perish in it."

Some Indians are fatalists, but not all, says Delgado (p. 310). The Visayans are generally careful, and watch out for the crocodiles. Those who have been devoured by those reptiles have always been evil, and were so punished by God for their sins. Mas says (p. 79), that this fatalism must have been imported from Asia.

78 Delgado says (p. 310): "This proceeds from their barbarous condition, and because the Spaniards commonly deceive them, and teach them things that are not very good, especially the convict guachinangos, of whom this country is full. But that they cannot be persuaded that it is a sin to steal from the religious or from the Spaniards, I regard as a misapprehension, or at least it is not common for this to happen, although his Paternity brings forward such evidence, that one cannot doubt him. For I have seen the contrary in many villages."

Mas (pp. 80, 81), says: "It is a fact that some Indians have but little scruple in stealing from Spaniards, for they say that all that the latter possess is of the Philippines and consequently theirs. But do not believe that they have any consideration for their fellow-countrymen. In its proper place we shall see that theft is the greatest part of the criminality of the islands.... It is to be noted that they generally rob on a small and rarely on a large scale; for their ambition is limited to satisfying a vice or to bettering their present condition, but not in changing it.

"The father provincial of the Augustinian religious, said in his printed report, in the compilation made concerning the causes of the insurrection in Ilocos in 1807:

"'The Indians of Ilocos have become highwaymen, like those of the other provinces. They steal cows, horses, and carabaos from their own countrymen; and those who are occupied in this trade are ready for all sorts of evil. It is not surprising that many of these should have come with the deserters who first rebelled in the mountains of Piddig, and that others should unite with them when the fire was fanned. But one can not call this a cause for insurrection, nor do I believe that for such thefts the means should be to take the stealers of carabaos to Manila so that they might be punished; but it is enough for the alcaldes-mayor to watch over their province and punish these thefts. By so doing they would succeed in lessening thefts, for the extermination of them is as impossible as is making an end of the classes of the thieves according to the proverb of the Indians, "When the rats die, then the thieves will come to an end."'

"It is true that perhaps one ought not to ascribe all this demoralization to a perverse disposition. One must not have lived among the Filipinos, or have been very blind in regard to them, to say that they are all thieves. There are very many who, although they could steal with impunity, do not do so.... The frequency of theft may proceed from other causes. Perhaps the system of mercy and impunity that has dictated and is dictating the sentences of the Audiencia of Manila has contributed thereto...."

79 M. and D. omit "of which I heard," and the latter reads "and I shall only tell of two of which I was a witness."

Spaniards also, says Delgado (pp. 310, 311), recount things that are not credible, and "it is not to be wondered at that some rude and ignorant people should believe such nonsense; and if they believe some things that are told them by some scholars, it is because of the authority of those people among them.... This happens commonly in other places, besides among the Indians."

80 See an account of this matter and the trouble caused by it, in Vol. XXXIX.

81 i.e., "Silver and gold have I none" — a reference to Acts III, 6.

82 M. and D. read "miners."

83 "When the ship 'Santa Ana' arrived at Manila in the year 1832 with 250 Spanish soldiers, it was rumored among the women of the tobacco factory that those soldiers were coming to take away their children in order to irrigate the mines in España with their blood. All were aroused and fled to their homes, took their children, and began to take refuge in the houses of the Spanish women, and they could not be persuaded that it was all nonsense. The house of Doña Dolores Goyena was filled with them. Also many men armed with spears came out on the streets; but the disorder gradually subsided." (Mas, p. 82.)

84 M. and D. add "for all the ministers cannot free them from this deceit."

85 This is not so in general, says Delgado (p. 311), but is true only of some individuals among the various nations.

86 M. reads "respect the Spaniard more."

87 The truth is that any Spaniard, with rare exceptions, has more penetration, more vivacity, more nobility, more talent, and more courage than a Filipino. This superiority can do no less than have its effect.... For the rest, few in Manila have an exact idea of the Filipino character. Their arrogance may be seen in the importance which the gobernadorcillos give to themselves. They go daily to the city hall, but they make two regidors go to their houses to get them. There the regidors wait until the gobernadorcillo is ready to come out, and the latter then goes in solemn state to the city hall, preceded by the regidors and the alguacils, with staffs in hand. When these officers reach the door of the city hall, they stop in order to allow the gobernadorcillo to pass between them; and he enters without noticing the salutes given him by the guards, who take off their hats to him. He immediately takes a seat which is on an elevated platform, and there he thinks himself to be on a throne; and even the Spaniards who enter casually, especially in the villages on the highroad, appear of but little importance to him. This is the place where the auditors of the Audiencia of Manila, and all others who have any share in the government of Filipinas, ought to come incognito, and as if in passing, in order to know the Filipinos—instead of forming an opinion of their character from the servants of their house, or from those who go to the capital with clasped hands and a downcast look in their eyes to ask some favor of them. The strange thing is, that the Indians do not learn from the alcaldes-mayor, who administer justice with the greatest equality, and who do not sit in an elevated place, or even sit down, and go into the street without any following. This aristocratic spirit may be observed in the church. All the principales, who consist of the gobernadorcillos, cabezas de barangay, and all others who have the title 'Don' and wear a jacket, seat themselves in the central aisle or nave; and the following order of etiquette is in general scrupulously observed: the gobernadorcillo; the ex-gobernadorcillos, who are called past captains, in order of their seniority; the actual first lieutenant, who must be a cabeza de barangay; the two lieutenants; and nine present officials; the ex-cabezas, in order of seniority. If any ex-captain from another village is present, he takes a seat among those of his class, and is given the first place, out of courtesy. When the lieutenants and officials leave their posts, they are not called principales, as are the others, but titulados." (Mas, pp. 83, 84.)

88 D. reads "petty sextons."

89 Delgado says (p. 311): "It is a fact that nature always inclines rather to evil than to good. But in order to correct their vices there are fervent and zealous ministers in all parts, who preach to and teach them."

Mas says (pp. 85–89): "In fact some Indians practice ceremonies in their marriages which date from before the conquest.

"On the birth of an infant, the newborn child is sometimes taken to another house in order to free it from the Patianac; and, when the child is taken out for baptism, aromatic substances and incense are burned for the same reason.

"When a person dies, they celebrate a novena in his house at night, where the relatives (and sometimes those who are not relatives) assemble. After praying, it is not seldom that they sit down to gamble. On the last day there is a great banquet, and sometimes a dance. These mortuary feasts are practiced even yet, in all their purity, in the mountains, as we have already seen.

"If possible, both men and women bathe daily in the river. The women enter the water wrapped in their tapices, taking care that the bosom is covered. When they are in the water they take that garment off to wash themselves. The men enter the water with wide pantaloons and the body bare. They enter the river at any hour and before everybody; but one must confess that they do it with great decency and modesty.... When I was in Santa Cruz de la Laguna, the cura published an edict ordering men and women not to bathe in the same place. That gave rise to many jokes and jests, and it is to be supposed that they continued their old-time customs. They consider us as not overcleanly, because they see us make less use than they of the bath.... It is also the custom for the families of the country and many Europeans to bathe together. During the outdoor sports of Manila, at the summer houses of Mariquina, or other neighboring towns, the chief diversion is the bath. The women generally enter the water wearing a kind of blouse, and the men with wide pantaloons and the body uncovered. Newcomers from Europa do not consider this amusement at all decent.

"They kiss by bringing the nostril near and drawing in the breath. This is the plain kiss in the mountains, but some Filipinos of the plains, especially of Manila, have also become accustomed to kiss with the lips; but they always put the nose to the face at the same time, and if they have a sincere affection, they always smell as if they were giving a deep sigh with their mouth closed.... When they look at a person from a distance, and desire to express their desire to kiss him, they constrict the nose in the manner of one smelling. A very extreme kind of kiss is given by rubbing the nose on the spot that they wish to feel, and drawing in the breath as long as possible.

"I am greatly surprised that no one of the writers on the Filipinos has spoken of this remarkable fact, which springs from their exquisite sense of smell. It is so great that a servant can tell his master's shirt, after it is cleaned and ironed, even though it lies with ten or twelve other shirts resembling it and belonging to other persons, by simply smelling them. They also assert that if a man be near a woman for whom he experiences a feeling of love, she knows it by the odor of his perspiration, and vice versa. As a pledge of affection, they ask for a shirt that has been worn—which they return after it has lost its odor, and replace by another, just as we beg for a lock of hair.

"They had the custom of circumcision, a custom which they did not acquire from the Arabs, since it is still practiced on the peaks of the independent mountains. They practice it still, and that against the will of the curas. Ancient customs have very great force. It is to be noted that the manner of operation is not the same as that practiced by the Jews, for the cut is made from the upper to the lower part.

"They had the custom that the suitor for a maiden's hand went to serve in the house of his future father-in-law for three or four years, and did whatever he was asked—in general, the most onerous duties. Then the parents of the bride had to give him a house, clothes, etc., and the marriage was celebrated. In many provinces, as for instance, in Bulacan, there is now no trace of this custom, because of the abuses which were committed. This custom, which we meet in the first pages of the Old Testament, could not have been acquired from the Mussulmans, who by their Koran hold laws diametrically opposed. This custom is still followed in Laguna, although the young man does not live in the house of his loved one, for the cura does not permit it. The friars have done their utmost to destroy this custom.

"They scarify new-born infants in order to draw blood from them; and then apply lighted matches to various parts of the body, which cause them burns, and serve the place of caustics.

"Women in childbirth they suspend by the hair in order to stop the flow; and, after parturition, they compress the abdomen, and press down with great force on both thighs at once, in order to make the organs return to their former position; and they perform other things of like nature, which we consider as injurious and nonsensical. But they hold one of their old women higher than the best Paris physician.

"They consider the balete tree as sacred. At marriage, they carry it dishes of food as an offering; and it is very difficult, or impossible, to make them cut one of them. It has happened that they have begged incense from the cura on various pretexts in order to go immediately and burn it under a balete tree.

"They are very fond of telling tales of love adventures, of witches, and enchantment, and everything else that is rare and marvelous, even though it be nonsense and against common sense.

"They believe that all diseases are cured by drawing out the air that has been introduced into the body; and, consequently, their favorite remedy is to supply a kind of cupping-glass of Chinese origin, which they drag over two palmos on any part of the body, and which leaves a great red streak.

"They respect their fathers and mothers greatly, and even the younger brothers the older. I have seen a married woman, on entering her house, kiss the hand of a sister older than herself.

"In order that a young man may marry, he must give the bride the money or other things up to her value; and that price is often kept by the parents. The parents would rather have their daughter remain single, even though she be with child, than to give her without a dowry. It is not seldom that one can hear a mother say that she will not give her daughter for less than one hundred pesos, or fifty, etc.

"In order to strike fire they take a bit of bamboo, and slit it down the middle lengthwise. In the hollow or inner part, they dig out one portion near the center, which leaves the bamboo much thinner. Then on the outside they open a chink, lengthwise. Then they take the knife, and scraping the upper part of the other half-bamboo, they make some very fine shavings. These they roll about between the two palms of the hands until they form a small ball, and that they place in the hollow of the half-bamboo. The latter they place on the ground, with the shavings below. Then with the other half bamboo, they rub (while singing) across the one which has the shavings below it, upon the same point where the shavings are placed, and in a few seconds they begin to smoke. Thereupon they rub faster and blow, and a blaze starts. All this is the work of one minute.

"On going out between people, or when passing in front of anyone, they bend the body and clasp the hands, which they then move forward as if they wished to open a path or cut the air. This is a sign of respect, or their method of asking leave to pass.

"The women ride horseback, not astride, but with a side-saddle, as do Europeans."

90 M. reads "most of them."

91 This is common throughout the world, says Delgado (p. 311). "That they do not know their age happens commonly among rude and wild people, wherever they may be; but their age is known very well by their datos and chiefs, in order to assign them their place in the tribute readily. In what pertains to their ancient beliefs, there is no doubt that these are preserved in some parts, and there is no lack of babailanes, who are their priestesses or diuateras; but one must consider that all these peoples of the Indias are new Christians, and the seed that the enemy had sown, and which had thrust so deep roots into them, has not yet been completely destroyed."

92 M. and D. omit "than the word of the whole world."

Mas says (pp. 90–96): "The superstitions of these people can be divided into three classes. The first consists in believing that certain monsters or ghosts exist, to which they give names and assign special duties, and even certain exterior forms, which are described by those who affirm that they have seen them. Such are the Tigbalan, Osuang, Patianac, Sava, Naanayo, Tavac, Nono, Mancuculan, Aiasip, the rock Mutya, etc.

"The *Antinganting* is any object which promises wealth or happiness, as we would speak of the girdle of Venus, or the ring of Giges.

"Many Spaniards, especially the curas, imagine that these beliefs are not very deeply rooted, or that they have declined, and that most of the Filipinos are free from them. This is because in the presence of such the Filipinos do not dare tell the truth, not even in the confessional, because of their fear of the reprimand that surely awaits them. I have talked to many about these things, some of whom at the beginning began to laugh, and to joke about the poor fools who put faith in such nonsense. But when they saw that I was treating the matter seriously, and with the spirit of inquiry as a real thing, they changed their tone, and made no difficulty in assuring me of the existence of the fabulous beings described above....

"The second class consists in various practices, like that of burning incense under the balete tree; putting ashes at the door of the house where a person has died, in order that they might recognize the tracks of the soul of the dead one; leaving a plate for the dead man at the table, etc.

"When Don G. Piñeiro went to Culamba in 1841, for the purpose of climbing a lofty mountain, he encountered innumerable difficulties in getting people to accompany him, in spite of the orders of the superior government; and he had to desist and climb from the village of Los Baños accompanied by the cura, who had the road opened for him. The reason for that, as the said religious assured me, was the fear of the Filipinos for the anito, although the excuses that they offered were quite different.

"In the said village of Los Baños, they believe that there is an antinganting in one of the hot water springs, which has water at 67° Reaumur. This consists in the Divine Child, who appears and hops about in the water on Good Friday; and he who catches Him obtains the antinganting. This last year, 1841, a man tried to get too near, and fell in. His entire body was scalded, and he was bled; but not one drop of blood could be drawn from his body, and he died on the following day.

"The third, and to me the most remarkable, class is found not in certain personages or superstitious and determined proceedings, but in sudden and capricious scenes, and in improbable and inexplainable apparitions.

"There is scarce a Filipino, even the most enlightened, who does not tell marvelous things that have happened to him—wondrous visions, mute and speechless; ghosts, goblins, strange figures; dead people; dogs, and fabulous and never imagined animals; castles, and balls of fire, that have appeared to him;

frightful noises of all sorts that have scared him; and, finally, the most improbable stories and bits of nonsense that could be invented by the most raving maniac.

"On hearing them recount so many of these extravagances, and seeing that they distinguish them from dreams, I have been unable to believe that they were deceits; and observing their faces very carefully during the narration, I have been convinced that they were intimately persuaded that they had seen the things that they described. Whence can this mental weakness come? It is not from ignorance, for I have noticed the same thing as in the others, in several clerics who have studied in the university for ten or twelve years. One day I was in a convent where the boards of the floor began to creak because of dryness, and the coadjutor became so frightened that he went away to sleep in another house; and the Christian reflections, jests, and anger of the Spanish cura could not restrain him.... The Filipino cura, Don J. Severiano Mallares, committed and caused to be committed fifty-seven assassinations, because he believed that he could by this means save his mother, who, he had persuaded himself, had been bewitched; and was hanged in the year 1840. The attorney on that cause talked in pathetic terms of the *indescribable and barbarous prodigality of blood shed by that monster*. Reflecting upon this phenomenon, I am inclined to think that it is based on their natural timorousness...."

93 In D., "indolent."

94 From the word "islands" to this point, is omitted in D.

95 "That they are tyrants, one over the other," says Delgado (p. 311), "I do not deny. They inherited this peculiarity from their ancestors, and it has as yet been impossible to uproot it entirely, as many others which they learned from their ancestors. However, these vices are not so common as they were formerly. And not only would the Indians of these islands have been consumed if the Spaniards had not come hither, but they would have been conquered and enslaved by the neighboring nations, such as the Borneans, Chinese, and Japanese, as we see in the books of history.

" ... The *principales* were the aim of the popular wrath in the Ilocan insurrection in 1807. 'Kill all the lords and ladies' was the cry, while the people hastened toward the capital to petition for the abolition of the monopolies and the fifths. The same thing happened in the year 1814." (Mas, p. 97.)

96 M. omits "and bring it back as cold as ice."

97 This is a general statement that is not true, says Delgado (pp. 311, 312), for the example given is merely from boys; and, besides, it never freezes in Filipinas.

98 This citation is missing in M. It is from Horace's Satires, book i, ll, 106, 107. E. C. Wickham (Horace for English Readers; Oxford, 1903, p. 163), translates

the passage as follows: "There is measure in everything. There are fixed limits beyond which and short of which right cannot find resting-place."

99 "That they need beatings and the rattan," says Delgado (p. 312), "as examples prove, is a fact, and they confess it; but they resemble all other nations in this particular.... But it must be employed with prudence and moderation, as the discipline is employed by our fathers in our own lands, regarding them as sons and small children, and not as slaves or as our enemies. For God has brought us to their lands, in order to watch over them, and maintains us here for love of them. We must note that the Indians are not so bad as they seem to us.... It must also be observed that there are many Spaniards, and even ministers, who are melancholy and crabbed, and so ill-conditioned and moody, that everything wounds them, and they are contented with nothing. All the actions of the Indians displease them, and they even believe that the Indians do them purposely to make them impatient and to jest with them. From such ill-conditioned people the Indians suffer much, and tolerate and endure much, because of their respect for them. Consequently what the reverend father says below, namely 'that it costs them more to be Christians than one would believe' is a fact and true."

"The Spaniards cry out and are in despair at seeing the continual and great acts of rudeness of the Filipinos, some of which are done maliciously, with the sole object of making us angry, when they contract hate for us. At times after they have wearied and disgusted the Spaniards grievously, and have caused the latter to give them a buffet, this is a cause for great sport among them, and they celebrate it in the kitchen amid great guffaws, as I have heard many times. Especially is it so if those who are made angry are women. But the Spaniards persist in not being convinced of this fact, nor will they ever learn how to treat this people. The old men of the country say that the Spaniard is fire and the Filipino snow, and that the snow consumes the fire." (Mas, pp. 97, 98.)

100 M. and D. add "His master chid him, but the lad replied that the hen had but one leg."

101 This quotation is lacking in M. and D.

102 M. and D. read "in love and esteem."

103 "I shall not at present enter upon a discussion of whether one ought or ought not beat the Filipino. I shall only remark, as a matter pertaining to this section, that the first thing that one sees in any of their houses is the rattan hanging in a corner. When a father places his son in any Spanish house, this is his charge: 'Sir, beat him often.' To educate the young people, or to establish order in any place without the use of the rattan, is a thing that they do not understand." (Mas, p. 99.)

It is said that even at the present day a Filipino father will not hesitate to chastise his son corporally, even after the latter has attained his majority.

104 This last phrase and the Latin quotation are lacking in M. Englished that quotation is, "The evil hate sin for fear of punishment."

105 This phrase is omitted in D.

106 In D. this is "even if it be a leaf."

107 Delgado says (p. 312): "But if his Paternity knows of this lack, how surprising that this and other things happen in regard to them, such as that all keep their faces turned toward him who confesses. If his Paternity would then preach them a sermon and correct them, I assure him that they would correct themselves, and these backward-looking dancers who are so immodest in the church, when they ought to be modestly thinking of their sins and repenting of them, would correct themselves, and would not cause wonder and laughter."

108 M. omits the remainder of this sentence. For "Januses," D. reads "worms."

109 Because some of the Indians are given to blasphemy, says Delgado (p. 313), it does not follow that all of them are blasphemous.

110 "I shall here attempt a delicate and interesting investigation, namely, the religiousness of the Filipinos. There are opposite opinions on this matter, and serious errors are liable to arise.... "The women always wear scapulars about the neck, and usually some sort of a small cross; and a reliquary, containing the bones of a saint and a bit of the wood of the cross. But this has become a part of the dress, like earrings or necklaces, and both the devout women and those who are not devout wear them.

"The walls of the houses are often covered with the engravings of saints, and on the tables are many glass globes and urns containing saints, virgins, and little figures of the Divine Child, which generally have the face as well as the hands of ivory, and silver clothes richly embroidered. In well-to-do houses there are so many that they resemble a storehouse of saints rather than a habitation. In many houses this is a matter of vanity and ostentation; and they regard valuable saints as they do bureaus and mirrors elsewhere.

"In the church great sedateness and devotion or silence reigns. In the villages the church is divided into three parts. In one end the women are seated, in the other the men, while the gobernadorcillos and principales occupy the center. However, this is not observed very strictly in some villages. In some churches there are men in the front half and women in the back half. When a small village is founded, in order to get the concession for a settlement and for a cura they offer to give the latter, in addition to paying the *sanctórum* tribute [a tribute paid to the Church by all Philippine natives of sixteen years and over], a monthly quantity of rice, eggs, fowls, etc., but they are afterward very remiss in living up to their offer. Many friars have had to have recourse to the alcaldes and to the officials of the district; and I have even heard of one of them who had to take a musket and kill the fowls in the yards, and carry them to the convent.

"They are very fond of singing the passion or history of the death of Jesus Christ, which is written in Tagálog verse. During the evenings of Lent, the young men and women assemble in the houses for this purpose. But although this was a religious gathering at the time when it was originated, at the present time it has been converted into a carnival amusement, or to speak more plainly, into a pretext for the most scandalous vices; and the result of these canticles is that many of the girls of the village become enceinte. So true is what I have just said that the curas have prohibited everywhere the singing of the passion at night; and some of the curas go out with a whip in order to disperse them—or rather, send the fiscal of the church to ascertain who is singing, and send for such person immediately to beat him.

"They say that all the saints are Spanish, since the patrons of their churches are always of this class. They would have no veneration for a saint with a flat nose and the physiognomy of a Filipino.

"When any sick person refuses to confess, his relatives request him to do so. In this case they do not tell him that he will be condemned, etc., but, 'Consider what a shame it will be; just think what people will say; consider that you will be buried outside of holy ground.' The idea of being buried on the beach is what gives them most fear. This can only be explained by saying that they have seen the cemetery and the beach and not hell, nor the other world, which, as one would believe, costs them much to conceive—although in reality they do believe in it, in the same way as many Europeans believe in it, but without understanding it, and only because the sages give assurance of it....

"In spite of this indifference regarding the future life, they generally order masses said for the souls of their ancestors, and not because of compromise or vanity, but true faith and devotion, although this does not argue much in favor of their religiousness. For the Igorots, who are the type of the Filipinos, although they do not believe in the immortality of the soul, have many superstitions in regard to the shades of the dead....

"In some places the curas have to lock the doors of the church after mass, so that the people will not depart without hearing the sermon, and this in places quite religious, as is Pangasinan. Many of those who are carried to Mindanao or to Jolo as captives become renegades with the greatest ease; and then they will not return, even though they may.

"Some make the sign of the cross as they go down the stairways. All stop on the street at the sound of the prayer-bell; and the same thing happens in the houses, where they often pray on their knees with true devotion. They all remove their hats when passing in front of the church, and many stop to pray. Nevertheless, all the curas assert that they make a false confession, for they only confess the three following sins: absence from mass, eating of meat during Lent, and vain blaspheming; although it is apparent to the curas that they have committed other greater sins. It is a great trouble to get them to take part in the procession, and those who can do so escape through the cross streets. In Manila it is necessary for the regimental heads to appoint soldiers to go to take part in this act, and to pay them one-half real; and, were it not for this expedient, it would sometimes be impossible to do it. The curas have considerable trouble in the villages in getting them to confess. They are given forty days of grace, and many come after being threatened with twenty-five lashes; while many of the degree of captain, and many who are not, get along in spite of all without confession. In the village of Lilio, on the brow of Mount Banahao, where there are 1,300 tributes, there were more than 600 persons who did not confess in the year 1840; and this has not been one of the most remiss villages in the fulfilment of its religious duties."

[Father Juan Ferrando, who examined Mas's MS., says that 'the Filipinos confess according to the instruction that is given them. In Manila, as I know by experience, they confess as well as the most fervent Spaniard, and I have heard many fathers say the same of many Indians of the provinces.']

"Very many of them also never go to mass in any village where the cura is not especially zealous. In the city of Vigan, where there are about 30,000 persons, not more than 500 or 800 went to church during my stay there on any feast-day, except one of especial devotion to celebrate a virgin patroness of the city. There has been and is much talk of the influence of the curas in the villages. No doubt there is something in it, but their respect and deference toward the parish priest is influenced not a little, in my opinion by their idea (and one not ill founded) of the power of the priest, of the employment that he can give; and of their hope that he will protect them in any oppression that they receive from the civil government or from the soldiers. In reality, the friar usually addresses his parishioners in the language of peace, which is the method which fits well into the phlegmatic Filipino. He constitutes himself their defender, even without their having any regard for him—now from the injuries that the avarice of their governors causes them, now from the tendency of these to acquire preponderance and to command, which is the first instinct of man. Consequently, the friars, by resisting and restraining in all parts, and at so great a distance from Madrid, the tyranny or greed of the Spaniards, have been very useful to the villages, and have been acquiring their love. And since the islands are not kept subject by force, but by the will of the mass of the inhabitants, and the means of persuasion are principally in the hands of the religious, the government is necessarily obliged to show the latter considerable deference. From this fact originates their influence in temporal affairs, and the fear mixed with the respect with which they inspire the people.

Three facts naturally result from all this. The cura, speaking in general, is the one who governs the village. Consequently, when a new village is formed its inhabitants do not care to be annexed or dependent on another village in regard to spiritual things; but desire and petition for a parish priest of their own, in order that they might have in him a powerful defender in their differences and suits with other settlements, or with the alcalde of the province. Lastly, the ascendency that the minister is seen to enjoy is perhaps as much civil as religious, if it is not more so. And in fact ... although they have often succeeded in pacifying seditions by their mere presence alone, and the insurgents, for instance, in Ilocos in the year 1807, surrendered to the friar the cannon that they had captured from a band of 36 soldiers and two patrols of the guard, who were routed, yet at other times not only have individuals but whole masses refused to listen to the admonitions of the religious, have completely lost respect for them, have insulted them, threatened them, wounded them, and even assassinated them, and have not lacked the complement of all this, profaning the churches. I shall not mention the thefts in the churches, such as one which happened in the capital of Pangasinan when I was there in that province; for these might be considered as single individual deeds, isolated and insignificant. I deduce then, as the resultant conclusion of all these observations, that there are many Filipinos, especially among the feminine sex, who have the true fear of God, but many others who feel a great natural indifference in this matter. They exhibit scarce a disposition toward religion, a fact that I believe must proceed from their little consideration of the wonders of religion ... which is a mark of their small amount of intelligence, for they show great indifference for the punishments of the other world, and even the ecclesiastical punishments of this. Nothing shows this so clearly as the insincere confessions which they make in order to finish with it. It is to be noted that almost the same thing happens at the hour of death, and that this is seen in the small and remote villages where Spaniards have never been. Neither can it be the result of errors of faith or philosophic reading, since the people know no other books than those of the doctrine or the passion.

"Combining the above data and observations with what I have heard recounted, and what we see in manuscripts and printed books about the method by which the old-time religious have maintained devotion in these islands—which has been by calling the list in order to ascertain those who did not observe their obligation to attend mass and confession, and by punishing in the church courtyard those who are remiss—I am inclined to believe that the law of Jesus Christ is learned here superficially; and that if the system adopted some years ago be continued, of obliging the curas to reduce themselves only to the means of preaching, prohibiting them rigorously from compulsive and positive means, before a century passes there will be but few pure-blooded natives in this archipelago who are true and devout Christians...." (Mas, pp. 100–106.)

111 M. and D. omit all of this last sentence and quotation.

112 A vice common to all the world, says Delgado (p. 313).

113 "Although they have but little honor, they have in effect only too much vanity. When one goes to their houses, they make a great effort to show off their wealth, even if they have to beg a loan in order to meet the expense. They do not care to bury their relatives for the love of God, although they try if possible to avoid the payment of the funeral expenses. A cura told me that after a man had paid him the burial expenses a baguio or hurricane began; whereupon the man came to get his money, saying that he wished the burial of a pauper, because in the end, no one would have to see it." (Mas, p. 107.)

114 Delgado (p. 313) utters a warning against judging on this particular, and says "that virtues are not so distant from them, as his Paternity writes."

115 M. omits this sentence to this point.

116 What fault do the Indians have in trying to get and defend their own? There may be excess in this matter, says Delgado (p. 313), but the Indians do not go to law only to cause trouble.

117 M. and D. omit this sentence.

118 In regard to this Delgado says (pp. 313, 314) that "there is no dish more relished in this land than defamation and complaint.... This is a country where idleness sits enthroned; for when the ship is despatched to Nueva España there is nothing to do for a whole year, but to complain and discuss the lives of others." Delgado does not believe that lust is the only feature in the intercourse between men and women. Neither does he believe that women are treated, as they deserve, with kicks and blows; nor that such treatment is in accordance with conjugal love, or with the text of women being subject to men. San Agustin's advice to Europeans is not good.

119 The Ayer MS. and M. read "Machiabelo;" D. reads "Macabeo," i.e., "Maccabæan."

120 From this point M. and D. read: "They call this mabibig, and this is a thing that will rouse up the entire village against one, the stones, and the land itself. Hence, the concubinages among them, and other evils, have no human remedy, nor can have; for no one wishes to be mabibig, for that is the most abominable fault and the only sin among them."

121 The Indians do not tell tales of one another for a more potent reason than that of being declared mabibig, is Delgado's commentary (pp. 314, 315)— namely, the fear, of private revenge. "But the prudent Indians always advise the father minister, if there is any scandal in the village; now in confession, so that it might be remedied without anyone knowing the person who has told it; now by a fictitious and anonymous letter, as has happened to me several times. One must exercise prudence in this matter, for all that is written or spoken is not generally true."

122 M. and D. read with some slight verbal differences, which translate the same: "For one might happen to have a servant or two who waste and destroy the property of their master, and no other servant, however kindly he has been treated by his master, will tell him what is happening."

123 "This league of the caste of color for mutual protection and defense from the domineering caste is very natural. The Filipinos are not so constant in maintaining it, however, that it is not broken by two methods: by offering money to the accuser, or by bestowing so many lashes on each one who is implicated in the crime." (Mas, p. 109.)

124 Delgado (p. 315) finds this very natural, and dismisses it by the reflection that liberty is dear.

125 In M. and D. this reads: "Therefore when they say that there is no more sugar or no more oil, it is when there is not [sugar] enough to make a cup of chocolate, or oil enough to whet a knife."

126 M. and D. read: "They will place the best cup and plate, [D. mentions only the plate] which are much different than the others, for the master, and will only look after him, and pay no attention to the guests."

127 M. and D. omit this sentence.

128 Spanish, sacabuches consistol y deresistol, a transcriber's error for con sistol y diastol (this phrase omitted in D.); a play on words, as the sackbut forms the various tones by lengthening and shortening the instrument. The phrase systole and diastole is now applied to the alternate contraction and expansion of the heart; San Agustin apparently uses it through fondness for a learned phrase.

129 The citation from Quevedo is lacking in M. San Agustin has slightly misquoted; though it translates the same as the correct version. The lines are as follows:

Galalon, que en casa come poco,

y á costa agena el corpanchon ahita.

The citation is from Quevedo's *Poema heroica de las necedades y locuras de Orlando el enamorado.*

130 That is, "Much good may it do you," an expression used at eating or drinking. San Agustin evidently refers in the following clause to the scanty fare supplied to those who row in the boats as compulsory service.

131 This is not a general rule among the Tagálogs, and much less among the Visayans. Neither are all the Indians forgers. (Delgado, pp. 315, 316.)

132 M. omits "alcalde" and reads "prudent and experienced man." D. reads "a prudent and experienced alcalde."

133 i.e., "I heard your evidence, and feared."

134 M. reads "some Indians;" D., "some erudite Indians."

135 Rabula, "an ignorant, vociferous lawyer;" cf. English "pettifogger."

136 This sentence is omitted by M. D. reads "all the alcaldes."

137 The Italian phrase fabro de calumina is used.

138 King Josiah or Josias was slain at Mageddo. See IV Kings (II Kings of the King James version), xxiii, 29, 30; and II Paralipomenon (II Chronicles of the King James version), xxxv, 22–25.

139 M. reads: "the Indians making use of a whole year in order to increase their calumny." D. reads: "Just see what subtlety and moderate arithmetic they use in order to make their accusation; the Indians lumping together a whole year in order to give pasture to one single horse;" and then adds: "And there are so many cases of this that if I mentioned them all I would never end."

140 We have thus freely translated the original sin afianzar calumnia, which is a regular law term.

141 "But a short time ago, when Señor Seoane was regent of the Audiencia, as the result of an urgent complaint against a Spanish cura, a verbal process was ordered to be made, and from it not the slightest charge resulted against the priest. Another judge was entrusted with the forming of another verbal process, with the same result. The supreme tribunal, being persuaded that the matter was not all calumny, sent an expressly commissioned judge from Manila, who found no more crime than did the others.

"I personally saw a representation signed by the gobernadorcillo and all the principales of a village, in which they affirmed that their cura had forced the wife of the first lieutenant; had punished the lieutenant for opposing her being kept to sleep in the convent; went out on the street drunk; went into the town hall to beat individuals of the municipality; and had not celebrated mass on Sunday for the same reason of being drunk. When a verbal process was made of it, all retracted.

I became acquainted personally with this friar, who is a fine fellow...." (Mas, pp. 113, 114.)

142 From this point, M. and D. read: "but it is to images of some new miracle. They have the habit of devotion, but they seek the newest and forget the old."

143 As to the Indians being fond of making pilgrimages to new and distant shrines where some notable miracle has occurred, Spaniards often have the same love. See Delgado, p. 316.

144 San Agustin is speaking of the Indians of Manila and its environs, says Delgado (p. 316): "For this is rarely seen in the other islands. Hence in the twenty-four years that I have lived in the Visayas, only in the city of Cebu have I ever seen any other than some religious drama [auto sacramental], or the pieces of the school children."

145 In M. escuitiles; and in D. miscuitiles.

146 The verse number is given correctly in M. San Agustin quotes incorrectly, the proper version being:

Segnius irritant animos demissa per aurem,

Quam quæ sunt oculis subiecta fidelibus....

The translation given by Wickham (ut supra, p. 349), is as follows: "What finds entrance through the ear stirs the mind less actively than what is submitted to the eyes, which we cannot doubt."

"They are very fond of seeing theatrical pieces. They make some translations from our dramas, and they make a piece out of anything although it is destitute of the rules of art. They are especially fond of very long comedies, that last a month or more, with many hours of representation daily. These are drawn from histories or from stories, and they stage them. In Tondo there was played, for instance, Matilde, ó las Cruzadas [i.e., "Matilda, or the Crusades"]. The Celestina was probably the origin of this taste. Filipino poets have written several dramas of this kind, as well as some epic, religious, and love poems. But in the epoch previous to the arrival of the Spaniards, it appears that there existed only a few love songs, of whose merits I cannot judge, as I know the language so slightly.

"They have verses of as many as twelve syllables, which are the ones generally used in their poems. They are divided into quatrains, whose four verses rhyme among themselves. The Filipino rhyme, however, consists in the last letter being a vowel or a consonant.... They read all their verses in a singing tone, and the quatrains of the twelve-syllable verse are read with the motif of the *comintan*, which is their national song. The custom of singing when reading poetry is a practice of China, and of all the Asiatic peoples whom I have visited. The kind of versification which I have just cited is evidently anterior to our conquest, as is also the above-mentioned air, which is adjusted to it. This air is melancholy and does not resemble at all any Chinese or Indian music that I have heard. There are several comintans, just as there are different boleros, Polish dances, or Tyrolian dances. Some of them have a great resemblance to the music of Arabia. On the slopes of Camachin [which is a mountain in southern Mindanao], I heard a song which is exactly and purely of that sort...." (Mas, pp. 115, 116.)

The *Celestina* mentioned by Mas is a noted dramatic story—probably written about 1480, and by Rodrigo Cota, of Toledo, and others—which has exercised a very strong influence on the Spanish national drama. It has great literary merit, admirable style, and well-drawn pictures of human nature; and it attained so extensive and continual popularity that even the Inquisition did not place *Celestina* in the Index until 1793, notwithstanding its grossness of thought and language. (Ticknor, *History of Spanish Literature*, i, pp. 262–272.)

147 M. and D. read "Christ our Lord."

148 "In the Visayas," says Delgado (p. 317) "very rarely do the Indians imitate the Spaniards in their dress; for almost all of them go barefoot, according to their custom, and wear long black garments that cover the entire body (which we call cassocks or lambong), very wide breeches, and the shirt outside. For they can never accustom themselves, as do the Spaniards, to gathering it inside, as is the custom of the country. I have seen the same among the Tagálogs, with the exception of some servants of the Spaniards, and some officials and clerks, among them. But these men do not make the rule for the other nations of this archipelago, who are numerous and different. I can truly tell what I see among the Spaniards of Visayas, who dress in the same manner as the Indians; and very rarely do they put on shoes and stockings or slippers, except on an important feast-day when they go to the church, for they cannot endure it any other way. It is a fact that the Indians do preserve somewhat their ancient customs in districts where there is less civilization and instruction; but where they are well taught and directed, they have almost forgotten these."

"A cura told me that he had surprised a man and three old women crouched down beside the corpse of the former's dead wife. The four people were all covered over with sheets, and were in the attitude of listening with the closest of attention to see whether the deceased would say anything to them. They practice many simplicities like this in all their solemn ceremonies, of which we have spoken. So general is this that in the ordinances of good government in force, there is an article that orders the persecution of idolatry and aniterias." (Mas, pp. 116, 117.)

149 "If father Fray Gaspar had been in Madrid, he would not have been so greatly surprised that those soliciting anything should send their wives to obtain

favors. Moreover, the Filipinos, not only fearing, but with full consciousness, generally send and even take their wives to the Spaniards to obtain some employment, or merely for money. The most direct means for a general to obtain the friendship of a married woman is to win over the husband, just as in order to get a single woman one must gain over the mother. I have known very intimately a steward who was very much in love with his wife, and was jealous even of her shadow. Nevertheless, at the least insinuation of his master he took her to the latter's apartment, and it appears that he desired her to go there very often. Upon thinking over this matter, I am convinced that a partial cause of it is the little importance that they attach to the act of love, and especially in the fact to which they are persuaded that no one of their women will ever love us; and they are only handed over for the profit, and are lent us as a personal service, just like any other; and when the woman goes away from us, she takes her heart with her, which is all for the Filipinos." (Mas, p. 117.)

150 M. and D. add "most."

151 This phrase is omitted in D.

152 It is not to be wondered at that they are literal and material in their conversation, for they know only their villages. See Delgado, p. 317.

"I have observed none of this, especially in the women to whom I have talked. Almost all of them are always attentive, courteous, and kind." (Mas, p. 118.)

153 M. and D. omit this sentence.

154 M. adds: "and run away, for he is the bugaboo, with which the children are frightened."

155 Dogs do not bark at the Spaniards only, in any country, but at those who are strange to them. Neither do the Indians detest the fathers from birth. The fact that the Indians yield to anyone who assumes a boasting attitude, especially if he be drunk, and have a knife, is not so much cowardice as prudence. "I believe that the reverend father was very melancholy, and tired of the ministry, when he began to write his letter." (Delgado, pp. 317, 318.)

"If our father had traveled, he would have known that dogs bark at anyone whose clothes are unfamiliar to them. In regard to their horror of white faces, he at least exaggerates. It is not at all strange that a child should cry at an object being presented to him that he has never had in his ken before. I have seen many children burst into sobs at the sight of my eye-glasses. It is a fact that some of them have just as little as possible to do with us, either for contempt, embarrassment, or antipathy; but there are a very great number who profess affection for us. When the government secretary, Cambronero, died in the year 1840, all his servants shed tears abundantly. A serving-maid of the Señora de Recaño was left desolate, when the latter embarked for España a short time ago. An old woman on the occasion of [the engagement of] Movales in the year 1823, gave Col. Santa Romana proofs of great affection and fidelity. During the same engagement, while Don Domingo Benito was haranguing his artillery sergeants and telling them 'I shall die the first,' one of them answered, 'No, Sir, I shall die before you.' When the Jesuits were exiled, the villages that they administered grieved exceedingly. In the archives of St. Augustine, I have seen the relation of one of the friars who went there for their relief, and he paints in lively colors the memory preserved of the Jesuits: 'Here they cannot look upon a white habit; notwithstanding the kind words that we speak to them, and the presents that we make them, we cannot attract to ourselves the good-will of these people; hence, when we call a child, he runs away instead of coming to us.' I have seen some servants ready and anxious to go with their master to any part of the world; and, if the Spaniards would take than, many would go to España. When some insurgents in the island of Leite put Alcalde Lara in the stocks, his servant feigned to be in accord with them. He made them drunk, and then took his master from the stocks. He fitted up a barangay quickly, in which they attempted to escape, but the night was stormy, and all were drowned. And finally, I myself have received several disinterested proofs of their good-will." (Mas, pp. 118, 119.)

156 "It is difficult to ascertain whether the Filipino is a brave man or a coward. On one side, we see any braggart terrify a multitude; and on the other, some face dangers and death with unmoved spirit. When one of them decides to kill another, he does it without thinking at all of the consequences. A man of Vigan killed a girl who did not love him, six other persons, and a buffalo; and then stabbed at a tree, and killed himself. Another servant of the tobacco superintendent killed a girl for the same reason, before a crowd of people, and then himself. A soldier killed a girl for the same reason while I was passing in front of Santo Thomás. A coachman, in November, 1841, tried to kill another man, because of a love affair; and, failing in the attempt, killed himself. Filipino sailors have committed many cruelties, and have a reputation throughout the entire Indian Sea as turbulent fellows and assassins. The [insurance] companies of Bengal do not insure at full risk a vessel in which one-half the crew is composed of islanders. When I was in the island of Pinang, at the strait of Malacca, I tried to get passage to Singapor, in order to go to Filipinas, in the brigantine "Juana" and to take in my company as a servant one of the seventeen sailors of Manila, who had been discharged from a Portuguese vessel because of a row that they had had with the captain. The commander of the "Juana" was a Chinese, and the crew Malayan; counting sailors and Chinese passengers there were about 40 persons aboard. Under no consideration would the captain admit me together with the servant, telling me: 'No, no, even if you give me a hundred pesos, I will take no man from Manila.' In fact, after much begging, I had to resign myself and leave him ashore, and take ship without knowing who would guide and serve me; for I understood

neither Chinese nor Malayan. At the same time, I have heard that the Filipinos are cowards in a storm. The infantry captain Molla told me that the captain of a pontín which encountered a heavy tempest began to weep, and the sailors hid in order not to work; and he had to drive them out of the corners with a stick, for which they began to mutiny and to try to pitch him overboard. Ashore they have given some proofs of boldness by attacking Spaniards to their faces.... Sergeant Mateo was boldly confronted in the insurrection of 1823. The soldiers have the excellent quality of being obedient, and if they have Spanish officers and sergeants, will not turn their backs on the fire; but alone they have never given proof of gallantry. In the war with the English, they always fled ... and the few Europeans whom Anda had were his hope, and the soul of all his operations. I have asked many officers who have fought with Filipinos, either against the savages in the mountains, or against ladrones; and they all have told me that when it comes to fighting, they preferred to have twenty-five Europeans to one hundred Filipinos. Many allege, in proof of their bravery, the indifference with which they die; but this is rather a sign of stupidity than of good courage. From all of the above data, we might deduce that the individual whom we are analyzing is more often found to be cowardly than impassive and fearless; but that he is apt to become desperate, as is very frequently observed. They express that by the idea that he is hot-headed, and at such times they commit the most atrocious crimes and suicide. He is cruel, and sheds blood with but little symptoms of horror, and awaits death calmly. This is because he does not feel so strongly as we do the instinct of life. He has no great spirit for hazardous enterprises, as for instance that of boarding a warship, breaking a square, gaining a bridge, or assaulting a breach, unless he be inflamed by the most violent passions, that render him frantic." (Mas, pp. 119–121.)

157 In M., "to a great degree;" and in D., "in a certain manner."

158 D. reads "on this occasion."

159 Delgado says (p. 318) that the sin of intoxication is overstated. Among the Visayans, intoxicating beverages are indulged in in differing degrees, while many are abstemious. "I would like to hear what the Tagálog Indians who live among Spaniards in Manila would say to this stain, that is imputed to them alone."

"Perhaps this may have been so in the time of Father Gaspar, as the Filipinos preserved more of their ancient customs than now, for we see that intoxication is very common in the independent tribes living in the mountains, but today it is not observed that the [civilized Filipinos] drink more than the individuals of other nations who are considered sober." (Mas, pp. 121, 122.)

160 Delgado denies that the Indians are robbers (p. 318).

161 Delgado says (p. 318): "This passage is absolutely malicious, so far as the Visayans are concerned; for no Visayan woman of good blood will marry with

other than her equal, however poor she be. And although all are of one color, they make great distinctions among themselves."

"The same thing is recounted by Father Mozo to be the case among the mountain savages." (Mas, p. 122.)

162 i.e., "At least as to manner."

163 D. omits this last clause.

164 An adaptation of an old proverb, probably meaning here, "Although sins are committed here, they are not so frequent as in other places."

165 San Agustin speaks without sufficient authority, says Delgado (pp. 318, 319), for he only remained a short time in Panay, and learned nothing of the other parts of the Visayans. "I know very well that what he imputes to the Visayan women is not absolutely true. For generally they detest not only Cafres and negroes, but also inequality in birth. They are not so easy as his Paternity declares in admitting any temptation, and there are many of them who are very modest and reserved." Bad women exist everywhere, even among the whites.

"There is no doubt that modesty is a peculiar feature in these women. From the prudent and even humble manner in which the single youths approach their sweethearts, one can see that these young ladies hold their lovers within strict bounds and cause themselves to be treated by them with the greatest respect. I have not seen looseness and impudence, even among prostitutes. Many of the girls feign resistance, and desire to be conquered by a brave arm. This is the way, they say, among the beautiful sex in Filipinas. In Manila no woman makes the least sign or even calls out to a man on the street, or from the windows, as happens in Europa; and this does not result from fear of the police, for there is complete freedom in this point, as in many others. But in the midst of this delicacy of intercourse there are very few Filipino girls who do not relent to their gallants and to their presents. It appears that there are very few young women who marry as virgins and very many have had children before marriage. No great importance is attached to these slips, however much the curas endeavor to make them do so. Some curas have assured me that not only do the girls not consider it dishonorable, but think, on the contrary, that they can prove by this means that they have had lovers. If this is so, then we shall have another proof that these Filipinos preserve not a little of their character and primitive customs; since, according to the account of Father Juan Francisco de San Antonio, it was a shame for any woman, whether married or single, before the arrival of the Spaniards, not to have a lover, although it was at the same time a settled thing that no one would give her affection freely.

"That they are more affectionate than men is also a fact, but this is common to the sex in all countries....

"That they rarely love any Spaniards is also true. The beard, and especially the mustache, causes them a disagreeable impression, and he who believes the contrary is much mistaken. Besides, our education, our tastes, and our rank place a very high wall between the two persons. The basis of love is confidence; and a rude Filipino girl acquires with great difficulty confidence toward an European who is accustomed to operas and society. They may place themselves in the arms of Europeans through interest or persuasion; but after the moment of illusion is over, they do not know what to say and one gets tired of the other. The Filipino girl does not grow weary of her Filipino, for the attainments, inclinations, and acquaintances of both are the same. Notwithstanding the Filipinos live, as I am told, convinced that not one of their beauties has the slightest affection for us, and that they bestow their smiles upon us only for reasons of convenience, yet I imagine that sometimes the joke is turned upon themselves—especially if the Spaniard is very young, has but little beard, and is of a low class, or can lower himself to the level of the poor Filipino girl." (Mas, pp. 123–125.)

166 M. reads "fishing."

167 D. reads "gloomily."

168 M. reads "For to define them categorically, with an essential and real definition." D. reads "For to define them categorically, with an essential and real substantial definition, awaits another."

169 M. omits the remainder of this paragraph; and the last sentence in D. reads: "But it they had undertaken the task of defining the Indians, they would not have been so successful."

170 This was the French poet and theologian John Barclay, who was born at Pont-à-Mousson, in 1582, and died at Rome, August 12, 1621. He refused to enter the Society of Jesus, and followed his father to England where he published a poem at the coronation of James I, which found considerable favor. While in London he was accused of heresy, and was summoned to Rome by Paul V. In London he published a continuation of his Euphormion, the first part of which had appeared in 1610. This consists of a Latin satire in two books. His Argenis was published in Paris in 1621, and there was a Leyden edition in 1630. It is a story, written in prose and poetry, of the vices of the court. It was very popular and was translated into many languages. See Hoefer's Nouvelle biographie générale.

171 Probably Joannes Rodenborgh, who wrote the fifth part of Logicæ compendiosæ (Utrecht, 1676).

172 See ante, p. 192, note 109.

173 See ante, p. 191, note 105.

174 i.e., "Passion does not come from custom." This is lacking in M.

175 i.e., "And infamous need." This is from the Aeneid, book, vi, line 276.

176 St. Antony of Thebes was the founder of monachism. He is said to have been born at Koma, Egypt, near Heraklea, A. D. 251, and to have died A. D. 356. In early life he retired to the wilderness, and lived in seclusion until 305, when he founded the monastery of Fayum, near Memphis and Arsinoë. He is the patron of hospitallers, and his day is celebrated on January 17. His life was written by St. Athanasius, a condensed translation of which is given by S. Baring-Gould in his Lives of the Saints (London, 1897, 1898), i, pp. 249–272. See also Addis and Arnold's Catholic Dictionary, p. 596; and New International Encyclopædia.

177 Formerly called Thebaica regio, one of the three great divisions of ancient Egypt, and equivalent to Upper Egypt. This district was famous for its deserts, which became the habitation of many of the early Christians, among them both Sts. Antony and Arsenius. See Larousse's Grand Dictionnaire.

178 St. Arsenius was a Roman of a noble and wealthy family, who became the tutor of the two sons of Theodosius at Constantinople. He fled to Egypt after the death of Theodosius, in shame at the poor results of his teaching. There he lived in the desert, where he was called "the father of the emperors." He died about 440, after a long life of seclusion. He figures in Kingsley's story of Hypatia. His day is celebrated on July 19, and he is especially revered in France and Belgium. See Baring-Gould (ut supra), viii, pp. 446–448.

179 D. reads wrongly "Theodorico."

180 D. reads "gético."

181 In the first line of the above citation, which is from the Epistolarum ex Ponto, book i, epistle 3 (to Rufinus) read "littore" in place of "frigore." The translation of the two lines is as follows: "What is better than Rome? What is worse than the Scythian shore? Yet the barbarian flees thither from that city."

182 i.e., "Though composed of many, it draws to itself the nature of the more worthy simple form."

183 "Among the Filipino Indians there are many who are very good, and are very capable of being directed and taught in good and holy customs; and because there are many bad ones, who govern themselves not by reason, but by the pressure of public opinion, it cannot be said rightly and conscientiously that all are bad." (Delgado, p. 320.)

"This paragraph appears admirable to me, and a more exact idea of the Filipino cannot be given in so few words—at least such as he is at present, either because of circumstances, or because of his physical constitution, or of the two things together." (Mas, p. 127.)

184 M. and D. add "it is in favor of their comfort, and they commit other greater acts of insolence, for."

185 i.e., "They enter into the joy of their lord;" a reference to Matthew XXV, 21, 23.

186 i.e., "Not as to the cause, but as the effect." D. reverses the position of the negative.

187 Heliogabalus the Roman emperor, who ascended the throne in 218 A. D., at the age of fourteen, and was assassinated after three years. He is known chiefly for his acts of madness and bestiality, and his cruelty.

188 San Agustin has quoted these lines incorrectly. They are found in ll. 527–531 of Marcus Annæus Lucanus's Pharsalia, and are as follows:

... O vitæ tuta facultas Pauperis angustique lares!

O munera nondum Intellecta deum! Quibus hoc

Contingere templis Aut potuit muris nullo

Trepidare tumultu Cæsarea pulsante manu?...

The translation of this passage is as follows: "O secure opportunity of life, and lares of the needy poor man! O gifts not yet recognized as a god! What temples could enjoy this blessing, or what walls be in confusion in any tumult, if the hand of Cæsar move?"

189 "All religious agree that they die with the utmost indifference, and that when they come to the bedside of the dying one, in order to comfort him, they remain cold upon seeing how little those people are changed by the words that their approaching peril inspires in them. Confessions at such a time are generally somewhat more sincere, but always very short and stupid. The relatives are not at all careful about talking of his death in the presence of the sick person—as, for example, one of them remarking to the cura in a very natural and quiet voice in his uncle's presence (who still fully retained his feeling and hearing): 'See, Father, it would be wise for you to consecrate the winding-sheet, for I think that he is about to die soon.' The same indifference is to be observed in a criminal condemned to any punishment. He is seated on his heels on a bamboo bench, smoking. Every few moments the religious enters to give him a Christian word, to which the criminal generally answers: 'Yes, Father, I know quite well that I have to die; what am I to do about it? I am an evil man; God so decrees; such was my fate;' and other things of this sort. He eats regularly, and sleeps as on any other day.... [This] is only one additional proof, and in my opinion, a not slight one, that the Filipino race is inferior, at least in spiritual matters, to our race." (Mas, pp. 128, 129.)

190 The location of the above quotation is not given in the Ayer MS., but is given in both M. and D.

191 D. reads "chatcere."

192 Possibly a reference to Proverbs ii instead of xx (where there is nothing that corresponds to this passage). The translation of the above is: "I walk in the ways of justice, in the midst of the paths of judgment, so that I may call myself diligent."

193 This is not quoted correctly, but should be: Venite ad me omnes, qui laboratis et onerati estis, et ego reficiam vos. The editor of D. has emended this passage.

194 This is the wrong reference. In the King James version, it is lxxii, 13, and in the Douay version, lxxi, 13.

195 i.e., "For to him that is little, mercy is granted." This is not in M.

196 The remainder of this paragraph, and all the next, are lacking in M.

197 i.e., "No sacrifice is more acceptable to God than the zeal for souls."

198 i.e., "Ye therefore, my friends who are in the world, proceed with security, and cry out and announce my will. I will dwell in your heart and in your mouth: I will be your leader on the way, and you consolation at death. I will not leave you. Proceed with eagerness, for glory increases from the labor." D. reads "audacter," "boldly," instead of "alacriter." M. gives but a portion of the citation.

199 This quotation is not exact, the correct version being as follows: Patientia enim vobis necessaria est: ut voluntatem Dei facientis, reportetis promissionem. It is not in M.

200 In D. "placing."

201 M. is the only one of the three versions of this letter that locates this citation correctly. We adopt the reading of the Latin Vulgate, as San Agustin has not quoted exactly.

202 M. and D. omit these last four words.

203 M. and D. read "variety of combinations of."

204 Of the remainder of the letter, Delgado says (p. 323): "In regard to all the rest that the reverend writer adds, concerning the manner in which those who live with the Indians ought to comport themselves, I have nothing more to say or to add. For it is all well written and noted, and those who come new to these islands will do very well to read it and to do as the reverend father prescribes, teaching the Indians to read and write and other knowledge, for they have great capacity for all and at the same time, civilization, which is very necessary to them;

and where they fail and sin, punish them as children, and not as slaves. By so doing they will obtain from them whatever they wish."

Mas says (pp. 130, 131) of the advice given by San Agustin "I would be very glad, and it would be very advantageous for them, if all the Spaniards would adopt this system which is both wise and unique. But quite to the contrary, many persons think that the Filipinos ought to understand them at the slightest insinuation and very readily. For any fault they become impatient and call the Filipinos brutes, and carabaos, and express themselves in the presence of the Filipinos in the most violent manner, and in the most insulting terms about the race in general, even to the point of wishing to destroy them and other barbarous and sanguinary ideas of which their heart is not capable. And they do not take note that such outbreaks of wrath only serve the purpose of confusing the Filipinos, rendering them more stupid, and rousing up hatred against them and all the Spaniards."

205 In M. "mildly."

206 M. gives the reference wrongly as the nineteenth verse.

207 i.e., "Care must, in fact, be taken that the teacher and the father and the mother give discipline to their subjects."

208 Not in M.

209 In D. "and the merit lies in the patience."

210 i.e., "Help the poor because of the commandment; and send him not away empty-handed because of his poverty, etc." M. and D. add the thirteenth verse, as follows: Perde pecuniam propter fratrem et amicum tuum, et non abscondas illam sub lapide in perditionem. The English of this is: "Lose thy money for thy brother and thy friend: and hide it not under a stone to be lost." To the above paragraph M. and D. add the following: "For the merit becomes greater in proportion to their ingratitude if we fulfil our obligation and if they act according to their disposition. For, as says the royal prophet David (Psalm xxxvi, 21), Mutuabitur peccator, et non solvet: justus autem miseretur et tribuet."

211 This paragraph is divided into two paragraphs in M. and D. and is very much abridged. It is as follows: "It is necessary that those Indians who are taken as servants, be shown no love if they are children, but always uprightness, for one must consider it as most certain that in proportion as they are better clothed and caressed, the worse they will become when they grow up. This is the teaching of the Holy Spirit: [the verse from Proverbs as above follows]. They must be treated with great uprightness and prudence, for otherwise they will gradually lose their respect to the character that God presents to them in the Spaniard. [The fable of King Log follows as above.]"

212 i.e., "He who blows his nose too violently generally draws forth blood."

213 M. and D. make two paragraphs of the above, and read as follows: "One must not press them to give more of themselves than they can, as we do with the lemon, for that which will be expressed will be bitter, and, as says the proverb [in D.—"and as says a law commentary"] Qui nimis emungit solet extorquere cruorem. We must remember in all this the teaching of the holy Council of Trent, session 13 [in D.—"3"] de reformat, chapter I, whose words, although they are very well worth reading, I omit on account of their length. It is not proper to go up into their houses, except when necessity requires it, keeping therein the evangelical precept (Luke x, 7 [wrongly cited as xx]): Nolite transire de domo in domum. For one will lose much in estimation, while their vices [in D.—"coldness"] do not make this a desirable diversion."

214 M. and D. add: "anything is entrusted to them." The remainder of San Agustin's letter is omitted in D.

215 M. and D. add here: "for thus does the Holy Spirit advise us."

"One day a friend of mine ordered a servant in my presence to go to a certain house to ask in his name for the last gazettes from Europa. I advised my friend to give the servant a note, since the latter would doubtless give expression to some bit of nonsense. He took no notice of me, and sent the servant. In fact, the man understood "aceite" [i.e., "olive oil"], for "gaceta" [i.e., "gazette"], and returned with a bottle of olive oil. His master was very much put out, while I burst into a roar of laughter. A peculiar thing is often observed in servants, namely, when one of them is ordered, 'Go to the house of Don Antonio,' before the message is finished the servant begins to go; and one has to call him back and say to him, 'But, man alive, where are you going?' and, if he is allowed to go, he reaches his destination and says that he has been sent there, and then returns whence he came, or utters some foolish remark." (Mas, p. 133.)

216 In the Vulgate, the last word of the Latin in this citation is eum.

217 i.e., "at least in passing." This is not in M.

218 M. reads "denude themselves of their customs."

219 M. reads: "For the Indian who is ordained does not give himself a trade because of the more perfect estate."

220 M. has instead of "from the oar," "from handling a bolo."

221 Spanish, la cuña del mismo palo; another application of an old Spanish proverb.

222 M. adds "and those farthest from Manila, where also the remedy is very far away."

223 Spanish, sobre quítame allá esas pajas—literally, "regarding 'carry away these straws from me,'" defined by the Academy's dictionary as, "about a thing of little importance or value."

224 Picota: "a column [the insignia of jurisdiction] or gibbet of stone, which is usually placed at the entrances of towns or villages; on which are ignominiously exposed the heads of persons executed or of criminals" (Bárcia, Dicc. etimológico).

225 M. adds "to the father cura." The reason for this letter may be found possibly in this paragraph, in the hostility of the religious orders to admitting the Filipinos to the priesthood.

226 M. reads "How well it could be subdued and composed."

227 M. adds "in his happiness."

228 M. reads: "And while they were all gallantly seated in the hall, and she was, very finely adorned with jewels, in the room, surrounded by many ladies."

229 M. reads: "The bride spied the mouse from a long distance, and, not being able to restrain herself out of respect for that function, she arose and began to run the length of the hall. She overthrew the people, and they were unable to restrain the fair bride, and cause her to desist from her undertaking. The angry groom said to them."

230 The rest of this sentence reads in M., "even though they should become bishops."

231 Matthew xxv, 21.

232 i.e., "The priesthood is the apex of all good things which exist among men."

St. Ignatius the Martyr was born about the middle of the first century of the Christian era, and is said to have been baptized by the apostle John. He was bishop of Antioch for forty years. Arrested by the Roman authorities because of his preaching, he was sent to Rome, where he was killed by wild beasts in the arena, probably about 107 A. D. He met the famous Polycarp while on his way to Rome. Many epistles exist which are said to have been written by him, although some of them are probably spurious. His day is celebrated on February 1. See S. Baring-Gould (ut supra), ii, pp. 1–5, and *New International Encyclopædia*.

233 i.e., "Concerning the dignity of the priesthood." M. adds: "Nihil est in hoc secula excelentius sacerdotibus [i.e., 'There is nothing more excellent in this world than the priesthood']; and above, horur igitur, et sublimitas sacerdotalis nullis poterit compurationibus adequari si regum fulgori compares, et principum Diademati longe erit inferius, quam si plumbi metallum aduri fugorem compares. [i.e., "Therefore the priestly reverence and height can be equaled by no comparisons. If it be compared to the splendor of kings and the diadem of

princes, the comparison is far more inferior than if the metal lead were compared to gleaming gold."] And of this Father Don Antonio Molina speaks at length in his admirable book."

234 St. Ambrose was one of the four doctors of the western church. He was born at Trèves about 340 A. D., and received a good education in Rome, and entered into the Roman civil service. Elected to the office of bishop of Milan, in what was regarded as a miraculous manner, he soon became one of the great strongholds of the young religion of Christianity. To him was due the honor of receiving the great Augustine into the Church. His death occurred in 397 A. D. His day is celebrated on December 7; and in Milan he is regarded as a patron saint. The Ambrosian Library of that city is named for him. See S. Baring-Gould (ut supra), xv, pp. 74–104; and New International Encyclopædia.

235 Antonio de Molina was a Spanish theologian, who was born at Villa-Nueva-de-los-Infantes (Castilla). Entering the Augustinian order, he taught theology, until he later retired to the house at Miradores, where he died September 12, 1612. He wrote a book called Instruccion de Sacerdotes, which was published in various places in Spain, and later translated into various languages, among them the Latin. See Hoefer's Nouvelle biographie générale, xxxv, col. 892.

236 Paulo Segneri, S.J. was one of the most illustrious men that the Jesuit order has produced. He was a native of Nettuno, Italy, being born March 22, 1624, and entered the Society December 2, 1637. He early became deaf through his excessive study. After teaching the humanities and rhetoric, he became a preacher and missionary, traversing Italy on his missionary journeys during the years 1665–1692. In 1692 he was called to Rome by Innocent XII, to take the place of his preacher-in-ordinary. His death occurred at Rome, December 9, 1694. His influence on Italy is ranked by some only second to that of Savonarola. His style in writing is regarded as of chief rank in purity and accuracy for his century. His writings were numerous, and have been translated into many languages, some of them into Greek and Arabian. The book mentioned in the text is Il parroco instruito: opera in cui si dimostra a qualsisia curato novello il debito che lo strigne, e la via da tenerse nell' adempirlo (Firenze, 1692). See Sommervogel's Bibliothèque; and Hoefer (ut supra), xliii, cols. 685, 686.

237 The dignity of patriarch in the Catholic church (leaving aside the papal rank) is the highest grade in the hierarchy of jurisdiction. Antioch early occupied a high place among the patriarchates, although with the lapse of time it lost its high position; and finally, after the schism between the eastern and western churches, the appointee to that dignity did not actually assume the office. See Addis and Arnold's Catholic Dictionary, pp. 35, 36, and 640. The patriarch mentioned in the text was the famous Cardinal Charles Thomas Millard de Tournon. See Vol.

XXVIII, p. 118, and note 56; Concepción, ix, pp. 1–123; and Crétineau-Joly, v, pp. 38–54.

238 These last two sentences are missing in M.

239 At this point the letter proper in M. ends with the words: "May God preserve you for many years," and no signature follows. This is followed by the questions for men and women of Murillo Velarde.

240 In the text, legitimos; probably a transcriber's error for ilegitimos ("of illegitimate birth").

Other papal letters give leave to dispense with the above classes, who could not, otherwise, be promoted to holy orders. Both classes could, also, be raised to church dignities, but only to minor dignities, and not to high ones as bishoprics, etc. The distinction between espurios and [i]legitimos seems merely to have been a legal one, as both terms mean the same in effect.—Rev. T. C. Middleton, O.S.A.

241 i.e., "It was lately related to us."

242 In the copy of this letter conserved in the collection of Fray Eduardo Navarro of the Colegio de Filipinas, Valladolid, Spain (of which we have the transcription of a few pages at the end), this word reads divina.

243 Antonio (not Pedro) Urceo, who was also called Codrus, was an erudite Italian, who was born August 14, 1446 at Rubiera, and died at Bologna in 1500. He was a good educator of youth, but of choleric temper. While acting as tutor in one of the noble Italian families, a fire destroyed most of his papers, which so worked upon him that he retired into almost complete seclusion for six months. In 1482 he went to Bologna, where he taught grammar and eloquence. Although during his life he gave doubts of his orthodoxy, his death was all that could have been wished. His works were published in four editions, the first being at Bologna in 1502, under the title In hoc Codri Volumine hæc continentur Orationes, seu sermones ut ipse appelabat Epistolae. Silvae. Satyrae. Eglogae. Epigrammata. The translation of the above citation is as follows:

"Although thou be freeborn and sprung from noble parents;

Still even yet thou mayst be a base beast.

Add that thou art an honor to thy country, and claim the noblest kin;

Still even yet thou mayst be a base beast.

Thou mayst have wealth, thou mayst have abundance of elegant furniture;

Still even yet thou mayst be a base beast.

In short, whatever thou shalt be, unless thou have prudence,

I declare that thou wilt ever be a base beast."

Of the native priests of the Philippines, Delgado says (pp. 293–296): "I know some seculars in the islands, who although Indians, can serve as an example and confusion to the European priests. I shall only bring forward two examples: one, the bachelor Don Eugenio de Santa Cruz, judge-provisor of this bishopric of Santísimo Nombre de Jesús, and calificador of the Holy Office, a full blooded Indian and a native of Pampanga. And inasmuch as the author of this letter confesses that the Pampangos are a different people, I shall name another, namely, the bachelor Don Bartolomé Saguinsin, a Tagálog, a cura of the district of Quiape (outside the walls of Manila), an Indian, and a native of the village of Antipolo. I knew his parents, and had friendly relations with them while I was minister in that village. Both men were esteemed for their abilities and venerated for their virtues, in Tagalos and Visayas." In addition, "those reared in any of the four colleges in Manila, for the clerical estate are all the sons of chiefs, people of distinction among the Indians themselves, and not of the timaua, or of the class of olipon, as the Visayan says, or maharlica or alipin, as the Tagálog calls the slaves and freedmen. The reverend fathers of St. Dominic or of the Society rear these boys and instruct them in virtue and learning; and if they have any of the vices of Indians, these are corrected and suppressed by the teaching and conversation of the fathers. Furthermore, when the most illustrious bishops promote any of these men to holy orders, they do not proceed blindly, ordering any one whomever to be advanced—but only with great consideration and prudence, and after informing themselves of his birth and his morals, and examining and testing him first before the ministry of souls is entrusted to him; and to say the contrary is to censure the most illustrious prelates, to whom we owe so much veneration and reverence. Furthermore, there are among these Indians, many (and perhaps most of them) who are as noble, in their line of descent as Indians, as is any Spaniard; and some of them much more than many Spaniards who esteem themselves as nobles in this land. For, although their fate keeps them, in the present order of things, in an almost abject condition, many of them are seigniors of vassals. Their seigniory has not been suppressed by the king, nor can it be suppressed. Such we call cabezas de barangay in Tagálog, and Ginhaopan in Visayan. They and their children and relatives lose nothing of their nobility because they serve the king in cutting timber, in the fleets, or in other personal services which are necessary in this land. As they lose nothing, it is also much honor for them that the king be served by them. Accordingly, there are sargentos-mayor, masters-of-camp, captains, governors of the villages, and lieutenants, and all are Indians of distinction. These would not go to row in a banca, and their hands would certainly be freed from handling a bolo or an ax in the cutting of timber, and their mothers, wives, and daughters would not have become spinners, if it were not for España. And although all the Indians seem of one color to the father, this color is well distinguished among them; and they are very respectful to their chiefs and much more so to their priests, even though these be Indians like themselves." Delgado continues by saying that, although some of the native priests have turned out badly, that is not sufficient to condemn them all. It is arbitrary to declare that the Indian enters the priesthood solely for his own comfort, and because of the respect shown him, and not because of the spiritual blessings. Many Spaniards also enter the ecclesiastical estate merely for a living. There are examples of Negro, Japanese, and Chinese priests. "Consequently, it is not to be wondered at that the most illustrious prelates and bishops should ordain Indians here and in Nueva España, and in other parts of the Indias."

244 The date of the Navarro copy is wrongly given as 1725.

245 Pedro Murillo Velarde was born August 6, 1696, at Villa Laujar, Granada, and entered the Jesuit novitiate at the age of 22. Having entered the Philippine missions, he was long a professor in the university of Manila; and later was rector at Antipolo, visitor to the Mindanao missions, and procurator at Rome and Madrid. He died at the hospital of Puerto Santa Maria, November 30, 1753. Murillo Velarde is one of the more noted among Jesuit writers. His principal works are the following: Cursus juris canonici, hispani et indici (Madrid, 1743); Historia de la provincia de Philipinas de la Compañia de Jesus (Manila, 1749); and Geographica historica (Madrid, 1752), in ten volumes. In the Historia (which work we have used freely in the present series, as material for annotation) was published his noted map of the Philippine Islands, the first detailed map of the archipelago; it was made by order of the governor of the island, Valdes Tamón, in 1734.

246 A kind of sausage composed of lean pork, almonds, pineapple kernels, and honey.

247 This sentence is missing in Father Navarro's copy.

248 Literally "lose a foothold."

249 Delgado here refers to the "Opinion" by Murillo Velarde which is prefixed to vol. i of San Antonio's Chronicas; this is dated at San Miguel, May 19, 1738, and contains a detailed description of the products of the islands— vegetable, animal, and mineral—from which we extract his description of the peoples therein, as follows:

"The natives of these islands are generally called Indians, because these islands are included in the demarcation of the Western Indias—although properly they are in the Eastern hemisphere, because, as they are distant from España more than a hundred and eighty degrees of longitude, which makes the half-circuit [of the globe], it necessarily follows that they must be on the side of the East. All the Indians resemble one another, especially in the yellowish-brown color and the flattened nose; and there is little difference between the individuals. In the island of Negros, between Cavitan and Sipalay, I encountered heathen blacks with crinkled hair, as if they were from Guinea. The people who are here called creoles are of a swarthy brown color, with withered skin, and are quite civilized and capable. As for the origin of the Indians, I am inclined to think that they originate from Malayos, on account of the similarity of their language; for by examining on various occasions a Malay (a native of Maláca) who could speak several languages fluently, and a Ternatan, and Lutaos and Subanos, I have ascertained the following: In the Malay, "sky" is called languit, and the same in Tagálog, in Lutáo, and Subáno; "man" [varon] is lalaqui in Malay, as in the Tagálog and Bisayan; "tongue" is dila in Malay, as in Tagálog; "white" is puti in Malay, as in Tagálog, Subáno, and Lutáo. In other words the difference is but slight; thus, in Malay "land" is nigri, in Tagálog lupa, in Lutáo tana, in Boholan yuta; and "man" [hombre] is in Malay oran, in Tagálog tavo, in Lutáo aa, in Subáno gatao. The Indians are exceedingly clever in every kind of handiwork, not for inventing, but for imitating what they see. They write beautifully; many of them are tailors and barbers, for they learn both these trades with little effort; and there are among them excellent embroiderers, painters, and silversmiths; and engravers whose work has no equal in all the Indias—and I was even going to place it far ahead of all the rest, if shame had not restrained me—as is very obvious in the many and excellent engravings which they are all the time producing. They are good carvers, gilders, and carpenters. They build vessels for these islands—galleys, galliots, pataches, and ships for the Acapulco trade-route. They are good seamen, artillerists, and divers—for there is hardly an Indian who does not know how to swim very well. They are the pilots of these seas. They excel in making bejuquillos, which are golden chains of delicate and exquisite workmanship. From palm-leaves, rattan, and nito they make hats, and petates or rugs, and mats, that are very handsome, and wrought with various kinds of flowers and other figures. They are noted as mechanics and puppet-players, and make complicated mechanisms which, by means of figures, go through various motions with propriety and accuracy. Some are watchmakers. They make gunpowder, and cast mortars, cannon, and bells. I have seen them make guns, as handsomely constructed as those made in Europe, although I do not think that they would be as substantial and reliable as those. There are in Manila three printing-houses, and all keep Indian workmen; and the errors that they make are not numerous. They have remarkable skill in music; and there is no village, however small, that has not a very respectable musician to officiate in the church. Among them are excellent voices—trebles, contraltos, tenors, and basses; almost all can play on the harp, and there are many violinists, and players on the oboe and flute. It is especially noticeable that not only those whose trade it is to make these instruments do so, but various Indians, through love [for such work], make guitars, harps, flutes, and violins, with their bolos or machetes; and they learn to play these instruments by only seeing them played, and without any special instruction. Almost the same thing occurs in other matters; and on this account it is said that the Indians have their understanding in their eyes, since they so closely imitate what they see. Such are the Indians, when observed on the outside surface of their aspect; but when one penetrates into the interior of their dispositions, peculiarities, and customs, they are a labyrinth, in which the most sagacious man loses his way. They appear ingenious and simple in countenance and words, but they are masters eminent in deceit and feigning; under an apparent simplicity they conceal an artful and crafty dissimulation. I believe that the Indian never fails to deceive, unless when his own interests are hindered. In their lawsuits and business dealings they are like flies, which never quit what they are seeking, no matter how much they are brushed away; and thus they surpass and conquer us. The Chinese say that the Spaniard is fire, and the Indian is water, and that water quenches fire. They neither resent an injury nor thank one for a kindness. If you give them anything, they immediately ask for another. There is no fixed rule for construing them; for each one is needed a new syntax, because they are anomalous. With them the argument is not concluded by induction, since no Indian resembles another, nor even is one like himself; for in the short round of one day he changes his colors oftener than a chameleon, takes more shapes than a Proteus, and has more movements than a Euripus. He who deals with them most knows them least. They are, in fine, a union of contrarieties, which the greatest logician could not reconcile; they are an obscure and confused Chaos, in which species cannot be perceived or formal qualities distinguished; and if I had to define them I would say:

"Obstabatque alijs aliud, quia corpore in vno

Frigida pugnabant calidis, humentia siccis,

Mollia cum duris, sine pondere habentia pondus."

250 Alluding to the irregular tides in the straits of Euripus, between Eubœa and Greece; during a large part of the month these tides occur as often as eleven to fourteen times during the twenty-four hours. Their irregularity occasioned among the Greeks a proverb, which Delgado here uses.

251 A name given by the inhabitants of Cuba to the natives of Mexico, and in Vera Cruz to those of the interior. The name is also applied to shrewd and brusque persons. (New Velázquez Dictionary.)

252 These two rules are respectively: "Evil once, evil is always presupposed;" and "Evil [may spring] from any failing."

253 These chains were also of Chinese manufacture; apparently the Filipinos took up this industry through their tendency to imitate.

254 The Lygodium scandens, also called Gnito and nitongputi, a climbing fern found throughout the Philippines. Blanco gives the name of the genus as Ugena. The glossy, wiry stems are used in the making of fine hats, mats, cigarette and cigar cases, etc. See Census of Philippines, iv, p. 166.

255 The balate is an echinoderm found abundantly in the Visayas, of which Delgado describes three varieties (p. 935): namely the Holothuria scabra (Jager), which is white; the Holothuria atra (Jager), which is black; and the bacongan or Synapta similis (Semper), which is of larger size. The second variety is most esteemed. It was sold dry in the Visayas or taken to Manila and sold, where they were worth thirty-five or forty or even more silver pesos per pico. The Chinese especially esteemed them (and do so yet) and large sums were paid for them in that country. The Filipinos occasionally ate them fresh, but only in the absence of fish.

The Native Peoples and their Customs

[San Antonio,1 in his Cronicas (Manila, 1738–44), i, pp. 129–172, has the following ethnological matter. We omit the side heads.]

Chapter XXXIX

Of the origin of the Indians

[After a brief allusion to the creation of man at the beginning of the world, the writer continues:]

384. Now, then, I have said as much as there is to say of the origin of the Indians, if we speak of the first and most remote. For to endeavor to determine the first settlers of these lands, whence and how they came, whether they were Carthaginians, Jews, Spaniards, Phœnicians, Greeks, Chinese, Tartars, etc., is reserved for God, who knows everything; and this task exceeds all human endeavor. And if such study obtain anything, it will amount only to a few fallible conjectures—with danger of the judgment, and without any advance of the truth or of reputation. And such is the notion (omitting many other absurdities that have been written), that the Indians were produced ex putre like unclean animals, or like the wild plants of the field. Others showing them great favor, assign the sun as their father, which produced them from some noble material. Others say [that they were produced] by the ingenious art of chemists or magicians; others that there were two Adams in the world, one in Asia, and another in the Western Indias, and that our Indians proceeded from one of them; others, that there were already people in the world before the creation of Adam; and that from them came the heathen, and from Adam, the Hebrews. All of the above, being so erroneous nonsense, and blindness from the devil, is already refuted, and is well refuted with contempt.

385. The only conjecture that can be made with some more visible foundation is the origin of our Indians, considering those who were found in these islands at the time of the conquest by the Spanish arms. In accordance with this, I shall relate what written records I have found (which is very little), and what I have carefully investigated, which will not be much, for the natives are not very capable of forming adequate accounts of this subject, and what we Europeans are reducing to treatises.

386. Father Colin (both learned and curious in the investigation of the matter which we are treating) reduces the people found in this land by our first conquistadors into three different classes. The first class consisted of those who ruled and governed as absolute masters; and these were civilized after their own fashion. The second consisted of black and barbarous mountaineers who inhabited the tops of the mountains, like brutes. The third consisted of men neither so barbaric nor so civilized as the other two classes; for, although they lived in retirement, they did not hate civilization and human intercourse.

387. This third class still remains in the same ancient condition. They live, as a rule, on the plateaus of the mountains, and at the mouths of rivers, and maintain themselves by hunting and fishing, and some agriculture. Most of them trade, and barter wax with the villages. These people are called Zimarrònes, Zambals, Ylàgas, Tìngues, Tagabalooyes,2 Manòbos, Mangyànes, and various other names, according to the difference of the sites where they live. Some or others of these have become Christians, through the efforts of the near-by evangelical ministers. The rest are heathen, but they have no determined rites, and are governed only by the customs of their ancestors, and those customs are mostly barbaric. Some of these people are accustomed to pay some sort of recognition or feudal due to our Catholic monarch, who is thereby bound to defend them from the invasions of their neighboring enemies. Such is done by the Tagabalooyes in the province of Caràga, who pay their annual feudal due in guinàras and medriñaques (textiles of abacá),3 in order to be defended from the Moros their neighbors. Likewise the Mangyànes of Mindôro (who number about seven thousand), who pay fifty-two arrobas and a half of wax annually, or 105 tributes; and some of the Manòbos in the mountains of Caràga (who are heathen and without number, although some are Christians—a people civilized and well inclined to work, who have [fixed] habitation and excellent houses)—pay tribute.

388. The origin of all these people (who are scattered throughout these islands) is inferred to be either the many civilized Indians who have retreated to the mountains in order not to pay tribute, or in order not to be chastised for any crime; or the many different nations immediate to this archipelago. For some bear traces of being Japanese mestizos, as do the Tagabalooyes, as I am well informed by religious who have had intercourse with them. Some are known to proceed from the Chinese; some from pure Indians, and some from other nations, as is declared by the circumstances of face, body, color, hair, customs, manner, and behavior—according to the experience of various religious, who agree that they are not of the pure race of the Indians, but mestizos as above stated. And even in five clans of Mangyànes

who are said to exist in the island of Mindòro, there is one which has a little tail, as do the monkeys; and many religious who have assured me of it, as witnesses. In Valèr, on the coast opposite us, a woman was found not long ago who had a long tail, as was told me by the present missionary; and he was unable to be sure of the origin of that race, unless it was a race of Jews.

389. I do not know whether those people who are found only in the environs of Manila, and are called Criollos Morenos [i.e., creole blacks], can be put in this mestizo class. The former are all oldtime Christians, docile, well inclined, and of sufficient understanding. They serve the king in personal duties, and always have their regiment of soldiers, with their master-of-camp, captains, and other leaders; and in this way they are outside the reckoning as Indians. It is difficult to assign their true origin to them. For some make them the descendants of those blacks, of whom we shall speak later, who were the primitive lords of these domains. But I do not see how this can be so, for they do not resemble those Negrillos either in their hair or in the members of their bodies, or in the qualities of their minds, in which these creoles have the complete advantage. And although it might be said that they have been bettered in all ways with the lapse of time, and the change of location to one more civilized and temperate, it is not credible that they would not retain some of their old vices, as is the case with various other races here, and as has been experienced in Nueva España. Some people make them the descendants of those slaves who were formerly held here by the petty rulers, brought by foreign traders in exchange for the drugs that formed their commerce and with whose price they made a good profit. Even yet they bring to our settlements a considerable number—so many, that it is necessary for one of the auditors to be judge of the slaves, and his duty costs him his time and patience. The creoles refuse to confess this origin, and it does not seem to me that they would be so well received and so well regarded if they had so vile an origin. Some believe that they descend from the free Malabars who come to these islands under pretext of trade. I incline more to this view, paying heed to the physiognomies and intellect of them all, for they are almost all alike in their clear dark color, aquiline noses, animated eyes, lank hair, docile disposition, and good manners, by which we may infer that those that there are now are Malabar and Indian mestizos.

390. At the present time, all this archipelago, and especially these islands of the Tagálogs, are full of another race of mestizos, who were not found at the first discovery, whom we call Sangley mestizos,4 who are descended from Indian women and Chinese men. For since trade with them [i.e., the Sangleys] has been, and is, so frequent, and so many remain in these islands under pretext of trade, and they are the ones who supply these islands with clothing, food, and other products, those who have mixed with the

Indian women in marriage are numerous; and for this purpose they become Christians, and from them have resulted so many mestizos that one cannot count them. They are all Christians, and quite commonly well disposed, and very industrious and civilized. They take pride in imitating the Europeans in everything, but their imitation is only a copy. They inhabit the same villages with the Tagálogs, but are not reckoned with them; since for the reckoning of the king they belong to a different body. The women are more like the Sangleys or Chinese, but the men not so much; however, these inherit from them ambition, in their continual industry.

391. There is also another kind of mestizo—the Japanese—who result from the Japanese who were shipwrecked on these islands in former years. They are of better conduct than the others, since they have a better origin. They are more esteemed here and have more privileges, for they only pay half as much tribute as do the others.

392. It is tradition that the Negrillos, who belong to the second class of people whom our first conquistadors found, were the first owners of the islands of this archipelago; and that, the civilized nations of other kingdoms having conquered them, they fled to the mountains and settled there, and from there it has never been possible to exterminate them, because their sites are impenetrable. There they have lived and brought forth children until the present. In former times they were so elated with their primitive power that, although their forces were not able to cope with those of foreigners in the open, they were very powerful in the thickets, mountains, and mouths of the rivers; and were accustomed to burst like an avalanche upon the villages, and compel their inhabitants to pay them tribute, as if they were the lords of the land, who were inhabiting it. And if the people refused to give it willingly, they killed right and left, collecting the tribute in the heads of those who were decapitated; as was written by one of our oldtime religious in the following words: "Even in my time, it happens," he says, "that they descended to the settlements and sought tribute from the Tagálogs, and at times took some heads for this purpose. Thus did it happen in Siniloan, which refused tribute at the approach of the Spaniards. The mountain Indians, having revolted, attacked the village; and they took three heads, and badly wounded a Spaniard who was defending them." Thus far the religious. At other times those people did not allow the Indians to make use of the wood and game of the mountains, and the fish of the rivers. For being very skilful in the use of the bow and arrow, and very swift and experienced in the fastnesses of the mountains and thickets, they inhumanly shot with arrows as many as approached their territories, without anyone catching sight or sound of them. For that reason, the inhabitants of the villages consider it wise to make an agreement with the Negrillos to pay

them a certain tribute, provided that the latter leave the rivers and fields free. And although this pact is not so apparent at present, I believe that it is practiced secretly because of the fear that the Indians have of them, and because of their dependence on them; since the Negrillos are the lords of the mountains which contain the most virgin forests, with woods of the greatest value. It is a fact, too, that those of the present day are as barbarous as their ancestors.

393. All of these people are black negroes, most of whom have kinky hair, and very few have lank. They are flat-nosed, and almost all of them have thick, projecting lips. They go totally naked, and only have their privies covered with some coverings resembling linen cloths, which they draw on from the back forward, and which are called bahaques. They make those bahaques from the bark of trees, pounded with heavy blows, so that there are some that look like fine linen. Wrapping a rattan around the waist, they fasten the bahaque to it by the two ends. As ornaments they wear certain bracelets of rattan of various colors, curiously wrought; and garlands on their heads and on the fleshy parts of their arms, composed of various flowers and branches; and as a means of greater distinction for some one person, a cock's feather or the feather of some other bird, as a plume. Their food consists of fruits, and roots of the mountain; and if they find, perchance, some deer, they eat it in that place where they kill it. That night they make their abode there, and after they grow tired of dancing, they sleep there—all helter-skelter, like brutes. Next day the same thing happens, and they sleep in another stopping-place. All their customs are the savage and brutish ones characteristic of barbarians; and they recognize no other laws, letters, or government than those of the heads of their families, at the most. They only care about defending their own territories, upon which they have lively wars, some Negrillos against others, with great mortality on both sides. At such times no natives dare enter the mountains, for the Negrillos kill them all, whether friend or enemy. Their most common arms are shield, bow, and arrow. If by a miracle any Christian is found among these people, and if perhaps the religious have reared some of them in Christianity from childhood, it very rarely occurs that he does not flee to the mountains whence he originated, when he becomes grown.

394. One of the islands of this archipelago which has a name, is the one called the island of Negros, because of the abundance of those people. It is located between the two islands of Zebú and Panày, and in it is established a Christian and civilized government. But at one point of this island, which lies toward the west, and is called the point of Sojotòn, there is a great number of the said blacks, and not one Christian. In the center of the island is a much greater number; therefore, it is along the beach where the Jesuit

fathers and the seculars administer, and where the Visayans or Pintados are settled.

395. The origin of these Negrillos is thought to have been interior India, or citra Gangen, which was called Etyopia; for it was settled by Ethiopian negroes, whence went out the settlers to African Etyopia, as Father Colin proves in detail. Consequently, there being on the mainland of India nations of negroes, and even in Nueva Guinea so many that their first discoverers gave the island that name because of the multitude of these people; and since the distance from those places to these islands and the Philippine archipelago is not great; nor was the land [of Nueva Guinea] which was five hundred leguas in length, entirely settled with blacks—whom the ships of Viceroy Don Antonio de Mendoza found in one of the capes of the strait of Magallanes: those blacks could very easily pass from one island to another, and their chief abode with their own name might be the island of Negros, as we have remarked. Thence they could extend afterward to dominate and settle the rest of the islands, without any opposition from other people, until the opposition came through other men more rational and civilized than they, who dispossessed them.

396. The third kind of people whom our Spaniards found in this archipelago were the civilized nations, who maintained their government or seigniory on the river banks, on the seashores, and in the other sites with the best locations in these regions, and in the locations most fit for healthful and safe dwelling-places. Among them there was another remarkable class of people, and their domination, scattered throughout the many islands of this archipelago, the chief of whom are the Tagálogs, Pampangos, Visayans, and Mindanaos. Other peoples are reduced to these, although they have various distinguishing marks. The Tagálogs, who are the natives of Manila and its archbishopric, with but little distance between their villages, were Malays, who came from a district called Malàyo; that is the origin of all the Malays, who are scattered throughout the most and the better parts of all these archipelagoes. They are located on the mainland of Malâca, and as that district is not far distant from the great island of Bornèy, it is inferred (and this tradition has been handed down from father to son), that the Malays went to Bornèy, and from Bornèy to settle Manila and its district; taking the name of *Tagàlog*—which is the same as *Taga Ylog*, which signifies, in their own language, "those who live on the rivers;" for the Tagálogs have always lived on the shores of the rivers.

397. That the Tagálogs originated directly from the Malays, is proved (in the opinion of all) by their language, which differs but little from that of the real Malays; by their color, and the shape of their faces and their bodies; by the clothes and vesture in which the Spanish conquistadors found

them; by their customs and ceremonies, all of which resemble those of the Malays—of whom the Tagálogs themselves said, and say always, that they are the true descendants. The coming of the Malays to this archipelago is not incredible, as we have so many examples of various accidents in these seas which have originated from the weather, by which we have seen brought to these islands unknown peoples, who spoke languages which no one could understand. For instance, a boat driven from its course, landed in the year 1725 on the opposite coast of Valèr and Casigùran, where our religious were in charge; it contained more than twenty men, whose language or garb had not been known until that time. But it is much more easily credible that the Malays came to these islands led by greed for their commercial profits—as, one reads in the histories of the Portuguese, happened in the regions of India with the Persians and Arab Moros, who, having entered under the pretext of trade, afterwards became masters of everything. The same thing is said here of the entrance of the Moro Malays.

398. The Pampangos (according to tradition) originated from the largest island of the Orient, which is that of Sumàtra or Trapobàna (although some apply the latter name to Zeilàn), which is located below the line. That island is seven hundred leguas in circumference, and is near the land of Malâca and Malâyo, and for that reason it is included in the Aurea Chersonesus. In the midst of that great island of Sumàtra there is a large lake, on whose surrounding marge many different peoples have their abodes. According to Father Colin (who himself examined him), a Pampango who had lost his way reached that place; and, having discovered that there were men there of his own build, language, and clothing, approached, and entered into conversation with them in his own elegant Pampango tongue. They answered him in the same speech, and one of their old men said: "You are descendants of the lost people who, in former times, left here to settle other lands, and have never been heard of since." From this it appears that one may infer the origin of the Pampangos. But it is not easy to determine whether they came from Sumàtra direct, or settled first in Bornèy, because of the nearness of its lands and domains, and thence passed on to settle the islands of this archipelago; although it appears from the statements of some who have been in Bornèy for a time that they even find there sufficient indications that the Pampangos originated, some from Sumàtra and others from Malâyo. It is certain that if the island of Bornèy was not a land continuous with that of these islands in past centuries (and arguments are not lacking for this), at least many islets are found lying in a row and near one another, with which Bornèy is closely connected.5 Such a one is Paragua, which extends in a northerly direction. Toward the east, Bornèy is extended by Mindanào. With this continuation and the short distances between these

regions, one can see the little difficulty in changing their abodes from one to the other; and it is believable that the Tagálogs, Pampangos, and other civilized races who were found in this archipelago, and who were almost alike in language, customs, bodily proportions, and clothing, as now we see them, came immediately from Bornèy, some from some provinces and some from others. That may account for the little difference that is found among them.

399. It is argued that the Visayans and Pintados—who are the ones found in the Camàrines, Lèyte, Samàr, Panày, Zebù, and other neighboring territories—came from the large island of Macasàr, which is very powerful and densely populated. It has its emperor, who is called Sumbanco, and many petty rulers. The basis of this argument lies, not only in the short distance from that island to this archipelago, for it is only distant about sixty leguas from the point of Samboànga; but also because in Macasàr, as is reported, there are Indians who adorn and tattoo the body as do the Visayans (who are called Pintados on that account). But it is not known with certainty where one and the other originated. We only know of a relation written by the chief pilot, Pedro Fernandez de Quiròs, of his voyage to the Salomon Islands and their discovery by Albaro de Mendaña de Neyra in the year 1595. That relation is addressed to Doctor Antonio de Morga, lieutenant-general for his Majesty of the Philipinas. The said Quiròs says in it that, finding themselves in ten long degrees south latitude, they sighted an island to which General Don Albaro gave the name of La Magdalena; and that from its port there came to receive them, he says, "with seventy ships, more than four hundred white Indians, of a very fine symmetry, tall, lusty, and robust, and so well built that they far surpassed us. They had fine teeth, eyes, mouth, the most beautiful hands and feet, and long hair. Many of them were very fair; and among them were the must handsome youths, all naked, and without covering over any part; and all their bodies, legs, arms, hands, and in some the faces, were adorned as among these Visayans." From this it is evident that they are Pintados Indians; and that they were not conquered, like those whom we call here Pintados Visayans. They live in south latitude, in the same parallel as that of the north, from ten to twelve degrees. But it is not easy to determine what might be the origin of the others; since, although it is known that this custom of tattooing and making figures on the body is found in Brasil, in Florida, among the Scythians of Asia, and the Britons of Europa, and even among the Moros of Africa, those nations are very remote from our Pintados; and so remote an origin cannot be conceded to the latter.

400. The large island of Mindanao took its name from a large lake (which is called Danào in the general language of these islands) which is found in that island, and into which many rivers flow. The same thing has happened

in that island as I have said of the others, namely, that its first owners and settlers must have been the ones who are now found on the uplands and in the fastnesses of the mountains and the crags. Since they are inclined to the mountains, they allowed the foreign traders to settle their seacoasts and rivers, as they were found uninhabited and defenseless; and when the latter had taken possession of the best of the territories and districts, the true owners were unable to expel the foreigners, since the latter were the more powerful and civilized.

401. From this fact comes the variety of tribes that have been found in that island of Mindanào: such as the Caragas, the Butuans, the Cagayans, the Dapitans, the Mindanaos, the Malanaos, besides the Tagabaloòyes, Manòbos, and Lutàos, and a great number of blacks, like those of whom we have already written. Of all of them, when we consider their first origin, there is no other inference than that it was in the neighboring islands of Bornèy, Macasàr, or the Malùcas, considering not only the Mahometan rites and their manner of dressing, but also the bonds of sympathy existing among them. For to this day they maintain their friendship and trade, and unite for the protection of one another, although they are not all Mahometans, and most of them are infidels, atheists, and total barbarians.

402. If we consider their more immediate origin, the Caragueños have the first place. They are so called from Caraga or Caràghas, which was formerly the name of all that coast which extended north and south from the point of Surigao to that of San Agustin, and then, turning toward the west, extended from Surigao and ran through Iligàn and as far as Dapitan, until in later times a division of districts was made. The Caragas are the oldest people in that island, and without the protection of any foreigners have maintained their location and their valorous courage—which was well known in former times, by the Visayans and even by all the islands of this archipelago. They have rendered greater their valor by the character of Christians (a fact which they owe to the burning zeal of the discalced Augustinian fathers, their first conquistadors), since their aid has been the most efficient and most formidable in the invasions of the Moros, in favor of the Church and its evangelical ministers. These people, if they are not Butuans, differ but little from them, and now they are united; by which we believe the origin of both to have been common.

403. The Butuans, worthy of eternal memory and thanks, as they were the first among whom the Catholic arms found shelter, come down from the village and river of Butuàn, the coast which looks to the north from Mindanào. It was the first soil where the famous Magallanes6 planted the domination of Jesus Christ and that of our Catholic king. All these, perchance, have the same origin as the Visayans and Pintados, because of their great

nearness to them. But they are the origin of the best blood and nobility of the Basilans and Joloans, for the king of Xolò even confessed that he was a Butuan. But he gives the lie to that by his barbarous procedure, for he has been the scourge most disturbing to these islands; while the Butuans have ever remained faithful, and have been vassals to God and to our Catholic monarch, following the example of the Caragas throughout.

404. The Cagayans take their name from Cagayàn el Chico [i.e., the little], which is [found by] following the coast from Butuan to the west and southwest. It is a bay with this name, which is not of ancient usage, but was given from the other Cagayàn, today a province in the upper part of the island of Luzòn, between Cape Bojeadòr and that of Engaño. These islanders are reduced and civilized, and differ but little from the previous ones [i.e., the Caragas] from which it is argued that they are not very different from them in their origin.

405. The Dapitans were a people who inhabited a closely hemmed-in strait between the island of Bohòl and that of Pànglao, and possessed the two shores of that strait. They conquered the Boholàns in a war, and assumed their name and territory. These new and triumphant Boholans left that island of Bohòl (the country having already been abandoned by the old Boholàns), and went to live in Dapitàn, located on the Mindanào coast, almost opposite Bohòl and Pánglao, whence they took the name Dapitàn. That name has been extended and preserved even to the present, because of their fortunate progress, and the friendly reception that our first conquistadors experienced from their noble loyalty and honorable valor. No other more remote origin is known of them, but it is conjectured to be like the others.

406. The Mindanàos and Malanàos are Moros, but they seem formerly to have been heathen (from which today they are considered as newcomers), and took their names from the celebrated lakes in their territories. Father Combès says that the Malanàos resemble the Visayans in their government, and the same is inferred of the Mindanàos; and, of both, that one must seek there their true origin. The Mindanàos have always remained Mahometans, and have not allowed the light of the gospel to enter. The Malanàos, with the district of Bayùg, were reduced to the yoke of Christ at another time, and were for some years constant to their baptisms by the discalced Augustinian fathers; but later they grew weary of it. At the present time some of those Moros have come to the governor of Manila with the title of ambassadors, from Bayùg and Malanào, in order to petition for the discalced Augustinian fathers as ministers of the gospel. This is not the first time when they have requested them, as well as the Franciscan religious, as I have seen in an original document. Since the fathers of the Society are those to whom those

places are adjudged for the preaching of the holy gospel, and since the disposition of that race is so faithless in their dealings, some suspicions have been aroused by those embassies, and we are endeavoring to probe their designs in coming.

407. The Tagabalòòyes take their name from some mountains which they call Balòòy, which are located in the interior of the jurisdiction of Caràga. They are not very far remote from and trade with the villages [of Caraga], and some indeed live in them who have become Christians. Others are being converted through the zeal and care of the discalced Augustinian fathers, who regard them as inhabitants of Baslig, which is their headquarters and priorate. Those people, as has been stated above, are the descendants of lately-arrived Japanese. This is the opinion of all the religious who have lived there and had intercourse with them, and the same is a tradition among themselves, and they desire to be so considered. And it would seem that one is convinced of it on seeing them; for they are light-complexioned, well built, lusty, very reliable in their dealings, respectful, and very valiant, but not restless. So I am informed by one who has had much to do with them; and all the above are qualities which we find in the Japanese.

408. The Lutàya nation, or the Lutaos, do not give much sign of their first origin, just as they do not evince any particular inclination for one kingdom or another. For since their natural disposition is one of self-interest and fickle, and delights in war, they make alliance now with the Joloans, now with the Basilans, and now with the Mindanaos—as quickly with one as another, and as quickly against their allies and with others. They show that they are Moros by the turban, the marlota,7 their arms, and their ceremonies; but they cannot be very ancient, since the Mahometans have not been very long in India and in these parts. The Lutaos could have come to these islands from the regions whence it is inferred that the others have come.

409. Of the mountain people without civilization or government, and with the life and custom of barbarians, it is inferred that they were some of these primitive possessors, who fled from the civilized foreigners. These people have various names in various settlements. In Yligàn and Sambòàngan, they are called Subànos; in Caràga, Manòbos; in Xolò, Guinuànos; in Basilàn, Sameacàs.8 And although some say that it is known that they are the descendants of the Malays, because their language is built on the general roots of the Malay language, there are religious (living today) who have lived there for many years, who assure me that they have not heard, in their method of talking with them, any Malay root. Consequently, since the islands are so strung out even as far as the islands of Bornèy and

Macasàr, and since the crossing is so easy, it is always inferred that their origin comes from that direction.

410. In the upper and northern part of the great island of Luzòn are the two provinces of Cagayàn and Ylòcos. Those people, as is inferred by Father Colin, are descended from Chinese or Japanese, because the graves of men of larger stature than the Indians have been found there, as well as some Chinese and Japanese jewels which have been preserved among them. If these should be slight indications—for they can proceed from various other circumstances, on account of the great nearness of China and Japan—they may aid in the foundation of that inference. But we cannot get any farther than conjectures, as in everything else, after so much toil. It serves only as a light, so that others may infer a truer origin. And the same is true of Pangasinàn, which lies next.

411. On this account, and without all the above serving as an obstacle, one can also conjecture the origin of other nations who are scattered through the innumerable islets of these archipelagoes; for they may proceed from all India extra Gangen and from its most renowned kingdoms, such as Siàn, Cambòja, China, Cochinchina, Tunquin, Japon, the Lequios, etc.—especially when not few affirm that the Chinese dominated all this archipelago, and that they were the first settlers of the Javas, as is mentioned by Barros. In fine, these are the conjectures that I have found. Other conjectures may be made from their customs and ceremonies, in the comparison of which the curious will find not a few strong arguments, if they read thoughtfully. But, at the last, God is the only one who knows the truth, to which our limited judgments cannot penetrate.

Chapter XL

Of the characteristics [genio] and genius [ingenio] of the Filipino Indians

[Paragraphs 412, 413, and a portion of 414 will be found in our Vol. XXVIII, pp. 220–223. The balance of the chapter follows.]

... They are the greatest enemies that the father ministers have. They are impious in the known necessities of their parents and relatives, and very charitable to a guest who comes to them and stays leisurely in their houses, without knowing him and without sending him away; and they do not even take warning by the experience of great inconveniences. Many other contradictions and contrarieties are found daily in these Indians by those who have communication with them and know them, so that in them vices are united to their opposed virtues, as if related. Only in the matter of lying there is no contradiction, for one cannot tell when they are not lying.

Neither does one know when they are thankful for any benefits received; for one could write by thousands the cases of their ingratitude which have been experienced—either not taking any account of the good that is shown them, regarding it as a justice due them; or paying with treachery pure and simple their greatest benefactors. All these are truths, and although (in the opinion of Terence) they gain hate for the one who states them, it is not right for the Indians who may read this to hate me; for I know it all by my own experience and that of other fathers of long standing—which indeed the Indians who know them recognize. In Nueva España and in Perû the same thing occurs, to about the same extent.

415. From this result other things, in the same father ministers, that seem also to be contradictions. For the minister of the Indians who loves them most would like not to have anything to do with them, but to be very distant from them; and if he succeeds in getting far away from them, then his love for them will not suffer it and he does not rest until he is with his Indians again. It is a providence of God, so that instruction may never be lacking to these wretched beings. This, I believe, appears like the discreet love with which Christ loved Judas, for an example to men; loving persons compassionately, and distinguishing their evil qualities, as things detestable. If all the above-mentioned contradictions of the Indians are malicious, or arise from their lack of understanding, let him who will examine it, for even in this have I found new contradictions. For some actions which appear simple are very doubly acts of malice; and quite the contrary also occurs at other times. In short, whether malicious or simple, their mental standpoint [*genio*] is incomprehensible, and consequently the merit that belongs to the ministers of instruction very great.

416. In regard to the mind [ingenio] and understanding of these natives, no general rules can be laid down; for there are rude and clever ones in all parts, although it be even among Spaniards and servants in courts. But speaking generally, all authors agree, and experience tells us the same, that the Filipinos are more clever than the Indians of other parts. They can learn any art at all with ease, and imitate with exactness any beautiful production that is placed before them. Consequently, they become so fine writers that the accounting-rooms are filled with them, as are also the secretariats, the courts, and the offices of private persons. But very rarely can one find the copy of an Indian which does not need revision, for they cannot cease lying even in writing; or else because of the little care with which they do it. This is very mortifying to those who dictate and correct. Some of them have been so capable that they have become officials in the accounting-rooms, and have served ad interim in the highest offices. Others serve as managers for alcaldes-mayor, and they have great knowledge of government business;

whether with a right conscience, God knows. There are others who have great cleverness for the management of a suit between litigants; and are so keen in entangling the parties that they cannot be disentangled with their laws, and recourse can be had to God alone. There are at present some of them who are printers, and they have sufficient intelligence. In their own political and civil government I have seen many Indians who are very capable, and who can discourse so powerfully, with their natural logic, that they convince. But as it is natural for them to be concerned only about the present time, they need some one to direct them so that they may not make any error in what they discuss. In short, their understandings are fastened with pins and attached always to material things, for they do not understand things with any depth. I believe that this is the reason why there is so little fruit produced from the constant repetition of sermons; for they are perplexed with abundant instruction, or else do not understand it. And although the sermon be very clear, and preached in their own native language, not one of them can yet repeat the substance of what he hears, although he understands it when it is preached. They are, however, very clever at handiwork, because of their great indifference in everything. On that account they can play well on all musical instruments; and their inclination for music is very great, and they make instruments. There are good singers among them, and these have positions, with a fitting salary attached, in all the churches, from the cathedral to the poorest ministry; and thus they are being trained, from the time when they sing soprano. They are fond of verses and representations. They are excellent translators, and can translate a Spanish comedy with elegance into verses of their own language. And thus, although all, both men and women, are fond of reading, they are indefatigable when verses are concerned, and they will act them out as they read them. Accordingly it results that they are clever for all things, in whatever duty they are set; and they would be more so if they were less lazy, or if their greed for temporal possessions were greater. On this account, they have always been, are, and will be poor, without caring for more than the food of the present day. I do not know whether this is a special providence of God for these poor wretches; for when they have a little wealth, as the vessel is so limited, immediately it swells out and then they do not know what to do; and, to let it be known that they are rich, they immediately waste it in expenses that are at best useless, until they remain as they were before. Thus their inclination [genio] is opposite to their judgment [ingenio] in this direction; and although they have sufficient intellect, they yield to their natural disposition [genio], which dominates them, and in this never allow themselves to be directed.

Chapter XLI

Of the letters, languages, and civilization of the Filipinos

417. Just as in Italia the Tuscan, Lombard, and Sicilian languages resemble one another, and in España the Castilian, Portuguese, and Valencian—for they all recognize one origin (namely, the Roman), although they are, strictly speaking, quite distinct among themselves—so it happens in the languages of these Philipinas Islands. The principal cultured languages found here at the conquest were six, namely, the Tagálog, the Visayan, the Pampanga, the Cagayan, the Ilocan, and the Pangasinan. It is a fact that all the languages here resemble one another, and he who knows one of them can easily talk the others, for the structure of them all differs but little. We trace them all to one origin, which cannot be other than the Malayan language, according to the comparison which has been made of words, and to the formation and construction of them all. Consequently, although these Indians have regarded their origin as distinct from that of various other nations, in the manner already mentioned, it is evident that the more immediate generations must have been Malays, since their letters and languages alone are found in these islands.

418. The vowels in the characters proper to their language are three in number, although they have the same value as our five in use; for the *E* and the *I* form one single letter, as do also the *O* and the *U*. The consonants are thirteen in number, but they are never used alone, for the vowel is always used with them. Thus by the use of the *C* and the *M* alone they write *cama* [*i.e.*, "bed"]. In order to pronounce words with other vowels, they make use of certain commas, placed either below or above. Consequently, as all the pronunciation of their writing for the most part makes it necessary for them to supply it at the expense of commas, the difficulty that was experienced was considerable, even in the natives themselves. On that account they have applied themselves so easily and willingly to our letters, in order to write in their own language.

419. Their own method of writing was peculiar, by writing the lines from top to bottom, beginning at the left hand and proceeding to the right. This bespeaks a very great antiquity; for the ancient custom of the Hebrews is to write lines, from the right to the left, as the Chinese do at the present time. But the latter write them from top to bottom, as was done in these islands. Diodorus Siculus, who wrote in the time of the emperor Cæsar Augustus, says that in an island of the torrid zone the people wrote from top to bottom, and employed only a few letters.

420. Before the people knew anything of paper in these islands they wrote on the smooth bark of bamboo, or on leaves of the many palms which

are found in these islands (and even yet this is done, in districts where there is no paper, or even that the schoolboys may not waste paper), the point of a knife or an iron, or some other material, serving as a pen (and now with birds' quills and ink). If it were a missive letter, they wrote it on palm-leaves, and folded it as we fold our letters. Some of them are much given to writing on the ground in a squatting posture, which is the usual way both men and women sit.

421. The cultured languages, as already stated, are six in number—for one cannot reckon the languages of the Negritos and mountain people as such, since each settlement has its own distinct language, which results from the lack of human intercourse. Among the cultured languages, the chief and mother languages are considered the Tagálog, the Pampanga, and the Visayan; and even among these the Tagálog is considered the most polished and powerful. That is not [for instance] because it lacks the *tu* [*i.e.,* "thou"]—which is well employed with their primitive pronoun *ycao* or *ca*, even with persons to whom the greatest respect is due—but on account of the *po* and *Po co*, which explains it, and signifies "Sir" [*señor mio*]. The first is used for men, and the second for women. Interwoven with the words, it shows reverence and courtesy; as, for example, in order to answer "Yes" to a woman one says *Oo, Po co*, an expression which without the *Po co* would be too familiar. In many other phrases in the Tagálog language is shown its seriousness and polish; those who write grammars of the language will be able to set them forth.

422. The natives of these islands employ innumerable other elegancies and courtesies, now in actions, now in words, now in names and titles, which they apply to themselves; these are various according to the difference of the provinces, and are too numerous to mention, for they are ceremonial, and they value their ceremonies highly. No one will pass in front of another, without asking permission, and in order to pass, he doubles the whole body with the most profound bow, at the same time lifting one foot in the air, and doubling the knee and lifting both hands to the face. If one has to talk to any person of higher rank, he shows all reverence and squats down [pone en cuclillas], with raised face, and waits thus, until he is asked his reason for coming; for to speak without being questioned would be a point of bad breeding. They employ many courteous acts and expressions in saluting one another when they meet; but these do not seem to me to be so many as in Nueva España, where people do not cease to use them until they lose sight of one another in the street. The Filipinos do this here with greater dignity and respect. When they write, they heighten their style with so many rhetorical phrases, metaphors, and pictures, that many who think

themselves poets would be glad to do as much; and yet this is only in prose. For, when it comes to poesy, he who would understand it must be very learned in their language, even among his own compatriots.

423. The names which they impose now are usually high-sounding. I know a Pius V, and a Philipe V; and, following this custom, they take as surnames the most honorable names of España. This is since they have known Castilians. But, even before, they could rival in this the kings of España; for just as the latter have been called "the Wise," "the Prudent," "the Chaste," etc., for the special virtues which have made them worthy of this glory, so here in the Philipinas, they called one "the Strong," another "the Splendid," and another "the Terrible," according to his deeds, or to those of his ancestors, or in accordance with various incidents that happened at birth. Now they are introducing the custom of taking the paternal name added to the baptismal name. However, when the first-born child comes to any one, the latter's Christian name is forgotten; for that instant they call the father by the name of his first-born for the rest of his life. If the name of the first-born is Rosa, the father is called Ama ni Rosa, or Pan-Rosa, which means "the father of Rosa." One must not then ask for such a man in any village by his Christian name (which is the one entered on the parish register), for there are many so named, so that he would not be known by that name. An author is not wanting to call this an instance of courtesy; but many times it serves as a dishonor, if they know him and call him, for example, "father of Judas." They employ many other names and endearing expressions in naming their children, relatives, and families, although I believe that the affection that they feel for one another has very little reality.

424. The "Don" of the Castilians is being rapidly introduced among the Indian chiefs, both men and women, of these islands. In olden times they did not lack a term proper to their own language by which they expressed it, as Lacan or Gat for the men, and Dayang for the women.

Chapter XLII

Of the physical features and clothing of these Indians

425. According to the differences in climate we find certain differences in the lines of the body and faces of the Indians, as has been stated above. But this difference amounts to but little. All of them are sufficiently corpulent, well-built, and well-featured, except that they are all flat-nosed; for the cartilage of the bridge of the nose does not come to a point as among Europeans. Consequently, there are no sharp noses among the full-blooded Indians. Some have tried to explain the color by saying that it is the color of cooked quinces, or brown, or an olive color. But it appears much stranger to me, and I have been unable to find a legitimate color to which to compare

it; for it is a brown color, but flushed with red.9 It is generally clearer in the women, and still lighter in all of the Visayans. The hair is black and lank, as is that of the Scythians, Getas [i.e., Getæ], and Turks, and is carefully tended with washings, and very fragrant oils, as was that of the Lycians. They assert that they do this in order to free it from grease (which is considerable), but a great part of it consists in vanity. Among the Tagálogs it is allowed to grow to the shoulders, among the Ilocans somewhat longer, and among the Visayans slightly longer or shorter, and done up; but the Cagayans leave it loose and hanging upon the shoulders. This custom must have appeared well to all of them, since everywhere they envy the one who has the longest and heaviest hair; and the same thing is seen among the women. It is indeed considered as an affront to cut the hair for any crime. The Zambals alone shave the head from the middle forward; and from the middle back, as far as the occiput, they wear a large shock of loose hair. Ribbons are never used to tie it, but with the hair itself men, women, and children make a knot near the crown of the head or the occiput, as do the Turks.

426. The eyes of all are very beautiful and large, either gray or black. The face is broad. The teeth are even and fine; formerly they covered them with ink or a varnish of a black color. Now that is no longer used except among the Tagabalòoyes of Caragà, of whom I have written; their beauty, lightness of complexion, and the features of their faces might deceive one, and they would be taken for Spaniards if they kept their mouths shut, and one did not see the black teeth. They also, especially the chief women, adorned the teeth with gold, with exquisite beauty. I do not know whether they waste the gold so now. All of the men are beardless in the face, but their bodies are sufficiently shaggy, as are those of all Asiatics. It is attributed to the temperature of the torrid zone in which we are. Who cares to study this more in detail would better read Fray Gregorio Garcia, the Dominican.10 In olden times the Indians removed and pulled out, as if it were a defect, any little hair that appeared on the face, with pincers of bamboo made for that very purpose. I have not read that they did this because they considered it a reproach to have a beard, as did those of Perù — who did the same, as I have read in the above-cited author.

427. The women (and in many parts the men, especially the mountaineers), have certain large holes in their ears, in which they place pendants and earrings of gold. They make the greater display of it according to the greater size and openness of the holes. Some women have two holes in each ear, for two kinds of earrings. This is usual among the Zimarrònes and blacks, for the civilized people have now adopted the custom of the Castilians in this regard.

428. In olden times the men wore their heads covered or wrapped about with a narrow strip of cotton or linen. Those who esteemed themselves as valiant men wore the two ends hanging to the shoulders. This they called the *potong*; and some wore this of colored cloth, to declare their chieftainship. No one could wear a red one unless he had killed at least one person, and he could not have it striped until he had killed seven. Now they wear neat white and black hats, which are woven from various materials which they gather in the field.

429. Of the mountain people it is already known that their own skin is their clothing, and that they only use the bahag, which is a linen or cloth which keeps in the privies. But the clothing of the men who live in villages is a half-shirt of linen, silk, or some other material—which, at the most, reaches to the navel; it is open to the air, and has wide sleeves without wristbands, and this is called the baro—and certain garments that they call saluàles, which correspond to our small-clothes or under-drawers. These are also loose and wide, and made of any kind of linen or other material; they do not open at the front, but at the side, and they are tied there. They never wear anything on feet or legs. The above is the whole amount of their clothing, and, at the most, a cord or belt at the waist, like a girdle, where they hang the knife. The chiefs and others wear, for church functions and other meetings of theirs, in addition to the said clothing, a long black garment reaching to the feet, with sleeves fitted at the wrists. This they call barong-mahaba, which signifies "long baro." It is an eminently modest and decent garment, and is worn loose and not girdled. For outside wear, these garments are of ordinary materials. For gala attire, they are of silk, and much worked with embroidery, except the long baro, which is always the same. Today the people of highest rank in the villages dress in the Spanish fashion, with coats, trousers, stockings, and shoes, although it is the most usual practice to wear stockings of natural skin, in the midst of all these adornments. In former times, their greatest care was exercised in supplying the lack of clothing with abundance of gold, with which they adorned all the body. That custom is still preserved, although not in the abundance of which we read earlier. In what they wore the full complement of their gala attire was a colored sash drawn up under the arm, which is no longer worn at the present time. All the clothing of the Filipino Indian is reduced to the above, and I believe that it is so throughout this archipelago, without any difference of special note.

430. The dress of the women is the baro already mentioned, but not so long, and only covering the breasts and hanging loose; and a garment as wide above as below, in which they envelope the body from the waist down, fastening one of the ends in the girdle in order to secure it. This garment is

called a tàpis. The mestizo women wear skirts with plaits and seams, with the opening at one side. The tàpis is the unchangeable costume of the Indian women of this archipelago, and this, at the most, is generally of silk, but of a modest hue, and of only one color. Upon their festival occasions the women—some for gala attire, or others, because they are more modest—wear white Spanish petticoats. Some wear an underskirt, especially within doors. But when they go abroad, the tàpis is [preferred] above all. Some of them wear garments resembling black mantillas, which they call cobìjas, with which they cover the whole body from the head down, in the manner of the mantillas of España. With this and the bits of gold that they wear on the body—in the ears, at the throat, on the wrists and fingers (and she who does not possess these ornaments must be very poor indeed)—they appear as Indian women in their wealth of gold, and are Indian women in their being and clothing. Now when the Indian women go abroad, they wear slippers embroidered with silk and gold; few and far between are those who wear shoes. Formerly, they wore a ribbon, of wrought gold which covered their foreheads and temples. Now, at the most, they usually wear a chased silver or gold nail, thrust through the knot of their hair. Women of a somewhat more advanced age and respect wear the long baro, which is made in the same manner as that of the men above described. It is certain that an Indian woman appears well in this manner, for there is no more modest dress for women that one can imagine.

431. The chief bodily adornments of the Visayans were the tattooing and designs which gave them the name of Pintados. They did this in the same manner as the Moro men and women, and it was the olden custom of the Huns, Gelones, and Agathyrsos; but the kind of the designs was according to the deeds and merit of each person. But that barbarous method of adornment was lost long ago, and has not been seen among them for many years. Perhaps they have erased those pictures with the water of holy baptism, since they embraced the true Catholic ceremonies.

Chapter XLIII

Of the false religion which these Indians held in their
heathendom; and of their superstitions and omens.

432. The great slothfulness and natural carelessness of these Indians is recognized by its results; for as yet not the slightest scrap of writing concerning their religion and ceremonies, or their ancient political government, has been found. Only by tradition and old songs which have been preserved from father to son, and from other things which they have still in use, has it been possible to trace somewhat of their antiquity by means of some careful ministers. The first who took his pen for this purpose, at the instance of the

superior government, was our venerable Fray Juan de Plassencia, one of the most zealous workers in the vineyard of this archipelago, in the year 1589.11 So great credence was given to him in this, that his relation of the customs of the Indians, having been received by the royal Audiencia, was imparted to the alcaldes-mayor of the provinces for their government. Later, in the year 1598, with but little difference in time, Doctor Don Antonio de Morga, auditor and lieutenant-governor of Philipinas, wrote his description. In it the same matter is treated, taken from the other. Our Fray Antonio de la Llave,12 afterward (in the year 1622) used this in his description. In the year 1660, Father Colin wrote his description, adding anew the best form. Since this is a matter in which we cannot exceed the ancients, yet with them all it will be necessary for me to write something, in order that I may not leave this treatise of my description faulty.

433. These Indians had various sorts of adorations: now to animals and birds, as did the Egyptians; now to the sun and the moon, as did the Assyrians. The Tagálogs adored now Tigmamanoquìn, which was a blue bird of the size of a turtledove; now the crow, which they called Meylupa, which signifies "Lord of the soil," as if he were the god Pan, or the goddess Ceres of the ancients; now the crocodile, which they called nono, which signifies "grandfather," to which they offered various sacrifices in order that it might not harm them. Sometimes they adored any old tree, especially the one they call balete, and even those now living show respect to it; now they adored and offered gifts to the stones, crags, reefs, and promontories of seas and rivers. All was the result of their natural fear, so that all these things should cause them no harm. Nevertheless, they had a knowledge of one sole God; and accordingly they adored Him as the principal God, and greater than all. The Visayans called Him Lauon, which signifies "ancient;" and the Tagálogs Bathalà Mey capal, signifying "God, the Maker, or Creator of all things."

434. Besides these they had other idols, which the Visayans called Diuata, and the Tagálogs, Anito, each of which had its special object and purpose. For there was one anito for the mountains and open country; another for the sowed fields; others for the sea and rivers; another for the house of their dwelling. These anitos they invoked in their work, according to the functions of each one. Among these they also made anitos of their ancestors, and to these was due the first adoration of all. The memory of this anito is not even yet erased. They kept some small badly-made figures of all these, of gold, stone, ivory, or wood; and they called them Lic-hà or Laràuan, which means a "figure" or "image" among them.

435. They also venerated as anitos those who came to disastrous ends, because either the lightning, or the shark, or the sword, killed them; for

they thought that such immediately went to glory, by way of the rainbow, which they call *balangao*. With such barbarous beliefs lived and died the old people, puffed up and vain, considering themselves as anitos. As such they caused themselves to be respected and worshiped; and buried after death in places set apart and of distinction among them all, as they were reverenced there. There are many cases of this known, and it required all the valor and zeal of the father ministers to destroy tombs, fell trees, and burn idols. But it is yet impossible to tear up the blind error of the *pasingtabì sa nonò*, which consists in begging favor from their aged dead whenever they enter any thicket or mountain or sowed fields, in order to build houses and for other things. For if they do not do this, they believe that their *nonos* will punish them with some evil result. This is found among an ignorant people without malice, who do not know why they do this, but only that they do it because they saw that their aged people do it here. The ministers labored hard to remove this error, especially in the remote villages; for in those that are now civilized the people at present laugh at it.

436. For all these adorations and sacrifices it is not evident that they had any common and public temple. For although these places had the name of simba or simbahan, which signifies "place of adoration and sacrifice," and the people attended them and resorted thither, they were not like our temples common to all, but, as it were, certain private oratories belonging to the houses of their chiefs, where those of their families, or their dependents, or those related by marriage, met to make a feast for any special object. For this purpose they made a bower in the house itself, which they call sibi, dividing it into three naves and lengthening the fourth. They adorned it with leaves and flowers on all sides, and many lighted lamps. In the middle was placed another large lamp, with many ornaments. Such was their simbahan or oratory. This feast was called pandot; it was their most solemn one, and lasted four days. During that time they played many musical instruments, and performed their adorations, which is called nag àanito13 in Tagálog. When the feast was ended and all the adornment removed, the place had no longer the name of church or temple, and remained a house like all the others.

437. Their sacrifices always redounded to the advantage of their bodies; for they were reduced to all eating, drinking, and making merry. In proportion to the motives, so were the ceremonies of their sacrifices. If it were only for the entertainment of their chief, they made a bower in front of his house, which they filled with hangings, according to their Moorish custom; and there they all ate, drank, danced, and sang. For this it was the usual practice to fetch a hog, which the catalôna or priestess ordered the

most graceful girl to stab with the knife, amid certain dances. That done, and the hog having been cooked according to their custom it was divided among all the company, as if it were a relic; and they ate it with great reverence and respect, with the other food of their feast. They drank more than they ate, as they always do. With this was ended the greatness of their sacrifice, without God to whom to offer it, or altar therefor.

438. If the sacrifice was for the health of some sick person, the priest of the sacrifice ordered a new house to be built at the expense of the sick one. That done (which took but a very short time, as the materials are close at hand, and many assemble for that purpose), they removed the sick person to it, and arranged what was to be sacrificed. That was sometimes a slave, but most generally some hog or marine animal; its flesh they set before the sick person, with other food according to their custom. The catalôna performed her usual dances, wounded the animal, and with its blood anointed the sick person, as well as some of the others among the bystanders. Then it was divided and cleaned, in order that it might be eaten. The catalôna looked at the entrails, and making wry faces and shaking her feet and hands, acted as if she were out of her senses—foaming at the mouth, either because she was incarnate as the devil, or because she so feigned so that credit might be given her. In this way she prophesied what would happen to the sick man, either adverse or propitious. If it were propitious, there was great feasting; and if adverse, means were not lacking to her to evade it—as they were also not lacking in case that her prophecy was not fulfilled. If the sick man died, she consoled them all by saying that their gods had elected him as one of their anitos, because of his prowess and merits; and she began to commend herself to this saint, and made them all commend themselves to him, and everything ended in drunkenness and rejoicing. Then the catalôna took all the gifts, which all had offered her according to their custom, and returned home, wealthier, but not with more reputation; for those who exercised that office among the Indians were held in no estimation, for they were considered lazy persons who lived by the toil of others.

439. When the sick person died, he was followed by the lamentation of his relatives and friends and even by other and hired mourners, who had that as their trade. In their lamentation they inserted a melancholy song, with innumerable extravagant things in praise of the dead. They bathed, smoked, and shrouded the corpse, and some embalmed it in the manner of the Hebrews, with certain aromatic liquors; and thus did they bury it, with all due respect.

440. The grave of the poor was a hole which was dug under the house itself, and was called *silong*. The rich and influential were kept unburied

for three days, amid the weeping and singing. A box or coffin was made out of one piece, which was the dug-out trunk of a tree; and the cover was tightly fitted on, so that no air could enter. There they buried the deceased, adorned with rich jewels and sheets of gold, especially upon his mouth. As the coffins were usually of incorruptible wood, which was used for this purpose, in this way some bodies have been found uncorrupted after many years.

441. The coffin with the body was placed in one of three places, according to the direction of the deceased: either in the highest story of the house itself, in a place like a cock-house, where they usually keep their treasures and other goods; or under the house, which is the silong, elevated from the ground; or if they place it in the ground itself, they dig a hole, and enclose it with a small railing and there they deposit the box with the body without covering over the hole. They buried others in the fields, and lit fires in the house, and then set sentinels so that the deceased should not come to take away the living with him. Others had themselves buried in a lofty place on the seashore, in order that they might be venerated and worshiped; and sentinels were posted so that no boats should pass there for a certain time.

442. Another box, filled with the best clothes of the deceased and various viands on their dishes, were set near the grave; if the deceased were a man, various weapons that he used were left there; if a woman, her loom, or other work-utensils that she had used. If the deceased had while living been employed in sea-raids, as a pirate, his coffin was made in the shape of a boat which they call barangay. As rowers they placed in it two goats, two hogs, two deer, or more, as they wished, male and female paired, with a slave of the deceased as pilot in order to take care of them all. Some food was put in for their sustenance, and when that food was consumed, they dried up with hunger and thirst, and all perished. If the deceased had been a warrior, a living slave, bound, was placed under him, and was left there to die with him. After the burial, although the lamentation ceased somewhat, the revelry in the house of the deceased did not cease. On the contrary, it lasted a longer or shorter time, according to the rank of the deceased.

443. On the third or fourth day of the funeral, all the relatives assembled at the house of the deceased, for they said that he returned that day to visit them. At the landing of the stairway of the house, they set water in a basin or tub, so that the deceased might wash his feet there, and rid himself of the earth of the grave. They kept a candle lit all that day. They stretched a petate, or reed mat, on the floor and sprinkled ashes on it, so that the deceased might leave the marks of his feet there. At meal time they left the best place at table vacant for the dead guest. They ate and drank, as at the most splendid banquet; and then spent the balance of the day in relating

and singing the prowess of the deceased; then each one went home. This ridiculous ceremony is called tibao. The Indians even yet retain the oldtime custom of this assembly, but all superstition and error have been removed from it, and they unite to pray for the deceased; but it is not without inconveniences that ought to be remedied.

444. The mourning consisted in fasting, and during the days of mourning they lived only on vegetables. This fasting or abstinence was called sipà by the Tagálogs. In dress the Visayans wore white, as do the Chinese in sign of mourning, and this is even yet the custom in some villages; but black is the most usual color for mourning in the rest of the islands. With this kind of mourning they cover all the body, so that the face may not be seen, especially if they are women and if the mourning is thorough. During the mourning the men may not wear a hat; but, instead, a black cloth wound about the head. They wear mourning for any deceased relative, even though he be related only very distantly; but the mourning is greater or less according to the degree of relationship, both in manner and in duration of time.

445. From the above is inferred the belief of these Indians in the transmigration of the souls of the deceased. In this they agree not only with the Chinese, who believe in this peculiar error, but also with other Indians whom Torquemada mentions in his second volume. The similarity that they might relate in rites, both with the Indians of Nueva España and Perû, and with other nations of greater antiquity, may be compared by the curious reader, by reading the entire book of the Origin of the Indians, and by tracing there that of these Indians.14.

446. It is an assured fact that the oldtime heathen of these islands knew that after this life there was another one of rest, or let us say paradise (for *Bathàla Maycapàl* alone in their belief lived in the sky); and that only the just and valiant, those who had moral virtues and lived without harming anyone, went thither to that place as a reward. In the same way, as all of them believed in the immortality of the soul in the other life, they believed in a place of punishment, pain, and sorrow which they called *casanàan*, where the wicked went, and where, they said, the devils dwelt. Consequently, the transmigration of the souls of their deceased to other living bodies was a sign of rest to them. Since no one desired his relatives to be numbered among the condemned in *casanàan*, the error of the Chinese found in them an easier entrance, for it was built upon the foundation of their own errors.

447. The superstitions and omens of these Filipinos are so many, and so different are those which yet prevail in many of them, especially in the districts more remote from intercourse with the religious, that it would take a great space to mention them. They merit tears, although they are all

laughable. They are being continually preached against, but we have not succeeded in extinguishing them; and the people obey the customs of their barbarous ancestors rather than the Christian prudence which the ministers teach them. And although I do not at this time consider it as an explicit error, ut in plurimum, yet the error implied in the tenacity with which these people follow the errors of their ancestors is dangerous.

448. Now they ask permission of the *nonos* for any task, with the *pasingtabi sa nono*. Now they have innumerable fears if the owl which they call *covàgo* hoots; if they find a snake in a new house, or on a journey that they have undertaken; if they hear anyone sneeze; if any rat squeals, or if the lizard sings, or if any dog howls; and other things like these. There must be no talk of fish in the house of the hunter, nor of hunting nor dogs in that of the fisherman; while in neither the one nor the other house must there be any mention of new implements for work, unless they have already been used. Sailors must name nothing of the land, nor landsmen anything of the sea: for all these were omens.

449. Pregnant women could not cut their hair, for they said that the children that they would bear would have no hair. When a woman is about to give birth, some men undress until they are stark naked. Then taking shields and catans, one takes his stand in the silong, and another on the ridge of the house, and they continually fence with the wind with their catans as long as the parturition lasts. I have removed some from this performance by force of punishment. They say that it is to keep the patiànac and the osuàng away from the woman. These are witches among them who come to obstruct the success of the childbirth, and to suck out the souls of children; and the people act thus in order to prevent them. He who does not wish to have this observed in public, through fear of punishment, removes his wife to another house for the parturition, if he thinks that the witch is in his. The procurer of this witch they say is the bird tictic,15 and that this bird, by flying and singing, shows the witch or osuàng the house where there is a parturition, and even guides him to work other misfortunes. Consequently, whenever they see or hear the tictic, they all grow melancholy, in their fear lest some harm come to them.

450. They greatly fear and reverence the tigbàlang or bibit. This is a ghost, goblin, or devil; and as it knows the cowardice of these Indians, it has been wont to appear to them in the mountains—now in the guise of an old man, telling them that he is their nono; now as a horse; and now as a monster. Consequently, the Indians in their terror make various pacts with it, and trade their rosaries for various articles of superstitious value, such as hairs, grass, stones, and other things, in order to obtain all their intents and free themselves from all the dangers. Thus do they live in delusion until

God wills that the evangelical ministers undeceive them, which costs no little [effort], because of the very great fear with which they are filled.

451. In order to discover any theft, they generally burn fresh rock-alum, and after it has vaporized and then crystallized they say that the figure which those crystals form is the living picture of So-and-so, and that he is the author of the theft. Since they believe such nonsense as easily as it is difficult to make them believe the divine mysteries, they all agree to that statement, even though the face should be that of a dog; and they make a charge in court against So-and-so, and impute the theft to him. Sometimes they take a screen or sieve (which they call bilào), in which they fasten some scissors in form of a cross, to which a rosary is hung. Then they proceed to call the name of each one who is present at this exercise. If the bilào shakes when the name of Pedro is called, then that poor Pedro is the robber, and pays for the theft, without having perhaps eaten or drunk of it.16 Sometimes they light a candle to the saint of miracles, my St. Anthony of Padua, misapplying his peculiar protection for all lost things; they believe that if the flame of the candle should flare up in the direction of any of those present at this act, he is thus shown to be the robber. For these and like deceitful artifices, there are not wanting masters, Indian impostors, both men and women, who, in order to gain money, deceive the simple-minded in this manner, without paying any heed to the claims of conscience in these wrongs.

452. The different kinds of these ministers of the devil in the olden days, so far as I have examined them, are twelve, and they are as follows, according to their own old names for them: sònat, catalònan, mangagávay, manyisalàt, mancocòlam, hoclòban, silàgan, magtatangàl, osuàng, mangagayoma, pangatahòan, and bayòguin.

453. The sònat was equivalent to a bishop among them; and they all reverenced him as one who pardoned sins, and ordained others as priests and priestesses. They expected salvation through him, and he could condemn them all. This office was general throughout these islands, but it was held only by the chiefest and most honored, as it was of great esteem among them. It is said that this office came from the Borneans. Some try to make out that he was the master of a kind of exercise that is not decent, but I have found nothing certain among the much that I have examined.

454. The catalònan (as remarked above) was the priest or priestess of their sacrifices; and although his office was an honorable one, it was only while the sacrifice was pending, for after that they paid but scant attention to him.

455. The *mangagàvay* were the sorcerers who gave and took away health and life by their sorceries. It was an office general throughout this archipelago.

456. The manyisalàt was the sorcerer appointed for lovers. The mancocòlam was the sorcerer or witch who belched forth fire from himself, which could not be extinguished with any application except by his rolling himself in the ordure and filth that falls from the houses into the silong; and the master of the house where he rolled himself died and there was no remedy. The hoclòban was another kind of sorcerer more efficacious than the others, since without any medicine he could kill, overturn houses, and work other destruction. This is in Catanduanes, but the two preceding ones are general.

457. The *silàgan's* duty was to draw out the entrails and eat them, from all persons whom he saw dressed in white. That happened toward Catanduanes; and it is not fable, since our Fray Juan de Mérida buried a Spanish clerk in Calilàya to whom this misfortune had happened. The *magtatàngal* is said to have been a man who left his body without head and intestines, and that the head wandered about hither and thither during the night in different parts of the world, and in the morning reunited with his body, leaving him alive as before. This story is current in Catanduànes, but it is regarded as a fable, although the natives assert that they have seen it.

458. We have already spoken of the *osuàng*. It is only added that human flesh is his usual food. They all saw this one flying, but this is told in the Visayas and not in Tagalos.

459. The *mangagayòma* was the sorcerer who made use of the natural remedies in his sorceries; but those remedies were often corrupted by pacts with the devil. The *pangatahòan* is the same as the soothsayer, who prognosticated the future; and this notion was general throughout this archipelago. The *bayòguin* was an effeminate man [*hombre maricon*], inclined to be a woman and to all the duties of the feminine sex.

460. This is sufficient as an index of innumerable other errors, superstitions, and omens, in which their ancients were submerged, and some of their descendants now follow their footsteps. However, I am of the opinion that it is born rather of their simplicity than of their malice, ut in plurimum. Yet I would not be so bold as to assert that there are not some who make their contracts with the devil; and, with or without contracts, it is certain that many enchantments are found here, whence follow deaths to some and extraordinary accidents to others. And although that can be attributed to the multitude of herbs of which they have good knowledge, they always leave suspicion of some diabolical art.

461. The oaths which were and are most usual in these Indians are execratory. Since they lie so much, I do not know why they are not brought to confusion in the promissory notes that are always furnished with curses. In the oath of allegiance which the people of Manila and Tondo took to our Catholic monarchs in the year 1571, they confirmed that promise of their obedience in this manner: "May the sun split us through the middle; may we be devoured by crocodiles; may our women not show us favor or affection"—if they should fail to keep their oath. Sometimes they took the pasambahan, which was, to draw the figure of any wild and monstrous animal, and ask to be torn to pieces by that animal if they broke their contract or agreement. Sometimes they lit a candle, and declared that, just as the candle, so might they be melted, if they did not fulfil their promise. Now this is somewhat better, but not, their perjuries; for with great ease and frequency one catches them in false oaths in legal instruments. This is well known, and therefore should be well punished.

Chapter XLIV

Of the former government and social customs of these Indians

462. I have already said that our brother and venerable father Fray Juan de Plassencia wrote in the convent of Nagcarlàn and signed (October 24, 1589) a relation describing all the old customs of these Indians, in obedience to a request and charge of the superior government. That relation appeared to all a very truthful statement, as, in order to make it, his examination and vigilance were rigorous.

463. Of this relation I have already used what I thought ought to be set down in their fitting places. Now I shall say in substance what he tells when speaking of the social customs of the Indians and their old-time government, with some additions which serve for the better understanding of the matter.

464. These Indians were not so lacking in prudence in the olden time that they did not have their economic, military and political government, those being the branches derived from the stem of prudence. Even the political government was not so simple among all of them that they did not have their architectonic rule—not monarchic, for they did not have an absolute king; nor democratic, for those who governed a state or village were not many; but an aristocratic one, for there were many magnates (who are here called either *maguinòos* or *datos*), among whom the entire government was divided.

465. In the olden days, when, as most of them believe, the Malays came to conquer these islands, they called the boat or ship by the name of barangay, which is well known and much used in these times. In this boat

came a whole family, consisting of parents, children, relatives, and slaves, under the government of one who was the leader, captain, or superior of all. In some districts, this man was called maguinòo, and in others dato. And in proportion as they continued to people this archipelago in this manner, it filled up with families and they appropriated their places of settlement, each of them seeking its own convenience for its maintenance and living. And there they lived governed by their own chiefs, not with a hard and fast rule, but all in friendly relations. By virtue of this friendship they were obliged to aid their chief, both in his wars and in the cultivation of his fields; and all to aid one another mutually. But no one was able to usurp the property which belonged to another, even though he were of the same barangay.

466. This barangay consisted of about one hundred persons, more or less, according to the number that they knew were sufficient for their territory. If perchance those of one barangay did any injury to another, cruel wars broke out between them, as broke out between the chiefs of Manila and Tondo when the Spaniards came in to plant with the faith the Catholic dominion, and with it the true peace, which now they enjoy with tranquillity. These chiefs or maguinóos, although some were so by inheritance, commonly did not get these offices by virtue of their blood, but by their merits; or because some one had more power, more wealth, more energy, or more moral virtue than any of the others. This method of government has always seemed so good to these Indians that it is the form followed in all the villages, and all the tributes are divided among various heads of barangays, in accordance with the enumeration of the villages; and those heads are the ones who look after the collection of the royal income, and see that the Indians live like Christians. They must also, by reason of their office, give account to the father minister and the alcalde-mayor of their province, in case there is any fault to find with their respective barangays.

467. No Indian could pass voluntarily from one barangay to another without the payment of a certain sum, which was established among them, and unless he made a great feast to all the barangay which he left. It was much more difficult if they were married. If a man of one barangay married a woman from another, the children had to be divided between the barangays, as was also done with the slaves.

468. The classes of people mentioned in that early age by our brother Plassencia (besides that of chief or dato) are three, as follows. One class is that of the nobles, whom they call mahadlìcas. This word signifies, according to the best vocabularies of the Tagálog language, those who are free, and who were never slaves. The second class are called pechèros; and the third are those who were slaves legitimately. Although I find in one vocabulary

that mahadlìca is rendered as "freedman," still I find that freedman is rendered by timava in most trustworthy vocabularies. And although in the common practice of the Tagálog speech, one now says minahadlìca aco nang panginoongco, that is, "My master freed me," I do not believe that it is so; for mahadlìca properly signifies "to give freedom to the slave," only because absolute liberty is its peculiar signification, and they make use of this term when it was given to a slave. Thus this term gives liberty, and the slave remains free from all slavery in the uttermost of its meaning. It is certain that the term timava is more correctly used to signify the freedman. Consequently, the Tagálog speech applies it and uses it, not only to express the liberty of the slave, but also for him who breaks the cord at the gallows and is freed from punishment; and for any fierce animal which makes sport of bonds. They only lengthen somewhat the accent of the last syllable in the latter sense, and say nagtitimavà .

469. The pechèros were the ones called alìping namamahay. Although in strictness, in the Tagálog, the term alìpin signifies "slave," the pechèro was not properly a slave, for he always remained in the house and could not be sold. Consequently, this term could only be applied to express their method of service, namely, an up-stairs servant, as I understand it. These pechèros were married. They served their masters, whether datos or not, with the half of their [time in the] fields, or as was agreed upon at the beginning; and served them as rowers. But they lived in their own houses with their wives and children, and were lords of their property, lands, and gold; and their masters had not the slightest liberty of action or dominion over those things. And, even though they should fall by inheritance to a son of their master, if the former went to live in another village he could not take them from their own native village; but they would serve him in their own village, according to their ability, as they served their former master.

470. The slaves who were strictly such were called alìping sa guiguilir. This term comes in strict Tagálog to mean the servants below stairs; for the term guilir signifies "the lower part of the house," or "its lower entrance." These were bought and sold, or acquired by war, although those who were born in a family were seldom sold, for affection's sake. Such served their master in all things; but the latter would give them some portion of his field, if they were faithful and zealous in their labor. If they gained anything by their industry, they could keep it. If they were slaves because of debt, a condition that was very frequent among them, when the debt was paid they were free; but they were also obliged to pay for their support and that of their children. At times it was usual to transfer the debt to another, for the obtaining of some profit; and the poor wretches remained slaves, even though such was not their condition. Much of this is found yet, although

not with the rigor of slavery, but by the force of obligation; but these poor pledged creatures suffer a certain kind of slavery in their continuous and toilsome service. The authorities ought to employ all their care for the uprooting of so keenly felt an abuse.

471. If perchance these slaves sa guiguilir acquired any gold through their industry, they could ransom themselves with it and become pechèros; and that ransom did not cost so little that it did not amount to more than five taes of gold, or thereabout. If one gave ten or more, then he became free from every claim, and became a noble. For this purpose a certain ceremony took place between the master and the slave, namely, the division between the twain of all the furniture that the slave used—and that with so great strictness that, if a jar was left over, they broke it and divided up the bits; and if it were a manta, they tore it through the middle, each one keeping half.

472. From the time when our brother Plassencia explained this difference of slaves, many acts of injustice which the Indians practiced on one another were remedied; for they made slaves of those who were never so, because, as the term *alipin* is so confused, and the alcaldes-mayor did not know the secret, they declared one to be a slave in all rigor, because the Indians proved that he was *alipin*, which signifies "slave," being silent, in their malicious reserve, as to whether he was *namamahay* or *sa guiguilir*. There were many such acts of trickery.

473. Those born of father and mother who were mahadlìcas were all also mahadlìcas, and never became slaves except by marriage. Consequently, if a mahadlìca woman married a slave, the children were divided. The first, third, and fifth belonged to the father, while the mother had the second, fourth, and sixth, and they alternated in the same way with the other children. If the father were free, then those who pertained to him were free; but slaves, if he were a slave. The same is to be understood in regard to the mother and her children. If there were only one son, or if there were an odd number, so that one was left over in the division, the last was half free and half slave. However, it has been impossible to determine at what age the division was made, or at what time. The slavery of these children followed the native condition of their parents in all things, and the children were divided as they pertained to them, whether they were male or female, as they were born. The same thing occurred when one was poor, and did not have the wherewithal with which to endow or buy his wife for marriage; and then, in order to marry her, he became her slave. Hence it resulted that the free children who belonged to the mother were masters and lords of their own father, and of the children who belonged to the father, their own brothers and sisters.

474. If the mahadlìcas had children by their slaves, mother and children were all free. But if the mahadlìca had intercourse with the slave woman of another, and she became pregnant, the mahadlìca gave the master of the slave woman one-half tae of gold because of the danger of the death of her who was pregnant, and because that her legitimate master was deprived of the services of the pregnant woman, by reason of him. When the woman gave birth, one-half the child remained free, and the father was bound to take care of its support; and, if he did not do that, he meant that he did not recognize the child as his, and it remained all slave.

475. If any free woman had children by any slave who was not her husband, all were free. If a free woman married a half-slave, the children were slaves only to the one-fourth part, and they considered that in the question of their service. The service was divided among all those who were considered as masters, by weeks or months, or as the masters might agree. But they had the right because of the parts that were free to compel their masters to free them for a just price, which was appraised in proportion to the character of their slavery. But if one were wholly slave, he could not compel his master to free him for any price, even if he became a slave only for debt provided he did not pay the debt at the expiration of the time.

476. Another form of servitude was found among them, which they called *cabalangay*; it included those persons who begged from the chief who was head of their barangay whatever they needed, with the obligation of serving him whenever they were summoned to row, work in his fields, or serve at his banquets—they helping to meet the expense [of these] with the tuba or quilàng, which was their wine. Thus did their headman give them what they needed, with this agreement.

477. This tyranny of slaves was so extensive in this archipelago that when our Spaniards conquered it, there were chiefs with so many slaves—of their own nation and color, and not foreign—that there were those who had one, two, and three hundred slaves; and most of these were not slaves by birth, but for slight reasons, and even without reasons. For since their best kind of property, after gold, consisted in slaves, as their own conveniences were increased considerably by their services, they expended care in nothing to a greater extent than in increasing the number of their slaves; now by usury and interest, in which they had no respect for their own parents and brothers and sisters; now by petty wars and engagements among themselves, in which the prisoners became slaves; now by the punishment for some slight crime such as for not having observed the interdict on speaking during the funeral obsequies, or if anyone passed by the chief's wife while she was taking a bath, or if, while the chief was passing by the house of any timava, some dust accidentally fell on him. Or they were made slaves because of

other reasons, as tyrannical, as trivial, such as are natural for those who have not the light of the holy gospel.

478. After this [report of Father Plassencia] was promulgated, the above abuse was so thoroughly removed that now there is not the slightest amount of slavery among the Indians, in accordance with apostolic briefs, which have been confirmed by various royal decrees of our Catholic monarchs. Thus we are all soldiers of one and the same divine Lord; all militia under the holy cross, which is our Catholic standard; and citizens and sharers of the heavenly Jerusalem, which is our kingdom. Thus do we live in these islands, Spaniards and Indians, all vassals of one Catholic monarch in regard to human matters. This point can be seen in extenso in the Politica Indiana of Solorzano in book 2, chapter i.17

479. The laws or regulations by which these Indians governed themselves were founded on the traditions and customs of their ancestors, which were not barbaric in all things as were they. For they were directed to venerate and obey their parents, and to treat their elders with the due respect; and individuals to follow the dictate of the community of the village; and to punish crimes, etc.

480. Their judges for this were the chief or dato aided by some old men of his own barangay, or of another barangay if necessary. Or they themselves appointed a judge-arbiter, even if he were of a distinct barangay or village. If there were a suit with rival parties, they tried first to come to an agreement. If they would not agree, an oath was taken from each one, who declared that they would do as the judges should sentence. Having done that, witnesses were examined summarily. If the testimony was equal for each side, then the litigants were reconciled. If the evidence were in favor of one of them, the suit was sentenced in his favor, and the defeated one was notified. If he would not admit the sentence willingly, the judge and all the others proceeded against him, and by way of execution deprived him of all the gold to which he had been sentenced. The greater part of it went to the judges of the case, and to pay the witnesses on the victorious side; while the poor litigant had the least of all, being content with only the glory of victory.

481. Criminal cases were judged according to the rank of the murderer and the murdered. For if the murdered man were a chief among them all his relatives went to the house of his murderer, and the houses of his relatives, and they had continual wars one with the other until—the old men stepped in and acted as mediators, with the declaration of the amount of gold that ought to be given as a payment for that murder. The judges and the chief old men took one-half that sum, and the other was divided among the wife, children, and relatives of the deceased. The penalty of death was never

adjudged except when the murderer and his victim were so poor and so destitute that they had no gold for satisfaction and expenses. In that case either his own chief or dato killed the criminal, or the other chiefs speared him after he had been fastened to a stake, and made him give up the ghost by spear-thrusts.

482. In the matter of thefts in which the thief was not known with certainty, and those under suspicion were many, they made a sort of general purgation performed in the following manner. Each one was obliged to bring in a bundle of cloth, leaves, or anything else in which the stolen article could be hidden. Then the fastenings were unwound, and if the stolen goods were found in any of them, the matter ceased, and no investigation was made as to whom the bundle belonged, or who had stolen it. But if the stolen goods were not found, the following means were employed. Each suspect was made to enter a river with a good bottom, staff in hand, and then all at once plunged under. The first one who came up, because he could no longer hold his breath, was regarded as the thief of the stolen goods, for his remorse of conscience, they said, took away his breath. On that account, many were drowned for fear of punishment. The other means was to place a stone in a vessel of boiling water, and to order the suspects to take it out with the hand, and he who refused to put in his hand paid for the theft. Another means was to give them each a wax candle with wicks of equal length, and of the same size and weight, all lit at the same instant; and he whose candle went out first was regarded as the culprit. Of all this, and in all the other suits and civil or criminal causes, the chief took half the gold, and the other half was divided among joint judges and witnesses; and scarce a bit was left for the poor creditor, litigant, or owner. This was one of the greatest sources of gain to the chiefs and datos, and offered the best opportunity for them to exercise their tyranny with the poor, even were the latter guiltless.

483. Adultery was not punishable corporally, but the adulterer paid a certain sum to the aggrieved party; and that was sufficient so that the honor of the latter was restored and his anger removed. They paid no attention to concubinage, rape, and incest, unless the crime were committed by a timava on a woman of rank. On the contrary, the committal of such sins openly was very common, for all of them were very much inclined to this excess; but I cannot find that they were addicted to the sin against nature in the olden time. Verbal insults, especially to chiefs, women, and old men, were regarded as deserving the severest kind of punishment, and it was difficult to obtain the pardon of the aggrieved.

Chapter XLV

Of other customs of these peoples, and in regard to their
marriage, dowries, children, and issue

484. It is not known whether these natives divided the time into hours, days, weeks, months, or years, or made any other division of time. As this was necessary to them for the reckoning of their commerce, trade, and contracts (in which they all engaged), they used for reckoning their times of payment, and for other transactions and business of their government—for the hours, the state of the sun in the sky, the crowing of the cock, and the laying time of the hens, and several other enigmas which are still employed in the Tagálog speech. To keep account of the changing of seasons, they knew when it was winter or summer by the trees, and their leaves and fruit. They knew of the division into months or years by moons. Consequently, in order to designate the date of payment, they said "in so many moons, in so many harvests, or in so many fruitings of such and such a tree." These were the methods employed in their trading and government.

485. The days were reckoned by the name of the sun, namely, arao. Thus the Tagálogs now reckon ysang árao, "one day;" dalauang árao, "two [days]," and so on until they have the difference of weeks, which they call by the name Domingo, saying "so many Domingos."18 The night is called gab-ì; and the day arao, from the name of the sun. The months were named and reckoned by the name of the moon, namely, bovan in Tagálog. Thus did they divide the seasons after their own manner, and in their own speech. Only there are no terms to indicate the hours of the clock [in their speech]; and now the Castilian [names of] hours are Tagalized, in order to indicate the hours of time. They call the clock horasan, that is, "a thing in which one sees the hours;" whether in its place or in the instrument made for it.

486. They expressed "the year" in their old speech by the word taòn. It is metaphorical, for it really means "the assembling of many," and that they have joined together months to make one year. They had a word to signify seasons and climates, namely panahon. But they never knew the word "time" [tiempo], in its general sense, and there is no proper Tagálog word for it; but they use the Spanish word only, corrupted after their manner, for they make it tiyempo.

487. Their business and contracts were for the greater part illegal, filled with usury, interest, and tricks; for each one thought only of increasing his own profits, and paid no attention to his nearest relatives. Consequently, loans with interest were very common and generally practiced (and even yet this archipelago is not free from this abuse, nor have the difficulties experienced in the confessional ceased); and the interest increases to a very

high figure, the debt doubling and increasing for so long a time as the debt is delayed, until it results that the debtor, his wealth, and his children, are all slaves. Their general business was the bartering of one product for another (and it is still much in vogue)—food, mantas, birds, stock, lands, houses, fields, slaves, fisheries, palms, nipa-groves, woodlands, and other similar products. Sometimes those products were sold for a price, which was paid in gold, according to the terms of the agreement. Thus they traded among themselves with the products of their own lands, and with foreigners from other nations for products peculiar to them; and for this they were wont to have their deferred payments, their days of reckoning, and their bondsmen who were concerned therein—but with exorbitant profits, because they were all usurers.

488. In regard to money of silver or gold they did not possess it in that [early] time. Those metals were employed in their trading only by the weight, which was used alone for silver and gold; and that weight they called talaro, and was indicated by balances, like ours. They reckoned and divided by this. And after they learned about money they gave to each piece its proper name, taking the coin that we call "tostòn," or "real of four," as the basis for greater sums. This they called salapì, although that is the common term for all kinds of money. They divided the salapì into two cahàtis, the cahàtis into two seycapat, the seycapat into two seycávalos, the seycávalo into two calatíos, the calatìo (which they call aliu) into the cūding, etc. All this division was regulated by tostòns in this manner: the cahàti signifies one-half tostòn; seycàpat, the fourth part; seycávalo, the eighth; calatìo is the Tagálog cuartillo;19 and so on. In order to say "three reals," they say tatlongbahagui, that is, three parts of the tostòn. From the tostòn on, they count up to ten, and from ten to twenty, etc. Consequently, in their language they use this expression for ours, saying, "I ask ten and one more," or "I ask one for twenty;" and so on. But now since they know what pesos are, that is, reals of eight, some of them reckon by pesos, which is more familiar to the Spaniards. But most of them do not forget their salapìs, nor the method of reckoning used by the ancients.

489. The gold, which they call guinto, was also reckoned by weight. The largest weight is the tàhel, which is the weight of ten reals of silver—or, as we say, of one escudo. The half-tàhel is called tingà , which is the weight of five reals. The fourth part is called sapaha, which is two and one-half reals. They also used other metaphorical terms (as the Spanish do the term granos), and said sangsàga, which is the weight of one red kidney-bean [frixolillo] with a white spot in the middle.

490. In order to weigh bulkier things, such as wax, silk, meat, etc., they had steelyards, which they called *sinantan*, which was equivalent to ten *cates*,

of twenty onzas [*i.e.*, ounce] apiece. The half of that they called *banal*, which was five cates; and the half of the cate they called *soco*. Consequently, these old weights having been adjusted to the Spanish weights by the regulations of the year 1727, one cale is equivalent to one libra, six onzas; one chinanta to thirteen libras, and twelve onzas; hence one quintal, of eighty of the old cates, corresponds to four arrobas and ten libras of our weight. A *pico* of one hundred cates is equivalent to five arrobas, twelve and one-half libras, in the new arrangement. As in the case of gold, one tàhel must weigh one and one-fourth onzas in our weight.

491. In regard to the measures of quantity which the ancients used, they were the same as those we now see: cabàn, ganta, half-ganta, and chupa. The city has regulated them by the Spanish measures in the following manner. The caban, which signifies "box" [arca] in their own Tagalog speech, is equivalent to one fanega of the standard of Toledo. The ganta (gantang in Visayan, and salòp in Tagálog) is equivalent to one half of a Toledo almud, which is the hal-zelemin in other territories. The half-ganta is equivalent to one cuartillo, which is called pitìs or caguiina in Tagálog. The chupa is the eighth of the half-almud of Toledo, which is called gàtang in Tagálog, and also gahinan, for it is the ration of cleaned rice sufficient for each meal of a man. The act of measuring in this manner is expressed by the word tàcal among the Tagálogs. When the king issues orders for rice, it is reckoned by cabàns of twenty-four gantas apiece; and now it is known that it is of pálay rice, which is rice with the husk and uncleaned. When vouchers are issued for the stipends and the support of the religious ministers, the reckoning is by fanegas, at the rate of two cabàns of twenty-four gantas each, of the said pálay rice uncleaned. And because his Majesty chooses that they give it to us very clean, it is now ruled in the royal accountancy that forty-eight gantas of the fanega of pálay is equivalent to a basket of twenty gantas of bigàs, which is the name for cleaned rice. Henge the king in his charity, in order to give us our sustenance in the rice without waste, gives valuation to the measure at his own pleasure, for the rice with husk, so that the quantity may be doubled. The estimation of the king in this is not the same as looking into the hollow measure in its strict capacity, as has been already explained.

492. They also measure by brazas and palmos (but for the vara, I find no proper Tagálog term, but only the Spanish). The braza is called dipa; that of the city is of sixty points, into which the six feet contained in it are divided. The palmo is called dancal. Tumòro is one jeme.20 Sangdamàc is the whole width of the hand with the five fingers. Sangdali is the width of one finger; and sucat is the act of measuring in this manner.21

493. So was their usage in their business. Although there are no arithmetical numbers among their characters, such as we use, they counted with little stones, making small heaps of them, and made use of the natural words of their own speech, which are very expressive in Tagálog; and they did not feel their ignorance of the numbers written in their own characters; for they could express the highest number very clearly by word of mouth.

494. The maritime folk were wont to go out upon many raids, and those ashore to set strange ambushes for their robberies, to the great loss of life. Their arms were bow and arrow, and a short lance resembling a dart, with the iron head of innumerable shapes; and some without iron, the points being made from the bamboos themselves, or from stakes hardened in the fire. They used cutlasses; large and broad daggers, of excellent quality, with sharp edges; and long blowpipes, through which they discharged arrows dipped in poison. Their defensive arms were wooden shields, breastplates of rattan or thick cord, and helmets of the same material.

495. Among so many barbaric customs, the universality of their vices prevailed; and they were infidel, tyrannical, and unchaste. They regarded virginity as an opprobrium, and there were men who received a salary for the office of deflowering [the girls] of their virginity. No woman, married or single, assured her honor and credit, unless she had some sweetheart; and although this was so honorable for the women, it was considered a dishonor to give the liberty of her body freely. Now the women are modest in their behavior, but easy, if they are sought, as the smoke from the fire of their beginnings still endures. At the birth of males, and even the females, the midwives themselves made easier for them the carnal act, by cutting off I know not what from their organs. And now that the midwives do not do it, there is no lack of the introduction of this abuse among the boys; but it is assured that this is not the circumcision of the Jews. The devil influenced them in other curious ways for the greater sensuality and duration in their carnal acts, methods which are now completely extinct. But they have sufficiently caught the plague of sodomy from the Japanese and Chinese; and I have already seen some persons burned, in my time. In short, men and women never think of being chaste, so that among the most holy all their thought is of their marriages.

496. At the present time we have always tried to see that the brides and grooms are always of equal rank and condition. It was not usual for them to have more than one own wife, and one own husband; but those who

were chiefs and wealthy were allowed to have some slaves as concubines, especially if their own wives did not prove fruitful. Only among the Visayans did the first religious ministers of the gospel find established the custom of one man having many legitimate wives, and that of large dowries, which was no small obstruction to the planting of the gospel. The general rule was for each man to have one legitimate wife; and they tried to obtain one who was of their own family, and even very closely related to them, barring out the first degree, for that was always a direct impediment to their marriage. Their marriages were not indissoluble, as are those of Christians. For if the consorts returned the dowry, one to the other, the one at fault to the one without blame, that was sufficient for repudiation; and they could marry others, unless the couple had children, in which case all the dowry was given to these. If profits had been made with the lapse of time, while they had lived together, those profits were divided between them both, if the gains were in common. But if they were the secret gains of one of them, then that one kept them.

497. The dowry, which is called bigaycàya, was always given by the man (and it is even yet given), the parents of the girl determining the sum beforehand, at the time when they discussed the marriage. The parents of the bride received that dowry, and neither the bride nor her parents contributed any fund. The dowry was set according to the rank of the contracting parties; and if, perchance, the parents of the bride asked more than the ordinary sum, they were under obligations to bestow some gift to the married couple to suit the occasion as, for instance, a couple of slaves, some small gold jewel, or a bit of cleared land—for cultivation, as I have seen practiced even yet, and which they called pasonòr. In this bigaycaya was included what they called panhimùyat, which was the sum that had to be paid to the mother of the bride in return for her care and labor in the rearing and education of her daughter. In it was also included the pasòso, or the sum that was to be paid to the chichiva, or nurse, who had reared her. At present, if perhaps there is no bigaycaya in any marriage, for any reason, they never fail to collect these revenues from the groom, upon which there is generally a suit.

498. This dowry or *bigaycaya* was and is given before the marriage with all the solemnity that they can muster up, amid a great concourse of maguinoos, relatives, and friends of the lovers. The latter are given the crosses on the money to kiss, which is counted and exhibited in public, in

confirmation of the pact; and then the marriage is immediately celebrated with feasting and rejoicing. The employment of this bigaycaya is not the same in all the villages. In some it is all converted into the property of the parents of the bride, by way of trade, they selling their daughter (as do those of Mesopotamia) for a reasonable price. If the men do not possess the wherewithal with which to buy them promptly, innumerable sins follow and the two live in improper relations, even to the knowledge of the parents themselves—the young man serving as a servant in the houses of the latter to do their will, but in the capacity of a son, as far as familiarity and permission for evil are concerned. Many efforts are employed to extirpate this diabolical abuse, but it still costs great toil. Under the title of *catipàdos* (thus they call those who are engaged for marriage) are some concubinages legitimate for all time, for which the bigaycàya is not necessary. Having given up the bigaycàya, the poor couple are left destitute, for the parents of the bride take charge of everything.

499. That money is better used in some villages; for it serves to provide all kinds of clothes for the bride, and for one-half the expenses of the wedding (which are generally very great), and the parochial fees of the marriage, so that scarcely any is left for the parents of the couple. This is the practice that I have seen observed where I have been. These and other ogalis (which are customs) can only have their origin in the past, and come from father to son, and even there is variety in them, according to their distinct origins.

500. That which in España is called "the exchange of rings," in order to give security to the marriage contract and the wishes of those who are to contract it, has also been observed here, the couple giving each other some jewel. This has been called *talingbòhol*. This was followed by the *habìlin*, which is the sign that they have given the dowry which they had promised. And this was like the sign in shops to show that the price was fixed and that the article could not be sold at another price. Some fathers have maintained the custom of asking the same price for their daughter as they paid for the mother when they were married; but as fortunes are unequal, this cannot be maintained inexorably, nor at all times, nor with all.

501. The dowry was never returned to the one who gave it, unless the son-in-law were so obedient to his parents-in-law that he should win their affection, in which case they returned him the dowry, at the death of any one; but this was rather a matter of charity than of obligation, as all confess.

If the woman who was to be married was alone, and had neither parents nor grandparents, she herself and no other received the dowry. At present, the greed of the Indians must be greater; for this poor lone woman is never without either the chichiva who gave her the breast, who will not be left without her payment, or uncle, aunt, or other relative in whose care she has been because of the loss of her legitimate parents. And since the above consider themselves as her parents in this matter (the pinaca ama, as the Indians call it) they take upon themselves the place of her parents, and get all the money, just as if they were the true parents.

502. All the relatives and friends who go to weddings were also wont to take each some little present. These gifts were set down very carefully and accurately, in an account, noting whatever each one gave. For if Pedro So-and-so gave two reals at this wedding, two reals were also given to him if he had another wedding in his house. All this money is spent, either in paying, if anything is due for the wedding, or as an aid in the expenses. Or if the parents of both the young couple are niggardly, they divide it and keep it. If they are generous, they use it in the *pamamuhay*, or furnishing of the house of the couple. Consequently, there is no regular custom in this. The nearest relatives give the couple a jewel as a mark of affection, but do not give money. These jewels belong to the bride, and to no one else.

503. Three days before the wedding all the relatives of both parties assemble at the house where it is to be celebrated, to make the pàlapàla, which is a sort of bower, by which they make the house larger so that all the guests may be accommodated easily. They spend three days in making this. The next three days are those customary to the wedding and its feast. Consequently, there are six days of expense, of racket, of reveling, of dancing and singing, until they fall asleep with fatigue and repletion, all helter-skelter without any distinction. Often from this perverse river the devil in turn gets his little harvest—now in quarrels and mishaps which have happened, and now in other more common sins; the greatest vigilance of the father ministers is insufficient to stop these wrongs, and there are no human forces (although there ought to be) which can banish these pernicious ogalis.

504. In the olden days they employed certain ridiculous ceremonies, which had but little decency attending the intercourse of the couple upon the night of the wedding, customs which have now been totally uprooted.

The least indecent was the coming of the catalona or babaylana to celebrate the espousals. They brought a hog for this purpose, and with it and on it performed their rites as in other sacrifices. The young couple seated themselves on their bridal bed, in the laps of certain old women who played the part of godmothers of the espousal. These women fed the young couple with their own hands from one dish, and they both drank from one vessel. The groom said that he loved the bride, and she that she loved the groom. Thereupon the shouts of joy broke out, and cries, and there was singing and dancing and drinking. Then the catalona arose with great gravity, and so many were the blessings that she showered down upon the young couple that, according to some that I have heard among these natives, they would exceed without any doubt the flatteries of our gypsy men and women, when they tell the fortune of one who has given them a large reward.

505. If the recently-married couple did not agree well, the groom danced, spear in hand, before a hog, and then gave it the death-thrust, praying meanwhile to his anito, and this was sufficient to make the young couple agree. Now the couple go in festal procession in the manner of a masquerade, to the house where they are to live. Then they form another such procession, in order to convey the godparents to their abodes, and with this the festival is at an end. And after so great expense, they usually remain indebted for the small parochial marriage fees, if the father minister has not been very prompt.

506. In regard to heirs, all the legitimate children equally inherited all the property of their parents. If there were no legitimate children, then the nearest relatives inherited. If one had two or more children by two wives, all legitimate, each child inherited what belonged to his mother, both of the wealth of her time, and of the profits made from it, which could have belonged to her. As to the dowry, it is inferred that the child's grandparents received it, and spent it at the time of the wedding. If there were other children who were not legitimate, who had been had by a free woman, they had one-third of the property, and the legitimate children the other two thirds. But in case that there were no legitimate children, then the illegitimate children of a free woman were the absolute heirs. Some property was given to the children of slave women according to the wishes of the legitimate heirs, and the mother became free, as has been stated above—as did the children also, in the manner already explained.

507. They were also accustomed to have adopted children, and they are still much addicted to this; but the adoption was purchased by the one adopted, who gave the adopter a certain sum of gold, and, without any other intricacies of law, the latter kept the one adopted, although otherwise he had his own legitimate father. This was the contract made in such cases. If the adopter reared the one adopted during his life (whether he had other children or not), the one adopted was to inherit the sum that had been given for his adoption—increased by a like sum, obtaining in the inheritance twenty, if ten had been given. But if the one adopted died first, the total obligation of the adopter expired, even to the heirs of the one adopted. Over and above the inheritance obligation, the adopter generally left the one adopted something else, such as a jewel or a slave, if his services had been good, as a reward for his faithfulness and affection. If however, the one adopted was disagreeable, the adopter gave him up by giving back the sum that had been given for his adoption, and the contract was annulled.

508. If children were had in adultery, they all lived with the mother. If the party aggrieved had been paid and satisfied by the culprit with gold, according to their custom, the children were declared legitimate, and inherited equally with the real legitimate children in the inheritance of the father; but they inherited nothing from the mother. But if the injury were not atoned for, they had no inheritance, and were not regarded as legitimate.

509. These children, and those had by one's own slave woman (notwithstanding the liberty which she and her children enjoyed), and much less the children had by a slave of another master (notwithstanding that gold was paid for her during her pregnancy), did not succeed to the nobility of their parents, nor to their privileges; but were always considered as people of low birth, and were enrolled among the timavas in the villages. The legitimate children alone could inherit nobility, and even posts. Hence if the father were absolute lord in one barangay, his sons succeeded to that office, according to priority of birth; and if there were no sons, then the daughters, and after them the nearest relatives; and it was unnecessary to appoint or name them in their wills. They have never had the custom of making wills, and at most leave a list of their wealth and obligations. However, the custom is now coming in of making some testamentary memoranda before the village clerk, so that it may be legal in court.

1 Juan Francisco de San Antonio was born in Madrid in 1682, and made his profession in the Franciscan order at the age of twenty. In 1724 he brought a mission band to the islands, and spent there the rest of his life. His lifelong employ was in preaching, and as instructor in theology—save fifteen years spent in Indian villages near Manila. He died in that city May 29, 1744, the same year in which the last volume of his Cronicas was published. See Huerta's Estado, p. 537.

2 These are the Tagablis or Tagabili, also called Tagabelíes, Tagabaloy, Tagabulú, Tagbalooys, etc. Murillo Velarde, in his map, places them west of Caraga and Bislig in Mindanao, but this district has been found to contain only Manobos and Mandayas. They are probably the heathen Malay people living between the bay of Sarangani and Lake Buluan, whence their name, meaning perhaps "people of Buluan." See Blumentritt's Native Tribes of Philippines (Mason's translation), and Census of Philippines, i, p. 476.

3 The cloth made from abacá alone is called sinamay; that made of abacá and pineapple fiber, jusi; and that from a specially selected grade of abacá, much finer and more difficult to extract than commercial hemp or that used in making other cloths, lupis. See Census of Philippines, iv, p. 19.

4 Zúñiga (Estadismo) mentions the Chinese mestizo population of Tambóbong or Malabón (now in Rizal province) as about 7,500. Some of them had acquired by trade property to the value of 40,000 pesos. The tribute collected from all the Chinese mestizos of Luzon numbered 10,500, over 8,000 of which came from the provinces immediately north of Manila—Tondó, Bulacán, and Pampanga. The Chinese mestizo element is very evident today in the provinces of Bulacán and Pampanga, and probably forms the principal element among the native owners of haciendas. See Census of Philippines, i, pp. 435, 436, 438.

5 Spanish, con que se da Borney la mano; literally "shakes hands."

6 An evident lapsus calami for Legazpi, such as has occurred in other writers.

7 A Moorish garment resembling a herdsman's jacket, with which the body is covered and girt. It is still used on some festive occasions. (Dicc. Academia, 1726.)

8 See ante, p. 123, note 48.

9 Spanish, amusco, pero encendido; the last word, encendido, is literally "kindled," or "glowing"—that is, as here used, evidently referring to a reddish tint given by the blood showing through the skin.

10 The name of this book is probably the Origen de los Indios de el nuevo mondo, e Indias occidentales (Valencia, 1607; 8vo). Garcia was also the author of a book entitled Historia ecclesiastica y seglar de la Yndia oriental y occidental, y predicacion del sancto evangelio en ella por los apostolos (Baeça, 1626; 8vo).

11 See this report in Vol. VII, pp. 173–196. See also Vol. XVI, pp. 321–329. But San Antonio quite overlooks the earlier relation by Miguel de Loarca (Vol. V, pp. 34–187).

12 Antonio de Padua or de la Llave went to the Philippines with Gomez Perez Dasmariñas in 1590. He took the habit March 17, 1591, and professed in the province of San Gregorio March 19, 1592, changing his former name of Gonzalo to Antonio. After studying in the Manila Franciscan convent, he became missionary in the village of San Miguel de Guilinguiling, in 1602, and afterwards in the villages of Paete, Santa Cruz, Siniloan, Lilio, and Pila. He acted as definitor ad interim, from October 7, 1634 to January 13, 1635, and after becoming missionary of Pila was appointed commissary-visitor, holding that office from June 12 to December 16, 1637. He served as definitor again in 1639, and finally died in the Franciscan convent of Mahayhay in 1645. He was the first chronicler of the province of San Gregorio, and wrote the annals of his order from its founding in the Philippines in 1577 to the year 1644, in two volumes; and a life of Gerónima de la Asuncion, foundress of the royal convent of Poor Clares in Manila. See Huerta's Estado, pp. 452, 453.

13 Possibly a misprint for magaanito, as it is called elsewhere.

14 See ante, p. 191, note 101.

15 Noceda and Sanlucar's Vocabulario de la lengua Tagala (Manila, 1860) defines tictic as the "song of a nocturnal bird called apira, whence the name was transferred to the bird itself. It is also known by the names of Lapira and Pirapira."

16 That is, evidently without having enjoyed any of the fruits of the theft.

17 The Spanish edition of Juan de Solorzano Pereyra's Disputationem de Indiarum jure (Matriti, 1629–39; 2 vols., fol.), and of which later editions were published. The title of the first edition of the Spanish work is Politica Indiana sacada en lengua castellana de los dos tomos del derecho i govierno municipal de las Indias Occidentales que mas copiosamente escribio en la Latina. ... Por el mesmo autor ... Anadidas muchas cosas que no estan en los tomos Latinos (Madrid, 1648, fol.).

18 i.e., Sunday, Domingo being the Spanish word; evidence that this method of styling the week was evolved after the conquest.

19 See Vol. III, p. 161, note 42.

20 The distance from the extremity of the thumb to the extremity of the index finger, when outstretched; hence a span.

21 For the above weights and measures, see Vols. III, p. 71, note 20; p. 184, note 50; p. 253, note 87; and XV, p. 179, note 116. See also Census of Philippines, i, p. 327; and iv, pp. 447–457 (a long list of weights and measures, with many tables, used in the Philippines).